T0287973

THROUGH THE MILL

Gail Cuthbert Brandt

THROUGH THE MILL

Girls and Women in the Quebec
Cotton Textile Industry, 1881-1951

Baraka
Books

Montréal

ISBN 978-1-77186-150-2 pbk; 978-1-77186-171-7 epub; 978-1-77186-172-4 pdf; 978-1-77186-173-1

Book Design and Cover by Folio infographie
Editing and proofreading: Elise Moser and Robin Philpot
Index: Brookfield Indexing Services

Legal Deposit, 4th quarter 2018

Bibliothèque et Archives nationales du Québec
Library and Archives Canada

Published by Baraka Books of Montreal
6977, rue Lacroix
Montréal, Québec H4E 2V4
Telephone: 514 808-8504
info@barakabooks.com
www.barakabooks.com

Printed and bound in Quebec

Société
de développement
des entreprises
culturelles
Québec

We acknowledge the support from the Société de développement des entreprises culturelles (SODEC) and the Government of Quebec tax credit for book publishing administered by SODEC.

Financé par le gouvernement du Canada
Funded by the Government of Canada | Canadä

Trade Distribution & Returns
Canada and the United States
Independent Publishers Group
1-800-888-4741 (IPG1);
orders@ipgbook.com

CONTENTS

ACKNOWLEDGEMENTS

I would like to acknowledge the invaluable contributions of the many individuals who made this book possible. First and foremost, I thank the wonderful women workers who so generously welcomed me into their homes and shared their time and stories. The information and perspectives they provided were crucial to my subsequent analysis and provided the basis for a far more interesting narrative than one constructed solely on the basis of written documents. The work of all academic historians is built on the essential foundation of the dedicated labour of countless numbers of archivists and librarians. I am indeed grateful to all who helped me during the course of my research at Library and Archives Canada in Ottawa (LAC), the *Bibliothèque et Archives nationales du Québec* in Quebec City, the diocesan archives in Valleyfield, and the archives of the Confédération des syndicats nationaux in Montreal. I would also like to note my debt to the late Madeleine Parent for granting me access to her papers held at LAC at a time when they were not open to the public.

Research funding for this project was made available by the Social Science and Humanities Reseach Council of Canada. Over the years a number of research assistants helped me mine the treasure troves of information these archives and libraries contained. They included Brigitte Grégoire, who not only conducted interviews but also transcribed the resulting notes and tapes, Susan Wismer and Michele Straka—all of whom were at York University—and Sarah Cairns at the University of Waterloo. Dr. Andrée Lévesque and Barbara Checketts kindly agreed to read the draft manuscript and made a number of suggestions to improve it. Turning a draft manuscript into a book is a complex process, and finding the right publisher is key to determining how smoothly this process unfolds. I was delighted to find in Robin Philpot of Baraka Books an encouraging collaborator whose many contributions as editor and publisher greatly enhanced the quality of the finished product. Elise Moser further improved the finished product through her careful copy editing, while Josée Lalancette put her creative talent into the design of this book. To these individuals and to my other colleagues and friends who have been unceasingly supportive, I am most grateful.

And then there is my family, both immediate and extended. To my husband, Bernd, and to my children, Nicole, Andrea, and Gregory, thank you for your patience and your love. I have dragged you to more project-related locales and engaged in more dinner conversations about this book than you probably care to remember.

INTRODUCTION

Growing up in rural southwestern Protestant Ontario, the first exposure I had to French-Canadian culture as a child was a dubbed version of *La famille Plouffe* that played on CBC's television network Friday nights in the late 1950s. Perhaps this experience was the start of my deep interest in French Canada, especially the working class, their family lives, and their day-to-day struggles. Since that time, I have had several opportunities to observe Quebec society up close, first as a student honing my ability to speak French in summer classes at the *Université de Montréal*, then as a waitress for a summer at Montreal's Queen Elizabeth Hotel, and later, as a researcher spending time in homes and archives in various parts of the province. The vibrancy and warmth of Quebecers I encountered over all these many years have made me into an unabashed *Québécophile,* and also, I firmly believe, into a better Canadian and a better historian.

What continually struck me as I sat in the kitchens of the women who are the focus of this book, or of Quebec farm women who were the subjects of another, co-authored work, is how much we had in common as we discussed family matters, women's issues, and economic and political matters. While this book is about French-speaking, Catholic women who worked in a specific sector of the textile industry in Quebec, many of their experiences were also common among women workers in low-paying, labour-intensive industries in communities across Canada in the late nineteenth and the first half of the twentieth centuries. More specifically, their working and domestic lives bear striking similarities to those of women textile workers in many other countries and times, including the present.

Given the historic importance of cotton-textile production in Quebec, it is not surprising that a phrase connected to millwork has entered popular speech in Quebec French—"*On est au coton.*" (I am at my wit's end; I'm fed up: I am worn out.) Celebrated Québécois filmmaker Denys Arcand cleverly used the expression as the title for his controversial documentary of the Quebec cotton industry, produced in 1970, precisely because it captured both the film's subject and the workers' situation. I have chosen the title *Through the Mill* because this phrase summarizes the many perspectives that this study seeks to capture. It was through the mill that girls passed from adolescence to womanhood; it was through the mill that their identities were forged as women workers, family members, and community participants; and it was through the mill that Quebec society was transformed from a traditional rural society to an increasingly urban and industrial one. And it is through the lens of the mill that we have an opportunity to explore the complex dynamics of gender, ethnicity, and class.

This book has been a very long time in the making. As so often occurs in women's lives, it has been put aside several times. Children and grandchildren were born, other research projects completed, a career in academic administration pursued, and volunteer duties with several organizations fulfilled. This long delay, while regrettable and frustrating in some respects, has been advantageous in others. Had I finished this manuscript in the early 1980s, as originally planned, this study would have been one of the very first to provide a detailed analysis of the lives of women industrial workers in Canada. The benefit of the delay in its completion, however, has been my ability to draw on a much more substantial and sophisticated body of historical literature dealing with working women's past experiences. This study is all the richer for having that increased body of work on which to draw.

When I began this project, the writing of Canadian women's history by professional historians was in its infancy. The primary focus at that time was on recovering the story of women's past political and social activism, especially through studies of middle class women's organizations and the suffrage movement. This interest was motivated by the need to explain why Canadian women in the 1970s were still struggling for economic, social, and political equality and to establish the historical roots of second-wave feminism, as it came to be called. Many of the questions related to women's equality in the 1970s pertained to paid work and issues such as occupational segregation in the labour force, equal pay, childcare for working mothers, and unionization. Even the notion of women's right to work outside the home, especially if they had preschool children, was still hotly contested. While there were a few pioneering articles about working class women and their labour force participation in late nineteenth- and early twentieth-century Canada, there were no in-depth studies of women industrial workers and of their experiences at work and at home. It was this gap that motivated me to undertake the research project that has eventually led to this book.

By the late 1980s and early 1990s, a small number of scholars, overwhelmingly feminist women, had published groundbreaking studies in labour history, a flourishing field at that time. However, historical preoccupations and trends rise and fall as a result of shifting social, political, and cultural concerns, and the influence of changing theoretical concepts and methodologies practiced in other disciplines. In the 1990s, domestically and internationally, the writing of history headed in a dramatic—some would say disconcerting—new direction as its professional practitioners drew inspiration from postmodernist theories widely employed by philosophers and literary studies specialists. This approach shifted the focus from debates in women's history about the relationship between patriarchy (the systematic subordination of women in society) and social class to ones about gender and gender identity and how both were socially constructed. "The linguistic turn," the emphasis on the power of language to mould and impact lives, deeply affected the field of labour history, as it did other areas of historical enquiry. This influence resulted not only in some rancorous debates within the field, but also increased focus on new areas of specialization such as gender history, cultural history, and the history of sexuality. As a result, nearly four decades after I began on this research journey, the number of books dedicated to examining the work and lives of women industrial workers in Canada remain few. It is my fervent hope that this long-promised work can still make a significant contribution to feminist labour history.

I chose to focus on the story of women who worked in the Quebec cotton industry for a number of reasons. To begin, the textile industry has been one of the earliest forms of industrial manufacturing in most countries, with cloth production moving from household to factory starting in Britain in the eighteenth century. Since children and women performed many of the tasks involved in the household creation of yarns and cloth, they accounted for the majority of early mill workers. In Canada, the first attempts to produce manufactured cotton goods occurred in Quebec in 1844. Although initial ventures were short-lived, following the implementation of the Conservative federal government's National Policy in 1879, the industry became well established in Quebec, Ontario, New Brunswick, and Nova Scotia. The combination of protective tariffs against textile imports, the construction of railways to transport goods nationally and regionally, and the creation of an enlarged domestic market through immigration and western settlement provided the necessary stimuli for the industry's expansion.

From 1880 on, Quebec established its pre-eminence as the centre for cotton textile manufacturing and would maintain it until the demise of the industry in the late 1990s. This dominance stemmed from its abundant natural and human resources in the form of impressive hydraulic power sites and a seemingly endless supply of cheap labour. The time period chosen for this book—from 1881 to 1951—covers the period when the cotton industry was most important for Quebec's economy and its citizens. These dates also align with publication years for Canada's decennial censuses that provide much of the statistical information about the industry and its workers. Although the Canadian cotton textile industry continued to exist for another half century, the numbers of workers in its employ and its share of the domestic market dropped dramatically. This decline was the result of increased foreign competition and consumer demand for new synthetic products such as polyester, acrylic, and spandex. For women in Quebec, cotton cloth production was the second largest manufacturing employer after the garment industry between 1881 and 1951. Within the French-Canadian working class, toiling in a cotton mill was a central life experience for thousands of girls and women.

At the core of this study are eighty-four oral interviews with some of those female workers. My research assistant, Brigitte Grégoire, and I conducted them throughout the summer of 1980 in Salaberry-de-Valleyfield and Magog, two communities with a long history as centres of cotton textile production. We started the process of finding our interviewees with the help of local union personnel who provided us contact information for a number of retired women workers. These people, in turn, provided us with names and addresses of other women who had already retired or were still working in the local mill. Dominion Textile, although suffering from intense international competition and with its economic and social influence much diminished, was still operating in Magog. This continued presence afforded us an opportunity to tour the mill and to witness first-hand many of the stages of cotton cloth production. Unfortunately, most of the impressive infrastructure of the Montreal Cottons complex in Valleyfield had already fallen victim to the wrecking ball and been replaced by a modern shopping mall.

As our list of interviewees grew through an informal, word-of-mouth process in both communities, we managed in the end to construct four cohorts of workers on the basis of their dates of birth. Fourteen were born between 1895 and 1904, thirty between 1905 and 1914, twenty-six between 1915 and 1924, and fourteen between 1925 and 1934. The oldest woman was nearly eighty-eight years old when we interviewed her and had started work at the cotton mill in Magog in 1906. The youngest interviewee, born in 1933, entered the same mill in 1949 and was still working there at the time we met her. Fifty-three were married and thirty-one were single. To preserve their anonymity, each interviewee was assigned a fictitious name. (See Appendix 1 for a short biographical sketch of each woman.) All of the interviews were conducted in French, and I have done the translating.

Our research conversations were structured around forty-five questions covering a range of topics including motivation for entering the cotton industry, family connections to the industry, occupational histories, work structures, working conditions and wages, union activities, marriage and family life, religious practices, and involvement in voluntary associations. Many questions were open-ended and provided the women with ample opportunity to add their own commentary. Since the interviews were conducted in their own homes, a level of comfort was achieved between the interviewers and interviewees that led to many informal conversations on subjects as diverse as jam-making, child-rearing practices, and Quebec nationalism. Primary documents located in national, provincial, and local archives, newspapers, periodicals, censuses, and government reports yielded a vast quantity of additional material about cotton-cloth and yarn manufacturing in Quebec. They have been used to corroborate and to complement the workers' own testimony. As well, scores of secondary sources relating to the history of Quebec and to the history of women have helped to shape this study.

Daughters, wives, mothers, French Canadians, Roman Catholics, workers—these are the multiple identities of the women who are the focus of this study. Over the course of their lives, each woman has combined at least four of them. The ways in which these identities coalesced and clashed in the context of Quebec society's expectations about how girls and women should live their lives in the late nineteenth century and first half of the twentieth century are examined. Major themes include the role of paid employment in women's lives, the gender dynamics of work both in the mill and at home, women workers' Catholicism, and demonstrations of workplace militancy.

The first part of the book covers the period from the mid-nineteenth century to the end of World War I, and the second, from 1919 to 1951. The first chapter in each part outlines major developments within the Quebec cotton industry during the period under review, why and how girls and women were recruited into the industry, and some of their common characteristics. The second chapters are devoted to an examination of working conditions and wages in the industry and their impact on women workers. The final chapter in each part focuses on their domestic lives and the ways in which they conformed to or deviated from prevailing ideas in French-Canadian society about proper roles and behaviour of girls and women. These factors are then explored for their possible influence on women workers' involvement with unions and workplace activism in general.

I began writing this book as a standard academic monograph, replete with discussions of relevant historiography, conceptual frameworks, and methodologies, and hundreds of carefully documented footnotes. In the end, I decided to strip away the scholarly apparatus and to write in a straightforward manner that will hopefully appeal to a broader public. It is my fervent hope that women and men who have earned their livelihoods in industry may feel as comfortable reading this book as professional students of history. Instead of using footnotes or endnotes, I have identified many individual sources within the actual narrative. This technique, along with the accompanying select annotated bibliography, should make it possible for readers with a more specialized interest in the subject matter to follow up readily on the underlying documentation.

PART 1
1881-1918

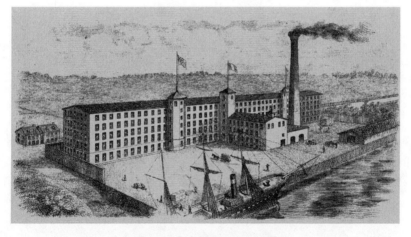

The Hochelaga Cotton Mill
In 1873 Montreal entrepreneur Victor Hudon established
this impressive, five storey cotton mill beside the St. Lawrence River in
the village of Hochelaga. The mill helped stimulate the rapid population
growth that led to the incorporation of Hochelaga into the city
of Montreal in 1883. (McCord Museum, M979.87.360.)

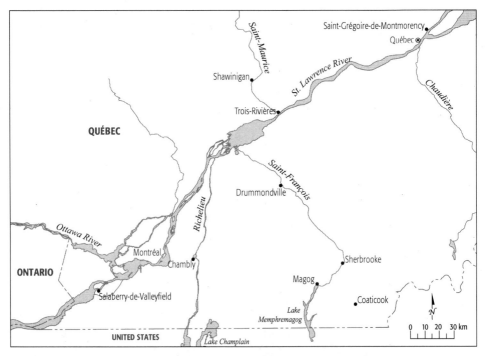

Locations of cotton textile mills in Quebec. (Map by Julie Benoît)

CHAPTER ONE

Developing the Quebec Cotton Industry: Girls and Women Wanted

In 1908 fifteen-year-old "Véronique" walked through the gates of the Montreal Cotton factory in Salaberry-de-Valleyfield, a town located sixty kilometres southwest of Montreal, to start work as a helper in the spinning department of the Old Mill. In doing so, she entered a work world familiar to thousands of young working-class women in Quebec and, like most, joined several family members already employed in the same establishment. In Véronique's case, they included her father, a sister, and three brothers. Drawn by the possibility of a better life, the family had migrated a considerable distance from Cap Saint-Ignace, situated some seventy kilometres east of Quebec City. For the next ten years, Véronique would continue to work in the twisting department at Montreal Cotton, until she left to get married and subsequently raise a family of eleven children.

There was a long tradition behind the work that Véronique and adolescent girls like her took up. For centuries girls and women had carded, spun, and woven cloth for their families. In seventeenth-century Europe, merchants subcontracted parts of the textile manufacturing process to individual families in their homes under the putting-out system of production. Labour performed by women and children was particularly important in the initial stages of cleaning, carding, and spinning of wool and flax,

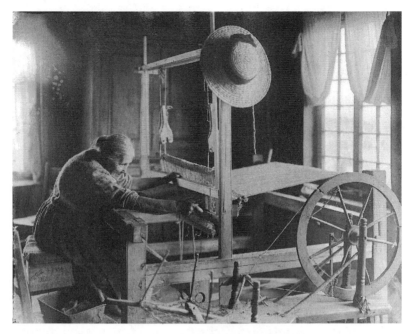

Weaving Homespun Cloth, 1898
This photo taken at Cap à l'Aigle in Charlevoix County shows an elderly woman labouring at her loom. The household production of woollen and linen cloth remained an important economic activity for rural girls and women in Quebec into the twentieth century. The burgeoning cotton industry took advantage of their skills by engaging them as spinners and weavers in its factories. (McCord Museum, VIEW-3237.)

and helped rural families earn precious cash that made it easier for them to subsist.

In Canada, historians have credited a woman with the development of pre-industrial textile production. Born in 1657 in Montreal, Agathe de Saint-Père was a successful businesswoman and mother of eight. To offset the shortage of woollen and linen cloth in the colony of Canada, she began to experiment with producing cloth from native plant and animal fibres. When the textile shortage worsened in 1705 following the sinking of a French supply ship, Saint-Père ransomed nine English weavers from their aboriginal captors and had looms constructed and apprentices trained under their supervision. Soon her household became the site of a cloth manufacturing enterprise featuring over twenty looms.

As forests gave way to permanent settlements, the colonists imported sheep from France and began to produce their own woollen goods. They also planted flax to make into homemade linen. As in Europe, cloth production became a standard component of household labour for children and women and a valuable source of family income. In 1886, when pioneer Quebec sociologist Léon Gérin visited a farm family near Trois-Rivières, he noted that the girls and their mother were busy with the laborious work involved in preparing the flax harvest for spinning and bleaching. During the previous winter, they had also spun forty-five pounds of wool produced by the farm's sheep that they then wove into cloth or knitted into clothing.

The rapid development of textile factories in England during the latter part of the eighteenth century, and subsequently in other industrializing countries, led to a dramatic increase in the demand for workers. This significant change in where cloth was produced afforded women and children the opportunity to transfer their skills from the hearth to the factory floor. Employers judged them to be highly desirable employees for many aspects of cloth production, considering them to be more dexterous, more easily controlled, and tidier than men. An even more important element in mill managers' hiring decisions was the well-known fact that women could be paid one-half or less the wages adult men earned. For women, employment in woollen and cotton factories was welcome, for it provided them with higher wages than they could earn as agricultural or domestic labourers. Although the working conditions in the mills were extremely taxing, the hours were shorter and the labour often lighter than was the case in the fields or in the home. By 1851, women comprised 49 percent of all British textile workers and 64 percent of cotton mill hands in the United States.

The general pattern of cloth production moving out of the household into the factory accelerated in Quebec and the rest of Canada as the cotton industry developed in the latter half of the nineteenth century. Employment of girls and women was central to the industry's expansion, and cotton manufacturing became one of the largest employers of women. Only the garment industry provided more jobs for Quebec's girls and women. By the end of the nineteenth century, girls and women would account for over half of the province's cotton-industry workforce.

The Early Years, 1844-78

The first company to manufacture cotton goods in Quebec was also the first joint-stock industrial company in Canada. The driving force behind the company was Adam Lomas, a skilled textile worker originally from Lancashire, England, who had become a mill manager in Massachusetts. Seeking new opportunities, he migrated to Sherbrooke, Quebec in 1842. Supported by a small group of shareholders including Sir Alexander Tilloch Galt, a prominent Upper Canadian businessman and future Father of Confederation, Lomas established a cotton mill in Sherbrooke in 1844 housing 1,200 spindles for the purpose of producing grey (unbleached) sheeting material. This first venture, unfortunately, was rather short-lived, for the mill was destroyed by fire sometime during the 1850s. Another cotton mill erected in Chambly, southeast of Montreal, also began operations in 1844. Within two years it produced some eight hundred yards of cloth daily, but its subsequent fate is unknown.

In 1853, Frederick Harris, a textile manufacturer from Vermont, was more successful in establishing a cotton mill in Montreal. Built on the banks of the Lachine Canal, the factory was equipped with 1,500 spindles and forty-six looms and produced primarily denims, tickings, and seamless bags. Within three years, there were over seventy employees, the majority of whom were women and children. By the mid-1870s, however, this company failed due to an inadequate local market and an inability to compete with lower-priced, superior-quality American and British products.

Despite continuing problems of this nature, the decade immediately following Confederation witnessed the realization of more ambitious, and ultimately more successful, projects in the primary cotton industry. In 1873 Montreal businessman and finan-

The Montreal Cotton Company, ca. 1900
Established in 1874 by a group of prominent Montreal businessmen,
Montreal Cotton was located on the Beauharnois Canal in Salaberry-
de-Valleyfield. By 1900 it employed some 2500 workers and was the
largest textile mill in Canada. (McCord Museum, MP-1985.31.9.)

cier Victor Hudon established the Hudon Cotton Company in
Hochelaga, a village of some one thousand inhabitants located on
the eastern half of the Island of Montreal. Built at a cost of
$200,000, the brick mill building was an imposing structure, fea-
turing five stories and housing eighteen thousand spindles and
three hundred looms. Drawing on the American model of cotton
factories, Hudon's mill integrated carding, spinning, weaving, and
finishing in one enterprise. As a result of rapid economic and
population growth arising from the presence of the Hudon mill
and other new industries, Hochelaga was transformed from an
agricultural village into an industrial neighbourhood and was
incorporated into the city of Montreal during the 1880s.

In 1874, a group of prominent Montreal business leaders, several of whom were involved in financing and directing the Hudon

mill, formed the Montreal Cotton Company, which became Montreal Cottons in 1911. Sir Hugh Allan, the famed banker, shipping magnate, and railway promoter who was already embroiled in the Pacific Scandal, served as the company's first president. The company built an impressive four-storey stone mill on the Beauharnois Canal in Valleyfield. Initially equipped with twenty-seven thousand spindles and 520 looms and boasting some of the most modern equipment on the continent, including machinery to bleach cotton cloth, the Montreal Cotton Company employed some 2,500 workers by the end of the nineteenth century. It soon became the largest textile mill in Canada.

Boom and Bust, 1879-84

With the return to power of John A. Macdonald in 1878 and the ensuing implementation of the Conservatives' National Policy, the Canadian cotton industry entered an era of rapid expansion. Seventeen cotton mills were established between 1878 and 1885, with six created in just one year, 1883. The 1879 tariff, one of the three prongs of the National Policy, raised duties on most imported cotton goods from 17.5 percent to 20-30 percent, thereby providing Canadian entrepreneurs a healthy level of protection against their British and American competitors. The construction of the transcontinental railway, the second feature of the National Policy, led to the building of many branch lines. They, in turn, facilitated the importation of raw cotton from the United States and the distribution of finished goods over a wider geographical area. The third component of the Conservative economic plan, the settlement of Western Canada, stimulated domestic consumption of cotton cloth products by creating new markets. In short, the National Policy can be credited with much of the spectacular growth occurring in the primary cotton industry in the late 1870s and early 1880s. Twenty-five cotton mills were operating in Canada by 1885.

Five of the new enterprises were established in the province of Quebec. They included the Coaticook Mills Company (1879), the Chambly Cotton Company (1881), and the Merchants Manufacturing Company, the Saint Anne Spinning Company, and the

Magog Cotton and Print Company (1882). The financial backers behind these mills were mostly drawn from the same group of Montreal merchants and capitalists, with men who had made their fortunes in the wholesale dry-goods trade dominating their ranks. Several were also directors of the existing Hudon and Montreal Cotton companies.

Civic officials, eager to promote the growth of their cities and towns by providing stable employment, invariably used incentives such as cash bonuses and twenty-year exemptions from municipal taxes to convince industrial entrepreneurs to build mills in their jurisdictions. The Saint Anne mill, another creation of Victor Hudon, received financial backing mostly from French-Canadian investors, including wealthy Montreal stockbroker Louis-Joseph Forget. As was the case with the earlier Hudon mill, it was located in the Hochelaga area of Montreal. The Merchants mill, founded by eight Montreal merchants and modeled on a Manchester, New Hampshire mill, was built on the banks of the Lachine Canal in Saint-Henri. Its function was limited to the production of grey cloth, while the Magog company built the first printing facility in Canada and turned out the first piece of Canadian calico print in June 1884.

Industrialists found Quebec very attractive due to the widespread availability of excellent hydraulic-power generation sites and an abundance of cheap labour. Starting in the early nineteenth century, Quebec experienced a prolonged demographic crisis as the population increased far more rapidly than the supply of arable land or jobs. Between 1851 and 1901, the population increased by 85 percent from 890,261 to 1,648,898; during the same period, over half a million residents emigrated to the United States, searching for an improved standard of living. One of Victor Hudon's stated purposes in establishing his cotton mill in Hochelaga was to help stem this population exodus.

The vast majority of those who left moved to the New England states and, in particular, to the textile centres located there. In towns such as Fall River and Lowell in Massachusetts, Manchester in New Hampshire, and Cohoes in New York, French Canadians developed distinctive "Little Canada" neighbourhoods. Here they

The Magog Cotton and Print Company
Located in Magog in the Eastern Townships, the company produced
the first Canadian calico print in 1884. This early photo
appears in *Commercial and Industrial Story of Magog*, Que.
published by Alexandre Paradis in 1951.

sought to preserve their cultural heritage through the establishment of their own churches, schools, shops, and social organizations. For many of these migrants, the Canadian-American border
was a meaningless political construct as they readily crossed back
and forth in pursuit of greater employment opportunities or
higher wages. In 1884, for example, the Merchants Company sent
labour recruiters to Cohoes due to a shortage of skilled cotton
workers in Montreal.

Cotton company profits attest to the general prosperity of the
Quebec industry between 1878 and 1883. As a later commission
investigating the textile industry, popularly known as the Turgeon
Commission, would report:

> The Hudon Company paid a dividend of 10 per cent on the common
> stock in 1878 and a stock bonus of 33 1/3 per cent in 1880, while cash
> dividends of 10 per cent were paid on the enlarged capital in 1881 and

1882. In 1883, while no dividends were paid, a common stock bonus of 10 per cent was given to shareholders on the basis of surplus accumulated to that time. The records of the Montreal Cotton Co. show that dividends of 11 per cent were paid in 1880, 20 per cent in 1881, 14 per cent in 1882 and 9 per cent in 1883.

Such profits, however, could not be sustained. Even as new mills were being constructed, production was outstripping demand. The Canadian industry soon had the capacity to supply unbleached cotton goods to a population twice that of the young nation. In an effort to rectify this dire situation, Andrew F. Gault, a managing director for the Hudon, Montreal Cotton, and Saint Anne mills, spearheaded the formation of the Canadian Cotton Manufacturers' Association in 1883. The participating companies agreed to limit production by reducing the number of looms in operation and also the number of days worked. As a result, the Merchants mill was idle from July 1884 until the following November. The increasingly difficult financial straits of most of the companies can also be illustrated by the case of the Magog Cotton and Print Company. It was so short of funds that it was unable to pay its employees in cash between June, when the cotton goods were produced, and November or December, when they were sold. In place of their wages, employees were offered scrip, a type of coupon redeemable for goods at the local store. This situation was doubly troublesome for the workers, since the cotton company's principal shareholder also owned the store.

Reorganization and rationalization, 1885-94

In addition to trying to limit production levels, cotton company managers sought to counteract the unsettling circumstances in the industry by diversifying production and manufacturing more bleached and printed goods. Yet another strategy was to establish export markets to absorb the rapidly expanding amount of cloth produced. With the completion of the Canadian Pacific Railway in 1885, manufacturers could ship cottons to Asia. In 1889, a group of investors led by Charles Ross Whitehead established the Montmorency Falls Cotton Company near Quebec City to produce fabrics for shipment to China and Africa. A further attempt to reduce domestic competition came in the form of mergers. In 1885, the Hudon Cotton Company and the Saint Anne Spinning Company amalgamated to form the Hochelaga Cotton Manu-facturing Company. By this time, Victor Hudon, founder of both companies, had lost control to the directors, who were mostly of British origin. With Hudon's departure, English replaced French as the language in which his original company's records had been kept.

By 1887, the Hochelaga enterprise, in conjunction with nearly all of the existing Canadian cotton firms, had established the Dominion Cotton Manufacturers' Association. The stated objective of this cartel was to regulate production and prices in an effort to stabilize the industry. Member companies had to post a bond that they forfeited if they sold their products below the prices the group had established. By 1890, the cartel had evolved into a new merger with the formation of the Dominion Cotton Mills Company, Limited. It brought together nine facili-ties including the Hochelaga, Saint Anne, Magog, and Coaticook mills in Quebec, and five others in Ontario, New Brunswick, and Nova Scotia. One year later, the Chambly mill joined the list of acquisitions. Incorporated under a federal charter, the new enterprise was the largest manufacturing company in Canada at that time.

The creation of Dominion Cotton Mills was the work of Montreal businessmen, several of whom were already promin-ent in the industry. Central to the group was Andrew Gault, who had initiated the 1883 cartel and, as president of both Hudon Cotton and Saint Anne Spinning, had brought about their initial merger into the Hochelaga Company. Born in Northern Ireland, Gault had moved to Canada with his parents and settled in Montreal, where he eventually entered the dry goods business and rose to the position of president of the family firm, Gault Brothers. With the implementation of the National Policy, he became so actively involved in the promotion of cotton factories that he earned the title the "Cotton King of Canada." In addition to serving as president of Dominion Cotton Mills, he became the chief executive officer of the Montreal Cotton Company and of Canadian Coloured Cottons, another merger created in 1892 by combining a New Brunswick mill with several located in Ontario. Gault also served as a director of the Bank of Montreal, the major financial institution behind the formation of Dominion Cotton. His primary collaborator in many of his cotton industry ventures was David Morrice, who had started his career as the pre-eminent importer of British textiles into Canada. Morrice's company served as the exclusive selling agent for over thirty-five cotton, woollen, and knitting mills located in four provinces, and he played a key role in the formation of Canadian Coloured Cottons.

The Montreal Cotton Company officially remained outside the newly formed cotton trusts. However, Gault and other directors of Dominion Cotton Mills, such as Louis-Joseph Forget and Charles Blair Gordon, head of a large Montreal-based dry goods company, also served on Montreal Cotton's board. Clearly the Valleyfield operation's relationship to the newly formed conglomerates was marked more by co-operation than by competition. Gault also controlled the Montmorency Cotton Company and served as its president.

The new amalgamations appear to have had their desired effect, and Dominion Cotton declared that 1892 was a particularly satisfactory year. Investors in the Montreal Cotton Company also enjoyed healthy annual dividends of 7 to 9 percent. By 1893, the capital invested in Dominion Cotton, Canadian Coloured Cottons, and the Montreal Cotton Company accounted for over 90 percent of the capital invested in the entire Canadian cotton industry. Two years later, exports of grey goods to China increased substantially from 1.7 million pounds to 3.5 million pounds. Quebec manufacturers already accounted for 43 percent of the value of the Canadian industry's products and 45 percent of the nation's cotton workers.

The influence the cotton companies exerted on the economic, social, and political lives of the communities in which they operated cannot be overestimated. With their sprawling and imposing late-Victorian industrial architecture, the Hudon and Saint Anne mills in Hochelaga and the Merchants facility in Saint-Henri physically dominated the landscape of their working class neighbourhoods. Similarly, in towns such as Valleyfield and Magog, the cotton companies were a striking presence. As well as occupying the equivalent of several city blocks with its mill complex and workers' housing, the Montreal Cotton Company possessed several hundred acres of land outside Valleyfield on which it ran its own farming operation, including a dairy to produce milk for its employees. For its part, Dominion Cottons also owned large tracts of land, amounting to some three thousand acres in and around Magog. It, too, operated a farm and sold the produce to its employees.

The relationship between the companies and the communities in which they located was often a strained one. Citizens felt both gratitude and resentment toward the companies—gratitude for the large number of jobs they provided, but also resentment for the tremendous power they possessed and the high-handed manner with which they often wielded it. During major strikes, the consequences reverberated throughout the community, for many workers barely survived on credit extended by grocers, butchers, bakers, and other merchants. Municipal assessments, land usage, and control of local hydroelectric power sites were frequent sources of contention. Most of the companies enjoyed generous municipal tax concessions in return for setting up their factories. The Hudon mill, for example, benefited from a twenty-year tax exemption, while the town of Valleyfield gave the Montreal Cotton Company a $50,000 bonus as well as a twenty-year tax holiday. In Magog, Dominion Cottons refused to pay its assigned school taxes of $5,000 after a special five-year arrangement that had allowed it to pay only $1,000 per annum expired.

The fact that the "foreign" capitalists who controlled the textile companies seemed indifferent to local citizens' interests, despite the efforts municipalities made to keep them happy, caused considerable bitterness. In April 1891, the editor of *Le Progrès de Valleyfield* complained, "The majority of the company directors are capitalists foreign to our religion and to our nationality. We never expected to be treated on the same footing as the directors' compatriots." He proceeded to report on a rumour

St. Anne Spinning Mill, 1909
Backed by some wealthy French-Canadian investors, in 1882 Victor
Hudon created a second company in Hochelaga, the St. Anne Spinning
Company. Three years later, Hudon's two companies amalgamated,
and he lost control to a group of prominent English-speaking
Montreal merchants. English replaced French as the operating language
of the newly created Hochelaga Cotton Manufacturing Company.
(McCord Museum, VIEW-4647.)

that there were two wage scales at the mill: one for English workers and another for French-Canadian employees, with the latter
receiving at the very least 25 percent less. He found this information particularly troubling, given that the company had
recently received a $4,000-a-year tax benefit, and alleged that
certain municipal politicians were in the company's pocket.
Quite simply, in his opinion the cotton company's influence was
"intolerable."

Expansion and Corporate Concentration, 1895-1904

Despite the impressive array of technological innovations and the extensive rationalization that took place in the industry, profits in the last years of the nineteenth century did not match those achieved between 1878 and 1883. Although Dominion Cotton Mills succeeded in paying annual dividends of 6 percent on its common stock between 1894 and 1900, these results were modest compared to those previously cited. The principal problem continued to be the limited size of the Canadian market. Only at the end of the century did Canadian consumption of cotton goods increase significantly, when per capita purchases rose from $2.30 in 1890 to $3.50 in 1900. This increased demand was undoubtedly attributable to a number of factors such as urbanization, increased economic specialization, and the acquisition of sewing machines by many Canadian households. The 1888-89 Eaton's catalogue introduced *The New Empress* sewing machine and, two years later, Butterick patterns became available. By 1900, Canadian women were opting more and more frequently to replace their family's heavy homespuns by the lighter, more easily maintained calicos, ginghams, and prints the domestic cotton industry was producing.

The rising popularity of cotton goods at the turn of the century seemed to ensure the future. Although the mills in Coaticook and Chambly were closed during earlier drives toward consolidation, other operations underwent significant expansions. In 1899, the Merchants Cotton Company in Montreal opened a new addition housing 750 more looms. Quebec's capacity to turn out white, dyed, and printed fabrics also increased with the establishment of the Colonial Bleaching and Printing Company the same year on the Lachine Canal in Saint-Henri, Montreal. Unlike its predecessors, it bought grey cloth from other mills rather than producing its own. As the new century began, the Magog mill added a thousand new looms. By this time, Magog had a population of some 3,500 and the factory and print works there provided work for approximately a thousand persons. In Valleyfield, a community of eleven thousand inhabitants by 1901, the local mill employed some two thousand workers, many of whom lived in company-

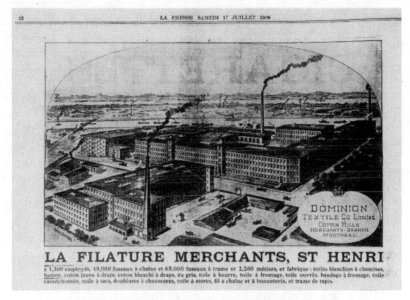

The Merchants Cotton Company, 1909
Established in 1882 by a group of eight Montreal merchants, this mill
was located on the bank of the Lachine Canal in the working class
district of Saint-Henri. The description below this image, published
in *La Presse* in July 1909, indicates that the mill employed 1300 hands
at that time and housed some 113,000 spindles and 2200 looms.
(Collections.banq.qc.ca/lapresse)

owned housing. The Montreal Cotton Company added two new
structures in the same year to house an additional forty thousand
spindles and 850 looms. According to one report, two-thirds of
the workers to be hired to tend to the new machinery would be
women. At Montmorency Falls, an additional 550 workers were
working in cotton textile manufacturing, and the company was
looking to increase its exports to China and Zanzibar.

According to the 1901 census, the value of products manufactured by Canadian cotton establishments had grown by 38 percent from $8.7 million in 1891 to $12 million. Increasingly,
production was concentrated in Quebec with the mills located
there accounting for over 50 percent of the value of Canadian cotton goods and for 45 percent of the industry's workers. Of the adult
workers employed in the Quebec cotton industry, 55 percent were

women while girls comprised 42 percent of adolescent employees under the age of sixteen.

Relations between the cotton companies and the municipalities in which they operated continued to be complex and sometimes antagonistic. Correspondence between the managers of the Montreal Cotton Company and the bishop's palace in Valleyfield between 1897 and 1908 reveals the many tensions existing between town and company. The managers, successively Louis Simpson and Fred Lacey, relied heavily on Monsignor Joseph-Médard Émard, the diocesan bishop, to arbitrate and to smooth relations, be they with workers, town council, or senior levels of government. Simpson, for his part, went to great lengths to keep His Grace informed as to the state of the cotton trade in general and the activities of the Montreal Cotton Company in particular. The circumstances in which Bishop Émard was asked to intervene on the company's behalf ranged from using his influence with Sir Wilfrid Laurier to oppose any reduction in the protective tariff for cotton goods— Simpson thoughtfully provided a complete draft of what the archbishop should say—to asking the nuns living in a convent near the factory to change the tone of their bells. It seems that the peal of the bells was too similar to that of the company's fire alarms and was frequently a source of confusion. The importance of the company to the welfare of the town, and consequently to the members of the bishop's flock, was a recurring theme in the managers' letters.

A major area of concern for the managers and investors at the turn of the century was the Liberal government's tariff policy. In 1897, in the glow of imperial sentiment occasioned by Queen Victoria's Diamond Jubilee, the Laurier government introduced a preferential tariff with Great Britain. This gesture of imperial solidarity resulted in a one-eighth reduction in duties on cotton goods that had previously ranged from 20 to 30 percent. In 1898, the government lowered customs duties on British manufactured goods by 25 percent and, two years later, by 33 percent. These reductions coincided with and encouraged an increase in the importation of British cotton goods.

To make matters worse, the price of raw cotton per pound rose to unprecedented heights with average prices of 16–16.5 cents per pound replacing those of 6–7 cents. The Boxer Rebellion in China in 1900 also led to an abrupt halt to the export of cotton goods to that country. To compensate, Montmorency mill directors approved the creation of their own bleachery, an act that only added to the surplus production of other Canadian mills. Yet another disruptive factor was a parting of the ways between Andrew Gault and David Morrice that effectively ended price-fixing between Dominion Cotton and Canadian Coloured Cotton.

In 1901, Dominion Cotton Mills' dividends were reduced to 4.5 percent, and from 1902 to 1904 no dividends were paid out. Similarly, the Merchants and Montmorency operations reported a stop to dividend payments. The following year Montreal Cotton was running at only half capacity during some months. Once again, British competition and overproduction brought on by mill expansions were threatening the stability of the Canadian industry. And the manufacturers once again turned to mergers and tariff increases to solve the crisis.

Consolidation and Expansion, 1905-18

In 1903, an attempt was made to amalgamate Dominion Cotton Mills with the Merchants Cotton Company and Colonial Bleaching and Printing, both of which had remained outside the 1890 merger that had created Dominion Cotton. Although not immediately successful, this initiative led eventually to the formation of the Dominion Textile Company in 1905. The new enterprise was the creation of a syndicate of thirteen of Montreal's most powerful capitalists including Herbert Holt, Senator Louis-Joseph Forget, David Morrice, David Yuile, John P. Black, and Charles Gordon. The members turned over $1 million to Royal Trust to act on their behalf and acquire shares in four existing companies—Dominion Cotton, Merchants, Montmorency, and Colonial—all of which were in serious financial difficulty. In return the syndicate members received half a million dollars' worth of the new company's preferred stock and $5 million of common stock. Through their exclusive control of the common stock, the syndicate had complete control over the direction of the new organization, which represented about half of all the spindles and looms operating in the Canadian cotton industry.

La Presse, Montreal's leading French-language newspaper, vehemently denounced the takeover as the latest example of the Forget interests' appetite for financial and commercial control of the Quebec economy. The newspaper claimed that since the capitalists in question could already exploit the inhabitants of Montreal through their control of the city's transportation and electrical distribution systems, was not their next step "to seize the citizen by the collar, and charge him a few more cents for the shirt he wears?" In its analysis of the deal as it related to the half-million-dollar investment in common shares, the *Canadian Journal of Fabrics* reported in 1906 that "a conservative estimate of the present value places it at $2,500,000 or a profit of $2,000,000 in a year and two months for the twenty-one holders of the stock."

Thirty years later, in writing his extensive report on the Quebec textile industry, Justice W.F.A. Turgeon concluded:

> The syndicate's $1,000,000 investment proved unusually profitable. One of the members of the syndicate. . . had retained all his shares, except some transferred as gifts to members of his family. The interest on the $500,000 of preferred shares has always been paid. The interest on the $500,000 invested in common stock has yielded an average annual return of over 98 percent, reaching a high point of 150 percent in several years and never going lower, after the first two years, than 50 percent.

It was certainly questionable whether the $4.5 million difference between the promoters' original $1 million investment and the $5.5 million par value stock they received could be justified as "good will" for their services in bringing about the deal.

A driving force behind the 1905 merger and the subsequent expansion of Dominion Textile into one of the world's largest primary-cotton-textile manufacturers was Charles Blair Gordon. Having risen from the lowly position of dry goods clerk to that of manager of the Standard Shirt Company, Gordon eventually became president and chairman of the board of Dominion Textile. In addition, he served as president of the Montreal Cotton Company, Hillcrest Collieries, Dominion Glass Company, the

Canadian Manufacturers' Association, and the Bank of Montreal. All told, he came to hold directorships on the boards of over thirty industrial and financial institutions. Gordon was also responsible for the purchase of the Penman Manufacturing Company by Dominion Textile in 1909 and for its transformation into one of the largest knit-goods manufacturers in the world. He served as president of Penman from its creation until his death in 1939. During World War I, Gordon headed up the Imperial Munitions Board and was knighted for his service. He also became a vice-president of the Bank of Montreal in 1916. While Gordon concentrated on the financial and administrative aspects of Dominion Textile and its components, it was Frank G. Daniels who ably oversaw the organization of the various plants. Another native Montrealer, Daniels had served as office manager and then mill manager of Montmorency Cotton Mills prior to joining Dominion Textile.

The Montreal Cotton Company in Valleyfield continued to remain officially outside the new merger, but Dominion Textile held a large block of its common shares, which meant that the two companies had interlocking directorships. Montreal Cotton's manager, Louis Simpson, proclaimed his satisfaction with the new arrangement, for it lessened competition and increased collaboration. Montreal Cotton could now print certain lines of products manufactured by other plants belonging to Dominion Textile.

From their strengthened position, the cotton manufacturers lobbied vigorously for higher protective tariffs. At tariff hearings conducted by the federal government in Valleyfield in 1905, Simpson led the procession of local politicians, businessmen, and farmers who argued that substantial tariff increases were necessary for the local cotton industry to survive. Simpson laid part of the blame for the need to raise tariffs up to 30 percent on "ladies of fashion and wealth in the larger cities" whose "constant demand for new things" and "higher grades of goods" resulted in shorter, more specialized runs, and higher production costs. However, as William Fielding, the minister of finance heading the commission of inquiry, pointed out, Montreal Cotton had succeeded in paying yearly dividends of 8 percent or more on its preferred shares despite all its alleged problems. By contrast, banks were paying only 3 percent interest per annum, and a 4 percent return on investment was considered an extremely attractive proposition.

Shortly after the incorporation of Dominion Textile, business conditions in the industry improved substantially. In response, Charles R. Whitehead, formerly president of the Montmorency Cotton Company and one of the organizers of Dominion Textile, established a new cotton company, the Wabasso Cotton Company, in 1907 in Trois-Rivières. The primary objective of this new venture was to supply the Canadian market with fine cotton goods using the latest British equipment, including a significant number of mule spinning devices. According to its directors, it was the only mill in North America to be furnished throughout by machinery fabricated by the world-renowned Platt Brothers Ltd. of Oldham, Lancashire. The *Annual Financial Review – Canadian*'s 1913 report documented the new company's initial success:

> The hopes of the promoters of this Company have been more than realized. Their goods have steadily gained ground and favor in the market, sales showing a remarkable increase from about $300,000 the first year to $400,000 the second year and to $600,000 the third. During these three years, the Company has added machinery and equipment from time to time as required.

Building on this success, in 1909 Whitehead and his associates established the Shawinigan Cotton Company in Shawinigan Falls, located thirty kilometres north of Trois-Rivières, to meet the growing demand of the parent company for cotton thread. This plant was particularly welcome in the community for it was expected to stabilize the adult male labour force by offering employment to women in their families. Curé Boulay, the local priest, helped arrange for the establishment of a hostel to provide accommodation for young farmwomen from the surrounding countryside. This residence, operated by a Dominican order of nuns, functioned for only a few years but is deemed to have played a role in facilitating the community's transition from a rural, agricultural way of life to the new industrial reality. It appears to have been the only instance in the Québec cotton industry during this time period in which boarding-house accommodation formed part of the strategy to recruit single young women..

Following the creation of its new branch plant, Wabasso continued its expansion. With the encouragement of an additional $25,000 grant and a twenty-year tax exemption from the municipality of Trois-Rivières, in 1911 the company announced that it would build a second plant, the Saint Maurice Valley Cotton Mills, in the city. The local newspaper, *Le Bien public*, reported in January of that year that the new mill was expected to engage at least two thousand workers.

In 1907, the same year that Wabasso launched its plant in Trois-Rivières, another new enterprise, the Mount Royal Spinning Company, opened on the Lachine Canal in the Côte-Saint-Paul district of Montreal. William Whitehead, brother of C.R. Whitehead, was one of its primary backers. Capitalized at $3 million and containing 1,200 looms and forty thousand spindles, it was designed to provide employment for eight hundred workers. In 1910, the plant was leased to Dominion Textile for a ten-year period and was later purchased by that conglomerate.

Under the guidance of F.G. Daniels, the newly appointed managing director of Dominion Textile, rationalization within the industry accelerated. An astute administrator, he ruthlessly closed down inefficient plants and consolidated most of the company's production in Quebec. Each remaining manufacturing unit was assigned its own special product lines. Bleaching and printing, formerly performed at six different facilities, were now centralized in Montreal and Magog, with the latter boasting the largest print works in North America. By 1911, the cotton industry had become increasingly concentrated in Quebec, where mills produced 66 percent of the value of the national industry's products and employed 63 percent of its workers. Women and girls, accounting for over half of the mill operatives, continued to play an essential role in the expansion of the provincial industry.

A Family Affair

While members of the Montreal business elite manipulated capital and effected mergers with pen and paper, hundreds of women and children operated the spindles and looms that transformed fixed capital into portable profits. In 1891, over half of all Quebec cotton workers were women and girls. In testimony contained in the 1889 report of the Royal Commission on the Relations of Labor and Capital, a witness reported that of the approximately one thousand workers employed at the Hochelaga Cotton Company, five to six hundred were women and about two hundred were girls and boys. Some of the children were ten years old or younger and had already been working for "a couple of years."

It is also evident from the testimony that Andrew Gault and other mill owners were completely indifferent to what actually transpired in the mills their companies controlled, as long as mill managers produced satisfactory financial results. As Gault unequivocally stated before the commission, "In the interior working of the mill I have taken I may say no interest whatever—that is no active interest." Indeed, he expressed his opinion that directors should not inquire too closely into daily operations. When questioned about the desirability of a legislated end to factory employment for boys under twelve and girls under fourteen, he responded:

> We would require two sets of hands, and it would be difficult to get them. Of course it is possible to do away with children altogether, and do the work by grown-up people and when we got accustomed to it we might perhaps do the work as well. It has, however, been the custom to employ young help in the cotton mills. The work is very light and there is not much labour about it and probably they are sometimes just as well in the mills as they would be about the streets.

In spite of growing concern about the physical and moral state of children and women in factories, it is clear from the evidence presented to the commission that there was no widespread opposition to their employment, provided that conditions were tolerable. In his submission, Cardinal Elzéar-Alexandre Taschereau, archbishop of Quebec, stated that he did not object to the employment of women and children. He stressed only the need to protect their morals and health. Confronted by a massive exodus of French Canadians from the Quebec countryside, the Catholic Church adopted a very pragmatic approach to industrialization. If industrial employment put bread on a family's table and kept it from leaving the province, how could such work be condemned? Indeed, the clergy were often key players in the establishment of local industries, as already noted in the case of Shawinigan. In Montreal, it was also Roman Catholic nuns who provided child-care services to enable needy married French-Canadian women to work for wages.

The cotton manufacturers relied extensively on family and kin networks in the rural regions and small municipalities of the province to recruit their workforces. Early in the nineteenth century, the American cotton industry had developed two methods of securing mill hands. One involved employing single young women who were lodged in company boarding houses, as in the case of Lowell, Massachusetts, while the other approach, more widely used in Rhode Island, focused on recruiting entire families. In Quebec, the former system found little favour. When the Hudon Company constructed its mill in Hochelaga in 1874, it also con-structed houses for its workers' families. By 1881, it owned and operated forty-six double-unit tenement houses.

The practice of providing company housing was copied in other textile centres such as Valleyfield, Magog, and Saint-Grégoire-de-Montmorency. In the latter community, the company built fourteen blocks of housing, each containing four tenement houses, over the course of the first two years. Housing was not only a way to attract and keep mill hands, but also a means to exercise a measure of control over them and provide long-term additional income. According to Andrew Gault, "While these cottages will pay the company a good rate of interest, it will give a control over the help which we could not otherwise have had and will in every way prove beneficial to the mill."

The decided preference for recruiting entire families was grounded in the demographic, economic, and cultural context of Quebec. To begin, there was a labour surplus in the rural areas. Given the prevalence of large families in the countryside, children of both sexes were available for waged labour off the farm. Moreover, the enthusiastic promotion of colonization movements by both the Catholic Church and the provincial government in the latter part of the nineteenth century resulted in the migration of thousands of families to the marginal agricultural lands of northern, southwestern, and eastern Quebec, lands that subsequently proved incapable of providing a satisfactory standard of living.

The high rate of mobility among rural families has been well documented in a number of studies. In his classic study of the émigrant déraciné (rootless emigrant), Léon Gérin described a household that in 1903 had twelve children and initially sought to eke out a living by doing waged agricultural work. Then the family migrated to New England where both parents and the older children found work in various textile mills. Nonetheless, the parents and some of the children returned regularly to the Montérégie region southwest of Montreal to pursue marginal farming. During a fifty-year period, the family moved twenty times, and its members eventually dispersed over two provinces and several American cities.

It was the same desire to escape the unrelenting toil and grinding poverty associated with subsistence farming that motivated thousands of other families to seek waged labour in Quebec's own burgeoning textile industry. Unlike the large numbers of single young Yankee women who left behind the farms of New England on their own or with women relatives or friends to take up work in that region's textile mills, the vast majority of single young Quebec women did not live apart from their families. In nineteenth-century Quebec, as elsewhere in Canada, public opinion was decidedly opposed to young women living outside a familial environment. As Andrew Gault put it, "We consider it an advantage that young women be with their families; it is with this very objective that we have constructed fifty to sixty workers' houses so that our employees have good and comfortable lodgings." Such views did not preclude the possibility of adolescent girls living away from their own nuclear families. It was essential, however, that they live with a surrogate family, be it in the form of a rela-

Two Sisters Holding Shuttles, circa 1890
This photo of two sisters was taken in an artist's studio before they
were about to leave Montreal to take up work in a textile mill in
Massachusetts. French-Canadian families regularly crossed back
and forth across the Canadian-American border in search of mill
employment. (McCord Museum, MP-1992-18.1.)

tive's family, an employer's family, or an institutional "family"
provided by a religious order.

The structure of the industry enhanced the suitability of family
recruitment for Quebec cotton mills. By the end of the nineteenth
century, Canadian manufacturers had achieved a very high degree
of vertical and horizontal integration. Companies such as Montreal
Cotton and Dominion Cottons encompassed all facets of cloth production in their operations. Cleaning, carding, spinning, weaving,
inspection, napping, dyeing, printing, and packaging were most
often carried on within the same complex. Since some of these

operations required a predominantly male workforce while women more commonly performed others, both sexes could easily find employment in the same textile enterprise.

As a result, cotton companies routinely sent recruiters into rural Quebec to encourage large families with several children of working age to move to the textile centres and to work in their mills. Already in the 1880s, the Hudon Company was sending agents into the Saguenay area to find cheap labour for its Hochelaga operations. The practice of company representatives travelling the back *rangs* (concessions) looking for interested families lasted well into the 1920s. A favourite recruiting ground for the Magog mill and print works was the Beauce region. In fact, one Magog neighbourhood was known locally as "la petite Beauce" because so many of its inhabitants had come from that area.

In some cases, families were offered company housing, but for those who had to find their own accommodation, the promise of employment for a number of family members was a sufficiently powerful incentive to move. Such was the case for the family of "Marie-Berthe." Contacted in Saint-Côme-de-Beauce by a company recruiter who promised work for all members of the family old enough, her father decided to move the family to Magog. Upon arrival there, Marie-Berthe, her mother, a sister, and one brother immediately went to work in the mill. It was, however, unusual at that time for married women who had children old enough to work in Quebec's mills and were not widowed to seek employment there as well. Some who did were women who had worked previously in American mills where working wives and mothers were much more common.

As younger children reached early adolescence, they tended to follow their parents and older siblings into the mills. They became familiar with the factory routine and work well before their official entry into the workforce, often as a result of carrying the midday meal to family members working in the mill and, while there, learning the tasks performed by their relatives. In this way family ties admirably served the interests of the mill owners, for not only did the family provide a continuing supply of factory hands but often initiated younger members into the world of the factory as well. For family members paid on a piecework basis, having another family member operate their machines while they were on their noon break also meant less lost time and more income.

While the companies relied on French-Canadian families to supply the vast majority of their female workers, they also sought out British women and teenage girls when there was a critical shortage of experienced labour. In November 1903, an article in the *Canadian Journal of Fabrics* noted, "Women agents, acting on behalf of mill owners of Valleyfield and other manufacturing locales in Canada, have been visiting Lancashire and Yorkshire in search of women weavers willing to emigrate to the Dominion. It is believed that passage money, in some cases, has been advanced and that a considerable number are coming."

During the first decade of the twentieth century, girls and women continued to constitute nearly half of the total workforce, but the extent of their presence varied enormously from facility to facility. Dominion Textile provided statistics in 1908 indicating that the proportion of women and girls in their employ varied from 13 percent in the Colonial Bleachery to 57 percent at the Hochelaga mill. When all facilities were taken into account, girls and women accounted for 45 percent of the company's labour force. For its part, Montreal Cotton reported that it employed 2,487 workers in August 1908. Girls accounted for 40 percent of workers under the age of eighteen, and women for 38 percent of the adult workforce.

Family and kin ties continued to be of paramount importance in the initiation of young women into the cotton industry. Nine of fourteen women interviewed in Valleyfield and Magog who were born between 1895 and 1904 entered the mills alongside, or in the footsteps of, several other family members. "Desneiges" began work in 1914 at the Magog factory when she was fourteen, joining her father, two brothers, and two sisters who were already employed there. The family had moved from Roxton Falls seven years previously to take advantage of the greater employment opportunities in Magog. Given the large number of workers one nuclear family might supply and the many years each individual worked, it was not uncommon for a single family to contribute well over a hundred years of service to a textile company. Family ties were important even in cases where young adults moved to the textile centres without their parents. In 1910, for example, seventeen-year-old "Rachel" was sent to Magog to live and work with her older sister, a young widow who needed to find work to support herself. Whenever their mother, who remained in the Beauce, fell ill, the two sisters took leave from the mill and returned home to render assistance.

It was parents who decided when their daughters would enter the mill. When "Ursule" went to work at the Montreal Cotton Company in 1915 at the age of twelve, she did so because she was one of six children, and as she explained, "I had to help my father." "Philomène" recalled starting wage labour in 1918 when she turned fourteen—"I was the oldest, I had to work. My father asked for me. He was a foreman at the Gault plant [in Valleyfield]. Mother had fifteen children. Being the eldest, I had to sacrifice my education to go to work."

In light of the early age at which they became wage earners, most women cotton workers received only a rudimentary formal education. All of the Valleyfield and Magog women interviewed who were born between 1895 and 1904 had left school by the age of fourteen. Several had fewer than five years of formal education. Moreover, each school "year" often represented less than six months of actual school attendance. Rachel, for example, started school when she was nearly seven years old and attended for only five or six months each year until she was about ten. Formal education for "Agathe" also ended abruptly at the age of ten when she was kept home to help her mother. Similar circumstances accounted for Marie-Berthe quitting school when she was only nine, for, as she explained, "My mother was ill and I was the oldest."

The Division of Labour in the Mill

The initial assignments given to inexperienced women and girls required little skill. Doffing (removing full spools from frames and replacing them with empty ones), stripping bobbins, threading shuttles, or removing cotton waste from machines were tasks frequently assigned to novices. As the worker became familiar with the machinery and the manufacturing process, an experienced hand would instruct her so that she could then assume responsibility for running her own set of drawing or spinning frames, looms, or other machinery. Girls and women were employed principally in the carding, spinning, spooling, drawing-in, weaving, inspection, and sample rooms.

Men and boys were employed exclusively in the heavy and dirty work of opening the raw cotton bales and operating the picking machines that removed impurities and formed the fibres into rolls (laps). In the carding room, the laps were separated into individual strands and any remaining impurities were removed. Many individual fibres were then placed in parallel formation to form a long cord about three-quarters of an inch in diameter. This cord (sliver) in turn was fed through a drawing frame in order to stretch it and make it as even as possible. According to testimony presented to the 1908 royal commission investigating the cotton industry, the carding division of the Hochelaga mill employed many young girls and boys, and about half of them were considered skilled workers.

In the spinning department, the coarse cotton, or roving, was twisted onto spindles to produce a finer, stronger, and more uniform thread. It was then subjected to repeated windings and twistings, the number and degree varying according to the desired type of yarn. In Quebec, when the spinning mule was the prevalent type of spinning device, the spinners were men. The enormous size and complexity of the machine, and the danger its moving carriage presented to women wearing long skirts, were reasons frequently given for the absence of women mule spinners. Patriarchy, however, also played a significant role in the exclusion of women from this type of work. The mule spinner could only accomplish his task with the assistance of at least one apprentice who performed the dangerous work of piecing together broken threads while the carriage was in motion. Since the mule spinner was paid on a piece-rate basis, it was clearly in his interest to obtain the maximum output from his apprentice, a result frequently achieved through an extensive use of verbal and physical intimidation. This custom of harsh discipline served to disqualify women from mule spinning since it was considered inappropriate for women workers to wield authority over men or discipline them, whatever their age. In addition, mule spinners were among the most skilled workers in the industry, and they used that status and their craft unions to keep women out of their ranks.

In the last quarter of the nineteenth century, however, the mule spinners' control over the spinning operation was increasingly undermined by the rapid expansion of ring spinning. From the manufacturer's perspective, the ring-spinning frame offered many advantages over the mule. A very simple drawing-and-twisting device that took up less floor space, it required little physical exertion to operate and could turn out approximately one-third more yarn per operator. Broken ends could be more easily repaired although, according to one analysis, thirty-two separate hand movements were still involved in mending such breaks. The principal qualification for the ring spinner was manual dexterity, and women were considered naturally endowed for this type of work. Consequently, from its inception, ring spinning was a female occupational preserve.

By 1905, there were 17.9 million ring spindles in American cotton mills, compared to only 5.2 million mule spindles. The replacement of mule spinning by ring spinning proceeded rather more slowly in Canada than in the United States. Like their British counterparts, Canadian manufacturers preferred the finer cloth achieved by the mule-spinning process. This was the reason why Wabasso initially used only mule-spinning devices in its operations. The early ring spindles produced yarn that was coarser, had more twist, and was better suited for warp thread than for weft or filling yarn. As a result of continued technical improvements, however, by the 1920s it was possible to produce finer counts of cotton yarn on ring spindles. Mule spinning was rendered obsolete, and its skilled practitioners disappeared from the mills.

Once it was spun, the cotton yarn used for weft thread was ready for weaving. Warp thread, running the entire length of the piece of cloth, required additional treatment so that it could withstand the friction of the shuttle moving back and forth during the

Mule Spinning in an English Cotton Mill, 1835
As this image shows, adult men, women, and boys were employed in mule spinning sheds in the early years of the British cotton industry. Note the boy piecing together broken threads below the mule device operated by the woman. One of the main reasons that women disappeared from mule spinning rooms by the latter half of the nineteenth century was the widespread belief that men, not women, should control young boys. That control included the administration of corporal punishment to ensure maximum production. Illustration from Edward Baines, *History of the Cotton Manufacture in Great Britain* (London, 1835).

weaving process. The three main components to this treatment were spooling, warping, and slashing. Spooling involved joining the thread from several bobbins to form a single, continuous thread, and required considerable speed and concentration on the part of the machine operator. According to a description published in the *Canadian Textile Journal* in July 1922, "the spooler—usually a girl or woman—must be alert and active, and especially nimble fingered." Yarn from several spools was subsequently placed on a large wooden roller called a warper's beam, and warper-tenders were also usually women.

The next phase in the preparation of the warp thread was slashing, the addition of sizing to the yarn to strengthen it. Slashers were usually men since it took considerable physical strength to install a set of warper's beams in the slashing machine. Moreover, the slasher's job was considered a skilled position due to the expertise needed to determine the appropriate quantity of sizing to be added. In the early years of the industry, this work was also very unpleasant since temperatures in the slashing room exceeded 100°F (38°C), and the stench of sour starch was constant.

After the warp threads had been sized, each had to be drawn through the loom harness to produce a sheath through which the shuttle could travel. This tedious and delicate work was performed by "drawing-in girls" who considered themselves to be an elite group of women workers, enjoying the safest and cleanest of working conditions in the mill. When the drawing-in was complete, the warp was installed on the loom.

In both Europe and North America, when cloth was domestically produced, weaving had often been a man's job, but with the introduction of the power loom and the transfer of weaving to the factory, women also found employment in the weave rooms. Technological innovations in the latter part of the nineteenth century, such as the introduction of the automatic loom and the electric stop, further facilitated the assignment of weaving to women. The Northrop Loom, available in North America after 1894, featured a bobbin-changing device that provided for the automatic transfer of bobbins to a loom shuttle that in turn was threaded automatically. There was also a warp stop-motion to keep the loom from producing inferior quality cloth. No longer was it necessary to stop the loom approximately every eight minutes to replace the shuttle when the bobbin became empty. Automatic threading devices also eliminated one of the major occupational hazards for weavers, "the kiss of death," the act of sucking the thread through the shuttle some five hundred to a thousand times per day. With each threading the operative inhaled cotton fibres, dust, sizing, and dyestuffs, and, not surprisingly, had a high risk of contracting fatal respiratory diseases.

The automatic loom netted manufacturers substantial labour savings. In the past a weaver had six to eight power looms to operate, but with the automatic loom, the same person could be expected to mind up to thirty machines. With the improved machinery, many traits associated with women were now considered desirable assets for the competent weaver. They included nimble fingers, slender hands, and the ability to concentrate on the minutest of details. However, not even the most experienced and gifted woman weaver was considered a potential candidate for the position of loom fixer. That job required mechanical ability, a trait pervasively regarded as "masculine." Since weavers were paid by the "cut" or the yardage of cloth they produced, the loom fixer directly affected the level of earnings of the weavers by his willingness, speed, and ability to repair their looms. As a result, he exercised a considerable degree of control over the work process in the weave room, a power deemed inappropriate for women to wield.

Ultimately the installation of automatic looms also led to a fragmentation of the weaver's work and the creation of a number of less skilled tasks, mostly performed by young women. Battery hands, for example, loaded full bobbins into the bobbin-changing device while doffers removed the finished cloth from the loom, and cleaners kept the loom free of dust and debris. In this way, new low-paid jobs for women and girls were created, and it was possible to substantially increase the output of each weaver.

The final stage in grey-cloth production was inspection. Each cut of cloth was carefully examined for flaws and graded according to its quality. Cloth inspectors were usually women, since the work was clean, light, and monotonous. The chief requirements for a cloth inspector were excellent eyesight, unlimited patience, and the endurance needed to stand on one's feet for over ten hours per day. Women repaired defects, folded the cloth, and packed it for shipment. By contrast, the finishing processes of bleaching, dyeing, and printing employed mostly men since the tasks involved in these operations were considered skilled.

Skill levels, gender, and ethnicity were inextricably linked. French-Canadian mill workers, of whom a significant proportion were women, worked at tasks that were considered unskilled, or at best semi-skilled, in the production of grey cotton cloth. The most highly skilled workers in the mills in both Valleyfield and Magog were the male loom fixers and mechanics, including many of English birth who had started working as lads in the Lancashire and Yorkshire mills. All of the managers, from boss foremen to mill superintendent, were English, while most of the assistant foremen (second hands) were French Canadians since they had to interact directly with the workers on the factory floor. In Magog, the ethnic division of labour was site-specific as well. The vast majority of French-Canadian women and girls toiled in the mill while most English women worked at jobs considered cleaner and more highly skilled in the print works across the street, although a few did work in the mill's carding and weaving rooms.

War Work

If family employment and a clear division of labour continued to be hallmarks of Quebec's cotton industry, so too was its volatility. The prosperity initially enjoyed after the establishment of the trust in 1905 was relatively short-lived. From 1913 to 1915, a serious nationwide economic recession crippled the industry and caused many girls and women to lose their jobs. Reporting on industries in the Eastern Townships in the summer of 1914, Factory Inspector R. H. Gooley noted that companies in his district were experiencing depressed conditions and were laying off employees in a "humane" way by letting go the unmarried and keeping on the heads of families. Needless to say, this practice meant that girls, boys, and women were the first to go.

Even the outbreak of war did not initially lead to significant increases in production and employment. As the *Canadian Textile Journal* noted in January 1915, "war contracts are not operating so heavy as in the case of other branches..." By 1916, however, sales soared as the fighting in Europe intensified and the Allied armies consumed millions of yards of khaki, canvas, and surgical dressings. The wartime demand for textiles permitted the cotton companies to reap impressive profits and achieve unprecedented annual surpluses. The 1916 fiscal report released by the Montreal Cotton Company stated unequivocally that business "was exceptional." The following year a fire destroyed the company's electrical plant and adversely affected production for at least the first quarter of 1918. Still, that year "a good" surplus of over $350,000 was produced. Dominion Textile similarly declared a surplus of over $350,000 in 1917 after all costs related to mill charges, repairs and improvements, dividend payments, and a reserve for war taxes were taken into account. The following year, the surplus was $745,000, although that amount would be subject to the newly created war-profits tax. One of the biggest wartime contracts came from the American government in 1918 as it sought to outfit its soldiers quickly following its late entry into the war.

While mill managers could draw satisfaction from the impressive gains in the industry after 1915, they had to contend with acute labour shortages. They attempted to resolve this problem by introducing into their mills the most advanced automatic machinery available and by recruiting yet more women. In fact, verbal testimony indicates that the number of women workers significantly increased as the war dragged on. As "Florida" recalled, "At that time [1916], it was easy to get a job because people left for the war." The companies encouraged young women to apply to offset the loss of men who had either been recruited into the armed forces or lured away to more highly paid war work. The same year that Florida entered the Magog mill, the editor of the *Canadian Textile Journal* penned a glowing tribute to "the great army of women" employed in the textile industry:

> Canada is fortunate . . . in possessing the most superior type of womanhood in the world. Today, thousands of these noble women have responded to the call of duty; not by taking their place on the firing line, but by entering the workshop. . . . They have thoroughly demonstrated their capabilities during the past months. Make the workroom healthy, both physically and morally. Elevate the character of the job and the textile mills of the Dominion would not lack intelligent workers.

Amélie Lemieux, one of the provincial women factory inspectors at the time, also paid homage to women for doing their part during the war "to elevate and relieve the masses" by taking on various forms of employment, including "in the factory where we meet them occupied with depressing tasks. The real woman, putting aside the impracticable theories of the zealots of the woman's movement, is currently astounding the entire world by her spirit of sacrifice and her devotion."

A bilingual recruiting pamphlet issued in 1917 by Dominion Textile's Magog branch indicated that the 575 girls and women there accounted for 47 percent of its workers. The total number of workers included the employees of the print works and the mechanical department, nearly all of whom were men. If the figures had been provided separately for the cotton mill, women would certainly have formed the majority of workers in that locale. In fact, women working in the Valleyfield and Magog mills at that time reported that, overall, women workers outnumbered the men. A feature of special interest for married women with children noted in the pamphlet was the existence of a childcare centre. Operated by a women's religious order, it could accommodate up to two hundred young children. According to "Hortense," it was the priest of Saint Patrick's parish, Curé Milaire, who arranged for a French order, the Sisters of the Holy Cross, to staff the daycare. Her testimony and that of other Magog women interviewed indicate that this was the same childcare facility that Inspector Gooley had singled out for praise in his 1910 report.

In its wartime promotional materials, Dominion Textile announced that it was looking for a hundred families to provide the labour it required, and pointed out the many advantages a family could reap by moving to Magog. They included attractive rents, excellent school facilities, inexpensive electrical lighting, and the possibility of purchasing basic staples such as potatoes, beans, and cordwood from the company's farm at cheap rates. In addition, the company boasted that it occasionally supplied its employees with coal, flour, and other goods at cost, thereby helping them to avoid the crippling inflation of the wartime period. In cases where transportation costs associated with moving to Magog might be a problem, the company also offered to help with travel arrangements. But above all, what Dominion Textile emphasized was the prospect of steady employment: "A man can always get work at good wages in Magog, and there are also places open for the other members of his family who are able to work. In this way, the family is able to obtain a large weekly income." It was promises such as these that led the parents of "Clementine" to leave Wotton, located between Victoriaville and Sherbrooke, for Magog near the end of the war. The need for mill hands was so great that, when her family arrived in the town on August 15 around 11 a.m., her three older sisters were told to report to work by 1 p.m. Since the truck with their clothing and other possessions had not yet arrived, their mother prevailed upon the company representative to let them start the next day instead.

Without access to records detailing the ratios of women to men in individual work areas, it is impossible to assess the extent to which the war actually caused a shift in the division of labour. Certainly none of the women interviewed indicated that work normally performed by men was significantly reallocated to women. Despite the increased need for women on the factory floor, the majority of the jobs they performed continued to be those usually assigned to women, such as doffing, twisting, spinning, drawing-in, weaving, and inspecting.

By 1918, Dominion Textile was a Canadian manufacturing enterprise of the first order, with several facilities employing approximately seven thousand hands in 1918. Its output, along with that of Montreal Cottons and Wabasso, ensured that Quebec was the foremost producer of cotton goods in Canada. Much of this success was directly attributable to women's work.

CHAPTER TWO

MILL LIFE

"The old work tool, over which the worker was the absolute master, has nearly disappeared today, given way to powerful machines, for which the worker is no longer more than a cog, a living part." So wrote the chief factory inspector of Quebec, Louis Guyon, in his 1893 report. Factory inspectors' reports, workers' testimony at royal commission hearings, and newspaper articles all indicate that cotton factories were difficult and dangerous places in which to earn one's living. Long hours of toil, low levels of pay, strict discipline, and multiple workplace hazards were central themes in descriptions of mill life detailed in these sources.

The textile trade journals and company executives, on the other hand, portrayed the work environment in an entirely different manner. They stressed that cotton factories, constructed according to the latest industrial architectural standards, featured high ceilings with many large windows allowing light to stream into modern workrooms. Strategically located near hydraulic power sites, the mills were among the first to utilize electricity to power their machinery and to illuminate their facilities. Industry promoters described much of the work as light and therefore easy for adolescents and women to perform. The fact that the industry offered employment to entire families, company representatives claimed, allowed working-class families to enjoy a better standard of living than those dependent on a single breadwinning man labouring in other industrial sectors. In addition, several of the cotton manufacturers boasted that they provided their workers with comfortable housing, numerous recreational opportunities, modern educational facilities, and even inexpensive foodstuffs from company farms. In the face of these starkly contrasting views, what can we conclude about working conditions in the cotton cloth industry, and to what extent had conditions improved by 1920?

Child Labour

Given cotton manufacturers' roles as industrial pioneers, major economic drivers in several communities, and employers of thousands of workers, the working conditions they offered were of significant interest to government officials and social reformers. Following the lead of Ontario, which passed its first factory act in 1884, the Quebec government introduced legislation the following year to set some limits regarding the employment of children and women in industrial establishments. The 1885 Manufacturers' Act covering factories with more than twenty workers prohibited the employment of girls under the age of fourteen and boys under twelve. However, girls between the ages of twelve and fourteen might still be hired, provided their parents or guardians produced a certificate attesting to the child's age and birthplace. It took three years before an inspection system was put in place to ensure that the law was being respected. Despite this legislation, ample testimony before the Royal Commission on the Relations of Labor and Capital (1887-89) bore witness to the widespread use of underage children for up to twelve hours per day in various Canadian industries, including the Quebec cotton industry.

In 1894, the Quebec government passed a new law, the Industrial Establishments Act, to replace the 1885 legislation. As the name change suggests, this act extended beyond manufacturing to include all industrial sectors, with the exception of mining and family workshops. Another change occurred in 1896 when the government appointed two women factory inspectors to visit manufacturing facilities employing significant numbers of girls and women. Louisa King was given responsibility for the western

Raoul Julien, Mule-Spinning Room in Chace Cotton Mill,
Burlington, Vermont, 1909

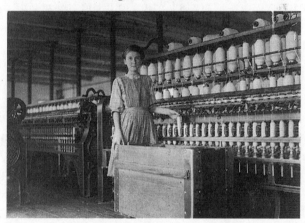

Adrienne Pagnette, Ring-Spinning Room in Glenallen Mill,
Winchedon, Massachusetts, 1909

These photos and scores of others taken by noted photographer, Lewis
Hine, document the widespread use of child labour in American cotton
mills. Many of the children were French Canadian, such as the two shown
here. According to Hine's captions, Raoul had been a "back-roping boy" for
two years, while Adrienne, described as "an adolescent French illiterate,"
was probably fourteen or fifteen years old. As many as ten of the seventeen
members of the Pagnette family worked in the same mill. Hine also noted
on her photo "stooping, reaching and pushing heavy boxes is bad for young
girls." (Library of Congress, Prints & Photographs Online Catalog,
National Child Labor Committee Collection, 01727 and 02315.)

area of Montreal while her counterpart, Louise Provencher, over-saw the eastern district of the city. However, the age provisions for starting employment went unchanged. It was only in 1903 that the minimum age for boys was raised to thirteen and then, in 1907, to fourteen while the minimum age for girls remained fourteen years. In 1906, the provincial government finally appointed a third woman factory inspector, Mademoiselle de Guise. She was based in Quebec City and carried out inspections in that city and sur-rounding areas.

Even with enhanced legislation on the books, a factory inspec-tion system in place, and growing pressure from social reformers for the eradication of child labour, the employment of underage children in Quebec's cotton industry remained a significant issue. Factory inspectors' reports throughout the 1890s continued to decry the presence of young children in the province's mills, although they also noted that the numbers of child workers were closely related to the state of industry. When economic downturns occurred, employers had less incentive to hire young workers, however low their wages.

Inspectors were more likely to blame parents who issued false certificates, rather than employers, for the continuing child labour problem. Louise Provencher, expressing concern in 1897 about the dangers that working alongside adults posed to children's morality, provided a typical explanation of the roots of the problem:

> Not that the majority of masters for the most part are to blame. . . .
> They do not covet these young employees, who, in most cases, boys and girls, are forced on them, by parents who abuse their authority and make their children work to exonerate themselves from all labor. . . .True, some families are in such great distress that it is bet-ter that the children should work than that they should pass their days on the street, the smallest school contribution being beyond the means of their parents, who moreover state that they are unable to clothe them properly.

It was, of course, the prevalence of the family wage model and the unrelenting struggle for working class families to ensure their survival that compelled most parents to send their underage children into the factories. Some government officials, including Chief Inspector Guyon, did recognize the strong link between parental poverty and child labour. In addition to expressing concern about the physical toll that factory work exacted on young, developing bodies, he and other inspectors consistently called for provincial legislation requiring children to attend school until the age of fourteen or to prove that they could read and write if they entered employment before this age. In his own 1902 testing of sixty-five young women factory workers between the ages of fourteen and sixteen, Guyon found that 20 percent were completely illiterate while another 28 percent could read but not write.

Beginning in 1907, the government did require factory inspectors to administer a literacy test to workers under sixteen. Children who could not read or write were supposed to attend evening classes if they wished to retain their jobs. The testing itself was of a very rudimentary nature, limited to having the young person sign her or his name and address and read from a card. Inspector P. J. Jobin reported in 1908 that he encountered more underage children than ever following the previous year's legislative amendments. In his opinion, the problem was fathers who were too lazy to earn a living, and the solution was to sentence those fathers to forced labour in a prison setting. He acknowledged that such action might be considered extreme, but it was "far from the brutality shown by heartless parents guilty of condemning little persons to work when they should be in school, of condemning them to become infirm, invalid, or degenerate, of condemning them to ignorance now and in the future."

Evidence presented in 1908 before William Lyon Mackenzie King's royal commission examining industrial disputes in Quebec's cotton factories reveals that Montreal Cotton Company employees who were under sixteen were being tested to determine their reading and writing skills. Lists compiled by the company one year earlier indicate the names and ages of the employees tested, the dates of the tests, the departments where the employees worked, and whether they could read and write. All together, there were 220 workers between the ages of thirteen and sixteen on the list, of whom two-thirds were boys and one-third were girls.

Among the boys, 14 percent were under fourteen, while 12 percent of the girls had not yet reached their fourteenth birthday. The latter number clearly indicates the continued presence of young girls in cotton mills, even after the law required them to be at least fourteen years old. While the lists contained some English as well as French names, most were French.

The proportion of boys and girls who could both read and write was very similar—76 percent of the boys and 74 percent of the girls. The illiteracy rate for the boys was slightly higher, with 17 percent described as being unable to either read or write, compared to 14 percent of the girls. The remainder could read or write, but not do both. Some individuals had the designation "night school" entered across from their names. It is not clear, however, if this notation meant that they were already attending night school or had been identified as needing such additional education. A significantly higher proportion of the boys unable to read and write received the "night school" designation (74 percent), compared to the percentage of illiterate girls (63 percent). This difference may well reflect the conventional wisdom of the time that it was more important for boys to acquire literacy skills to enhance their work opportunities, while girls were expected to marry at a young age and leave the workforce. The night school requirement was difficult for inspectors to implement since many communities did not have any night schools, while others had schools only for boys, not for girls. Whatever their gender, there was little reason to believe that sending them to night school would be very helpful. Inspector James Mitchell noted in his 1908 report, "I am not sure that it will be a boon to the illiterate who must attend night school after working between ten and eleven hours in a cotton mill. This is almost perhaps beyond the physical endurance of a child of fourteen years."

Despite the rudimentary nature of the required testing, it took at least eight days to administer the test to young cotton workers just in the Montreal district during the 1912-13 inspection year. "How do you suppose," Guyon wrote four years later, "that, in the middle of the deafening noise of a cotton factory, an inspector might make a child, already greatly intimidated by the presence of the boss, the inspector, and his co-workers, read and write?" He and his fellow inspectors called on the government to transfer responsibility for determining literacy levels to the schools by making it a requirement for workers under the age of sixteen to obtain a certificate from their local schools attesting that they could both read and write. They also lobbied for compulsory schooling up to the age of fourteen. In a province where the Roman Catholic Church jealously guarded its control over the education system, the call for compulsory schooling would go unheeded until 1943.

Fifteen percent of all employees in Quebec's cotton mills in 1901 were under sixteen years of age, and that level was exactly the same ten years later. Factory inspectors regularly reported that they were sending home underage children. In a speech to an international conference of inspectors held in August 1904, Lomer Gouin, minister of colonization and public works, noted that the largest number of underage children was to be found in textile mills. In its various assemblies and in its communications to mill managers between 1906 and 1908, the Fédération des ouvriers textiles du Canada (FOTC; Federation of Canadian Textile Workers), the province's largest textile workers' union at the time, also made frequent reference to the issue.

Factory inspectors could require children working in factories to undergo a medical examination and, on the examining doctor's advice, could order the child's dismissal on the grounds of being underage or not sufficiently strong. Chief Inspector Guyon continuously researched how other jurisdictions were dealing with the issue of child labour. His 1907 report contained tables compiled in Scotland showing the deleterious effect of working ten hours a day in a jute mill for the physical development of children under fifteen. He argued that the French-Canadian families who were "swallowed up" in New England and Quebec textile mills were showing the same tendency toward an "alarming physical decline," a deterioration commonly noted in American mills by experts there. He personally favoured the prohibition of all children under fourteen from factory work.

In his 1909 report King also expressed concern over the number of underage children who were brought before his commission.

"Some of these children," he wrote, "were so immature and ignor-
ant that they were unable to tell the year of their birth, or their age.
One little girl did not know the meaning of the word 'holiday,' and
when it had been explained to her, stated that the only holidays she
had known were Christmas and Epiphany. She had never received
a week's vacation." Louis Simpson, the manager of the Valleyfield
mills, complained to King that it was parents who were to blame
for any underage children in his mills. He told of one company
blacksmith who had presented false certificates on behalf of two of
his daughters. Although the worker "pleaded as his excuse that he
was poor," Simpson put him on notice as a warning to other workers. King appears to have accepted the explanation of mill managers
that they were personally opposed to the hiring of underage children, but were sometimes duped by selfish parents. In his final
report, he recommended that no child under fourteen be employed
and that legislation be enacted requiring children between the ages
of ten and fourteen to attend school.

By this time, the consequences for issuing a false declaration
regarding a child's age could include a fine of up to $100 and costs,
or a prison sentence of not more than six months, if the convicted
felon could not pay the fine. These conditions were printed on the
reverse side of the age certificate that the parent or guardian
signed. Nonetheless, parents continued to issue false declarations
and, if they were brought before a magistrate, were usually given
only a small fine. For this reason, Quebec's chief inspector called
on the government to require an official certificate supplied either
from church baptismal records or from the province's birth regis-
try. An amendment to the 1907 legislation that gave factory
inspectors the right to demand an official birth certificate cut
down appreciably on the number of false declarations provided
by parents regarding the ages of their children. Still it was possible to provide an underage child with the birth certificate of an
older sibling. By taking this route, Agathe was hired to work in the
sample room of the Magog print works in 1909 when she was only
twelve.

While most inspectors reported that they sent home any underage workers they found during their factory visits, some urged the

minister of labour to grant them greater discretion in applying the law. It was particularly hard to insist on the dismissal of youngsters whose mothers were widows or whose families were in crisis. In 1910, the inspector for the Eastern Townships cited the case of two widows who did not have the financial resources to keep their underage children in school and who pleaded with him to give permission for them to continue to work. Like the mothers, he felt the children were better off in the factory than roaming the streets unsupervised, but the law dictated that he send them home.

Louisa King also reflected on the difficult decisions she had to make: "I feel almost guilty for having taken bread from orphans because two or three dollars a week is a lot in a poor household. . . . It is nearly impossible for working class parents to raise their children properly and to save enough to ensure the well-being of the family in case of a father's death." Clémentine Clément described in her 1911 report how she reluctantly required the dismissal of a young boy whose mother had died and whose father was in the hospital. The boy was the only provider for himself and his younger brother. Another major problem for the inspectors was that there were thousands of children working for wages who fell outside the provincial legislation setting minimum ages for employment. They could be found hawking newspapers, shining shoes, acting as messengers, or working in small sweatshops and grocery stores. When the inspectors had underage workers fired from the manufacturing establishments, they knew that many of them would end up working under worse conditions.

Given the acute labour shortages and the sharply increased cost of living that occurred during World War I, it is not surprising that the provincial minister of public works and labour, Louis-Alexandre Taschereau, reported increases in child labour in Quebec factories during the latter stages of the war. His conclusion was based on numerous factory-inspector reports to this effect. The scarcity of workers led employers to ease their scrutiny of the proof-of-age certificates young workers provided, while inflationary pressures on family budgets prompted parents to send their children out to work, especially as wages increased.

Cotton factories, according to Inspector Alfred Robert, merited "continual surveillance" due to the large number of children they employed. His own solution upon finding underage children in poor health or performing tasks beyond their physical capacities was to require the employer to transfer them to lighter work. In this way, he attempted to protect them and the families who relied on their wages to make ends meet.

Interviews conducted with eight women from Magog and Valleyfield who began working during the war reveal that seven of them were fourteen years old or younger when they entered the mills. Three were actually under the legal age limit. "Ursule" was only twelve when she began working as a piecer in a Valleyfield spinning room in 1915. Hortense, whose family lived in Magog, entered the mill there in 1915, about six months after her thirteenth birthday. One year later, "Gabrielle" was hired as a battery hand in Magog at the age of thirteen. All three gave economic necessity as the reason for beginning employment before they had reached the legal age. According to Hortense, it was around 1918, following an accident involving an underage worker, that the Magog mill authorities began to insist that adolescent employees produce baptismal certificates to verify their ages. Nevertheless, a significant number of underage girls continued to find employment in the industry, as working class families sought to offset inflationary food and housing costs during the war and its aftermath by increasing household income.

Hours

According to the 1885 legislation, the length of the normal workday for children, adolescent girls, and women in workplaces with over twenty employees was not to exceed ten hours, nor was the workweek to consist of more than sixty hours. Employers had to provide the same classes of workers a one-hour break for their midday meal, but it was not counted in the ten-hour total. No such legal requirements applied to the number of hours male teenagers might work or the length of their meal break until 1909. Then it became illegal for industrial employers to employ boys under eighteen for more than sixty hours per week. Any such limitations on adult men's working hours were considered an unnecessary interference with the rights of both capital and labour. Only the weak—those under the age of eighteen and women—were considered deserving of a paternalistic state's intervention.

Employers were permitted to rearrange weekly hours of work in order to provide a half-day holiday on Saturday. This option became standard in the textile industry, but in order to earn this half-day of rest, employees had to work eleven hours each day from Monday to Friday. In some instances, their midday break was also reduced to a mere half hour. Several of the factory inspectors expressed their opposition to this provision in the law, considering its effects particularly deleterious for women and children. As Louisa King wrote in 1907, "To get to work at 6:30 in the morning means rising at 5 for those who reside at a distance from it: it means a long walk at an hour when the cold is more intense in winter, it means an interval of six or seven hours between a hasty breakfast and a cold dinner, but above all it means a long, frequently arduous workday—a day too long for women and growing children." Chief Inspector Guyon had summarized their criticisms a year earlier by calling for a major change to existing practices that allowed managers to begin operations as early as six o'clock in the morning and to prolong them beyond six o'clock at night.

Not surprisingly, mill managers did not share these concerns. Appearing before Mackenzie King's commission in 1908, Louis Simpson claimed that sixty hours of work was not too much for children and women, especially in a factory such as his, since it had excellent hygienic conditions. What was more astonishing was the admission by the superintendent of the Hochelaga and Saint Anne mills that, although he had worked for Dominion Textile for thirty-five years, he was not familiar with the provincial law that regulated hours of work. Since he personally worked from 6:15 a.m. until 6 p.m. and suffered no ill effects, he could not conceive how his employees could be adversely affected by working similar hours. Despite the factory inspectors' repeated urgings for change, it was only in 1911 that provincial legislation began to

Workers Leaving Wabasso Mill, circa 1914
Workers stream out of the Wabasso Mill in Trois-Rivières, either at lunch
hour or at the end of their long shift. The number of young women,
walking in groups, is noticeable. They seem to have heeded the frequent
admonitions of the factory inspectors to wear their hair up to avoid
entanglement in the mill machinery. (McCord Museum,
M2011.64.2.2.197.1.)

require cotton- and woollen-textile manufacturers to restrict the
workweek for women and children to fifty-eight hours. Two years
later, the normal workweek was reduced to fifty-five hours for the
same groups of workers, with a compulsory half-day holiday on
Saturday. Commenting on the shortened workweek in 1914, Louis
Guyon explained that the government had "wished to relieve the
very arduous work of employees in one of the most depressing
industries, work that taxed to a very high degree the strength of
young employees."

Even after these reductions were put into effect, as provided
by the original 1885 law, manufacturers could continue to seek an

extension of the workweek for children, adolescent girls, and women to as many as seventy-two hours, for up to six weeks in a given year. The adjusted workday, however, could not begin earlier than 6 a.m. or extend past 9 p.m. This legislative provision enabled employers to make up for production time lost as a result of mechanical problems or to fill orders for their goods during times of high demand. Requests for longer workweeks were not uncommon among textile companies whose machinery was frequently damaged by spring floods and whose orders for goods fluctuated significantly according to seasonal demand.

To secure the necessary overtime permits, manufacturers had to petition the local factory inspector, who had the sole responsibility for either granting or denying the request. It is obvious from the remarks of some of the inspectors that they did not automatically grant such requests, but rather sought to weigh the economic arguments of the companies against the welfare of workers who were already working extremely long hours. James Mitchell, the inspector for the eastern district of the city of Montreal and fifteen counties to the south, was in part guided by the weather in making his determination, refusing to grant special permits when it became hot. "Ten hours of labour a day," he explained in 1902, "is quite long enough for anyone who works in a mill, but especially during the summer months, when fresh air is indispensable for the preservation of health, the restoration of physical strength or the mental faculties." It is equally obvious that other inspectors were much more willing to grant extensions of the workweek, arguing that they had no choice but to approve the various requests because they met the requirements of the law.

The economic fortunes of the province can be roughly traced by the number of requests submitted for supplementary hours. When times were good, there was a dramatic increase as employers sought to take advantage of market conditions. Between July 1910 and June 1911, for example, nearly every cotton cloth manufacturer in the Quebec City inspection division obtained special permits covering the maximum number of weeks provided by the legislation. During the same period, R.H. Gooley issued an unprecedented number of permits (twenty-four), almost half of them to textile manufacturers in the Eastern Townships.

The practice of extending the workweek for children, young girls, and women increased in ensuing years, even as the length of the normal legislated workweek declined. As might be expected, the factory inspectors issued record numbers of extensions during the war years. Gooley, for example, granted seventy of the seventy-two requests submitted to him from July 1914 to June 1915. Most of these requests came from textile companies. In the following twelve-month period, he consented to all eighty-nine requests. Furthermore, he argued that the inspectors should have the authority to issue permits even if the workday went beyond 9:30 p.m., given the importance of filling war orders. It would appear that he did give permission for girls and women to work past the prescribed hour, since Hortense recalled working at night in Magog during the war. Employees responded by launching more protests against the use of overtime permits, but to little avail. As long as the petitioning company's circumstances accorded with those set out in the statute, most inspectors felt compelled to concur. In June 1918, moreover, the government modified its ban on night work for girls and women when it introduced legislation allowing the minister of labour to issue permits for the employment of women over eighteen on night shifts. However, this change was meant to apply only to munitions factories and only for the duration of the war.

Wages

The continued presence of children in the mills attests to the ongoing strategy of working class families making ends meet by having several family members actively engaged as wage earners. Wages varied substantially depending on the state of the industry, the length of the workweek, the nature of the work performed, and the age and gender of the worker. Weeks of short time routinely occurred during economic slumps, and entire mills were sometimes shut down for weeks or even months at a time. Such was the case at the Merchants mill in Montreal in 1884 when production ceased in July and only restarted in November. For part of the previous year, managers of the Hudon mill had initially suspended all Saturday work and then ceased production for three additional days each week. On the other hand, when the industry was booming, cotton hands could work excessively long hours but received no premium for hours worked above those associated with the standard workweek.

There were significant wage differentials as well among those who nominally performed the same tasks, since skill levels and experience played an important role in determining the earnings of pieceworkers. Moreover, the individual worker's wages rose and fell according to the quality and count of yarn worked on. In 1904, for example, there were thirty-one piece rates for drawing-in at the Saint Anne mill, depending upon the type of cloth that was being prepared. Even the weather was a factor in determining wages. The foreman of the card room in Montreal Cotton's Empire Mill reported in 1907 that the wages of female workers under his supervision declined because increased humidity levels made it necessary to add more twist to the fibre strands. The workers' output was also adversely affected by the substitution of Sea Island cotton by Egyptian, for "the Sea Island cotton is combed, while the Egyptian is not and there is always more money in running combed work than in running carded work." For their part, the women and girls alleged that the company had changed the gearing so that their daily production would be lowered.

The fortnightly wages of certain categories of women workers, such as weavers, were also dependent upon how co-operative skilled men workers such as loom fixers were. Since weavers were paid by the cut, any disruption in their production due to mechanical problems was costly, and so it was important to have their looms repaired quickly. Some evidence shows that loom fixers abused their power in relation to women weavers. In one instance, the manager of the Montreal Cotton Company reported that he dismissed a loom fixer who had struck a woman because she wanted her loom repaired.

Another potentially significant factor in the determination of women workers' earnings was the system of fines overseers imposed for work they considered unsatisfactory. This form of punishment was applied to children and women, over whom foremen exercised great authority. Given the patriarchal social structure both outside and within the factory, it was definitely more acceptable for foremen to impose fines on women and children than on other adult men. The superintendent of the Hudon and Saint Anne mills reported to the Royal Commission on the Relations of Labor and Capital that nearly $3,000 had been collected in fines in 1887 and specifically provided an example of this system of punishment being applied to female workers. Foremen levied fines not only for faulty work and dropping material on the floor, but also for behavioural "offences" such as refusing to work overtime or engaging in conduct that vexed the overseer, such as talking or laughing. Fining was clearly a way of reinforcing male power and of moulding the behaviour of women and children. Ironically, fining lowered the wages of those workers least able to absorb a reduction.

Due to the complicated wage schedules, most employees were unable to either predict or to verify their weekly earnings. In an attempt to work his way through the byzantine wage structure, Mackenzie King required companies to submit detailed evidence to his commission regarding rates of pay. Subsequently, his staff produced a series of tables indicating average wages, but they are of limited use. In the first place, there is no way of knowing how representative the single two-week pay period chosen by the companies to calculate average weekly incomes actually was. Furthermore, the groupings of workers for which these average wages were calculated varied, and so exact comparisons are impossible to make. It is possible, however, to establish an overall hierarchy of wage rates and to document important general increases and decreases in wages.

While men and women sometimes performed the same work, for the most part the gendered division of labour in the mills resulted in men controlling the most highly paid positions. Men workers earning the highest wages included electricians, mule spinners, loom fixers, machinists, carpenters, and slasher tenders. Many of these positions, formally recognized as skilled, were paid on an hourly basis. The primary exception was the mule spinners, who were paid by the piece. Conversely, while increasingly women employees were paid on a piecework basis, some received hourly wages. In their case, it was the least skilled jobs, such as doffing and cleaning, which were paid on an hourly basis. Since boys and men were sometimes employed in these same positions, it is impossible to conclude that all men were highly paid hourly employees and all women, the lowest-paid, least-skilled workers. Nonetheless, no women held jobs that were considered highly skilled and paid on an hourly basis.

Most studies of women's industrial wages prior to World War I have indicated that, on average, they were half of those earned by men. The cotton textile industry provides an intriguing example of simultaneous equality and disparity for women with regard to wages. Several of the textile managers and employees interviewed were proud of the fact that, from the very beginning, the industry provided equal pay for equal work. To some extent this was true. Girls who doffed or cleaned were paid at the same rate as were boys, and women weavers were paid on the same basis as their male counterparts. Still, women were excluded from the most remunerative positions in the industry.

A detailed document submitted by Dominion Textile to Mackenzie King's royal commission provided a listing of the men and women employed in each department at its Merchants mill and of their average daily wage, after a wage reduction took effect in May 1908. What is striking is the degree of occupational seg-regation. Of the fifteen departments indicated, eight employed only men while another was composed almost exclusively of men. Women comprised over two-thirds of the workers in three work areas, and, in three others, the numbers of men and women were roughly equal. The latter included the slashing, weave, and cloth departments. Yet even within these three departments, jobs were clearly assigned on the basis of gender. In the slashing department, all the slasher tenders and harness cleaners were men while all the drawing-in workers were women. Similarly in the weave room, both women and men wove, but only men fixed the looms. All the trimmers in the cloth room were women but all the nappers were men.

Workers in the Magog Cloth Room
This photograph dates from the early days of the Magog Cotton and Print
Company and was likely taken in the 1880s. The workers are identified
as being among the first to be employed in the cloth room. Two thirds
of them are women. (Alexandre Paradis, *Commercial
and Industrial Story of Magog*, Que. (Magog, 1951).)

According to evidence submitted by the Montreal Cotton
Company, the average daily wage for a ten-hour day for mule spinners was $2.27. By comparison, the wage for female ring spinners
for the same number of hours was only 94 cents. Among women
employees, weavers earned the most with an average of $1.36 per
day. A comparison of average daily wages for Dominion Textile's
mule spinners, ring spinners, and weavers for seven pay periods
between September 1905 and January 1908 suggests that ring
spinners earned on average 47–61 percent of what mule spinners
earned, and weavers, 57–87 percent compared to the same male
occupation. Women ring spinners' and weavers' wages expressed
as a proportion of the mule spinners' average wage actually
declined during this time period. Between April 1906 and August
1907, nearly all cotton workers managed to win significant
increases in their wages. For their part, mule spinners were able

to use their strategic position within the production process and their unions to obtain a higher level of increase than was the case for most cotton workers.

These and other data clearly show that most women cotton workers in Quebec would have found it impossible to survive on their wages alone. After the wage increases of 1906-7, weavers were earning a daily wage in the range of $1.30–$1.70 while ring spinners brought in approximately $1.00 a day. For doffing, the work assigned to most women learners, the hourly rate was approximately 6 cents an hour. Interviewees who did this work before 1914 reported that their pay packets contained only between $6.00 and $7.00 every two weeks. As "Rachel" recalled, "To start with, we didn't have a very big salary. I know it took time to save up some money."

After the imposition of a general 10 percent wage cut across the industry in May 1908, it became even more difficult to make ends meet. Marie Blanchet, who worked as a weaver, reported to the royal commission that she made $17 per fortnight running six looms before the wage cut, but only $10 per fortnight after the reduction, even though she was now minding eight looms. Her drastic loss of earnings stemmed mainly from a reduction in weekly working hours that took effect at the same time as the wage cut, from sixty hours to forty hours. Another weaver, Albina Corbeil, testified that her fortnightly earnings fell from $18 to $9 although the number of hours per week remained constant at forty. Delima Viau, a sixteen-year-old girl employed in the card room at Montreal Cotton, said she earned only 40–50 cents a day after May 1908. This amount was well below the $1.50 per day named by another witness as "sufficient to live on very modestly." According to the list of average daily wages for the Merchants mill in Montreal after the May 1908 wage reduction, a list that clearly distinguishes men and women workers, no group of women employees earned as much as $1.50 per day. The closest were the women weavers and slubbers (card room operatives) at $1.20. Spinners earned $1.05, and spoolers, 90 cents. The lowest daily wages were earned by the doffers and back tenders in the card room, who were paid only 49 cents a day.

When questioned about the 10 percent general wage reduction and the effect it had on their employees, managers refused
to acknowledge any responsibility to pay a living wage. As
Dominion Textile's superintendent Taylor bluntly put it, it was
not his concern. What difference could it possibly make to him?
While admitting that the board of directors of the Montreal
Cotton Company had paid an 8 percent dividend on the company's stock in 1908 and that management salaries had been
maintained at their existing levels, Louis Simpson stated that
he had ordered the 10 percent cut due to the depressed state of
the cotton trade.

During World War I women workers' wages did improve somewhat as the labour shortage gave them and their co-workers
increased power. According to Dominion Textile records, wages
increased by 21 percent in 1917 alone. Still, wages for starting positions remained abysmally low. When she began as a doffer in
Magog in 1914, fourteen-year-old "Desneiges" earned only $6.30
for working 110 hours over the course of two weeks, an amount
equivalent to a daily wage of less than 60 cents. "Ursule," like
many of the other women interviewed, remembered the exact
amount of the first fortnightly pay she earned in 1915 in Valleyfield.
In her case it was $17.86 ($1.62 per day) for preparing warps. For
her part, Hortense recalled taking home approximately $18 every
two weeks ($1.64 per day) in 1917 for her work as a spinner with
more than two years of experience in the Magog mill. However,
by this time spinners were minding more frames, sometimes
working nights, and eating their meals at their machines. Longer
workdays and increased wage rates help explain the improved
earnings for women during the war years, but so too do machinery speed-ups and increased production quotas.

Even during wartime, when women were replacing men in
many work settings, women cotton workers were denied any
meaningful form of occupational mobility that would have netted
them significantly higher wages. For the women interviewed in
Valleyfield and Magog who began working prior to 1920, the
answer to the question of whether women ever got promoted was
quickly answered. Women did not get promotions because, as

Rachel succinctly stated, "They didn't exist. Promotions were more for the men."

Overall, the low wages paid to women operatives in the textile industry appear to have generated little public concern. Since the vast majority were young, single, and lived at home, they were considered secondary wage earners whose wages, however meagre, more than sufficed when added to those of other family members. Such thinking was of cold comfort to women who remained single, wives with unemployed husbands, or widows whose wages were crucial for their own survival and that of their families.

Workplace Safety

Cables, straps, pulleys, gears, flywheels, drive shafts, propeller shafts—these were the muscle and sinew of modern industry that permitted each worker to achieve unprecedented production levels. Overhead, huge drive belts strained as they turned wheels and pulleys connected to scores of smaller belts supplying power to individual machines. On the mill floor, thousands of exposed machine parts whirled away, capable of bruising, cutting, or crushing body parts, or even killing the hapless worker. Add to these dangers the dust, grime, heat, and noxious fumes that permeated most nineteenth-century factories, and one begins to form an image of the environment in which workers of all ages and both sexes spent the vast majority of their waking hours. Small wonder that Chief Inspector Guyon declared in 1908, "Modern industry is a veritable battle ground, with its dead and its wounded."

Judging by the accident reports factory inspectors submitted, cotton factories were particularly perilous establishments and provided more than their share of the gruesome annual litany of injuries befalling Quebec's industrial workers. For 1899-1900, for example, Inspector James Mitchell submitted a detailed list of seventy-six accidents that had occurred within his district. Forty percent of the accidents he noted occurred in cotton mills, although they represented only 1 percent of the industrial establishments he had visited. Given the size of the cotton factories and the large number of machines and workers located within them, it is not surprising that they were sites of a substantial number of accidents. It is also obvious that the cotton companies took the legal requirement to report all accidents, however minor in nature, to the government authorities more seriously than did smaller employers.

Girls and women appear to have been underrepresented among those injured, no doubt because they were less likely to operate the heavier, more dangerous machinery. Perhaps they were also more prudent than the men, whose manly pride and greater familiarity with machinery might have led them to take more risks in making adjustments while their machines were in motion. Nonetheless, women were routinely victims of serious mishaps, ranging from fingers and hands crushed in machinery, to cuts caused by straps that suddenly broke, and loss of eyesight produced by flying shuttles. Women cotton workers referenced in Louis Guyon's list of 147 industrial accidents occurring between July 1900 and May 1901 included Edeia Taillefer, age fifteen, who had a finger crushed after getting her right hand caught in the gearing of a spinning frame; Mary Thériault, age sixteen, who received a serious blow to the head from a pulley that broke; and Corinne Boucher, age twenty, who lost a finger while cleaning a machine in operation. Another Taillefer girl, age fourteen, suffered a lacerated finger from leaning on a machine.

It was no doubt incidents such as the latter two that led most inspectors to place the blame for accidents squarely on the victims themselves and, more particularly, on their lack of caution. In fact, they frequently used the word *imprudence* (carelessness) to describe the cause of an accident. In her 1900 report, Louise Provencher clearly stated her belief that the victims themselves played a part in their misfortune through their carelessness and insubordination, and claimed, "Very frequently the employer is far from being the more guilty." No consideration was given to the fact that the majority of workers were poorly paid pieceworkers who could ill afford to stop their machines to clean or adjust them.

The factory inspectors' attitude is hardly surprising since the provincial legislation pertaining to industrial establishments laid

Estelle Poiriere, Granite No. 1 Mill, Fall River, Massachusetts, 1915
Estelle was a fifteen-year old doffer whose hand was mangled in a card
machine. According to Lewis Hine's notes, she was still not working six
months after the accident. Children in Quebec's cotton mills regularly
suffered accidents that resulted in serious lacerations and broken bones.
(Library of Congress, Prints & Photographs Online Catalog, National
Child Labor Committee Collection, 03078.)

much of the responsibility for accident prevention on the workers,
rather than on the employers. Women inspectors frequently complained that girls and women working in factories ignored the legal
requirement that they wear their hair up. No doubt their concern
was motivated by terrible accidents such as that recorded in a cotton mill in Cornwall, Ontario in 1902. Nineteen-year-old Lily Steacy
had her entire scalp torn off when she bent down to pick up a scrap
of waste beside a machine in the carding department. Despite the
sanguine prediction of the official textile industry newspaper that
the young woman would recover, she died two months later, after a
series of operations to graft skin from other parts of her body.
Inspector King criticized "a sentiment of vanity natural to youth"
that led the young machine operators "to run the risk of being
scalped rather than appearing a little less pretty." She ordered that
the hair regulation be printed in large letters and prominently displayed as a constant reminder to the women workers. For her part,
Mrs. Provencher maintained that some young women gave up their

positions and sought work elsewhere, "rather than submit to a measure which was so clearly enforced in their own interest." Legislators, manufacturers, and bureaucrats were united in putting the onus for factory safety on the individual worker.

Manufacturers were nonetheless slowly being held more accountable for safety in their factories. In his 1899 report, Dr. C. N. Stevenson, inspector at that time for the Eastern Townships, urged the government to deal severely with manufacturers who persistently failed to provide protective devices for dangerous parts of their machinery. This admonition was undoubtedly greatly appreciated by Stevenson's superior, Guyon, who was leading his own campaign to obtain safer working conditions. One of his pet projects was the creation of a permanent exhibition of safety devices that were available to manufacturers. He took great pride in announcing in 1901 that, as a result of viewing this collection, the manager of one of the province's largest mills had promised to install protective devices on all carding machines and weave looms in his establishment. Similarly Guyon took credit two years later for the fact that a judge awarded $1,800 to a young woman who had lost an eye as a result of being hit by a flying shuttle in a cotton mill. According to him, it was the factory inspector's testimony about the availability of shuttle protectors that influenced the judge's decision, since previously there had been several court cases involving accidents with shuttles, but none had been successful.

It took more than educational exhibits and gentle persuasion, however, to get employers to take their responsibility for worker safety seriously. As the chief inspector was forced to admit in 1910, "Protected by an accident insurance company, many employers and most of the large corporations do not pay enough heed to the accidents that might happen [to] workmen. To the good traditions of law which require that an employer should treat his employee as a father, the manufacturer replies, 'I am not my brother's keeper....'" Thus it was with great pleasure that he noted the provincial government's passage of workers' compensation legislation in March 1909 that made employers more directly accountable for worker safety and provided some automatic compensation for injuries sustained. Prior to the enactment of this law, injured workers or their families had to pursue court cases, often lengthy and costly, in the fragile hope of establishing negligence on the part of the employer and entitlement to company compensation.

Some mill workers could access medical services through their workplaces. By 1906, the Montreal Cotton Company provided a form of medical insurance to its nearly three thousand employees, by exacting a fee of 10 cents each fortnight from employees who earned more than 75 cents a day, and 5 cents from those who earned less. These payments entitled the workers to consult doctors, retained by the company, at no cost. Not all workers were satisfied with this "benefit," however, since they were obliged to contribute to the scheme. They could not consult the physician of their choice, and the time available for consultation appears to have been very limited. The union newspaper, *Le Fileur,* reported in November 1906 that as many as one hundred workers would want to see a single company doctor on call between 7 and 9 p.m., and so the quality of the care was questionable.

While factory inspectors reported progress toward the creation of safer workplaces, especially in larger industrial establishments, the number of workplace accidents increased significantly during the war years. Officials attributed this upsurge to a number of factors including the intensification of production to meet war orders, the general labour shortage that resulted in the replacement of older, seasoned workers by younger, inexperienced ones, and overcrowding in workrooms. According to Inspector Gooley, the cotton mills in his Eastern Townships district were particularly affected by these trends. Many experienced girls left their mill jobs "to take others in the munitions industry where the lure of higher wages offset the certain knowledge that their new employment situation would not extend beyond the war."

If government officials were initially slow in laying the burden of responsibility for workers' safety on employers, they were quick to identify the moral dangers that working in industrial settings posed for girls and women. Certainly the moral state of working class women who toiled outside the home was of overriding concern to the commissioners appointed to the Royal Commission on the Relations of Labor and Capital in the late 1880s. However, both of the reports issued by the commission—one by the conservative, "paternalist" faction, the other by the pro-labour representatives—concluded that immorality in the factories was not a serious problem. According to the pro-labour report, the commissioners took special care to investigate morals in the cotton mills and judged "the moral character of the working women in Canada to be as high as that of other classes." To keep it that way, they recommended the provision of separate "conveniences" for female workers to reduce the potential for "scandal." The belief that the mingling of the sexes at the workplace and, more specifically, the lack of separate toilet facilities, posed a serious menace to women's morality would preoccupy middle class reformers for many years to come.

Commentary on the moral state of women mill workers sometimes took a curious form. In a startlingly sarcastic column published in July 1896, the editor of the Valleyfield newspaper, himself a textile worker's son, poked fun at mill manager Louis Simpson for publicly criticizing a male overseer for offensive language he had used with women employees in his charge. Simpson had characterized the foreman's behaviour as insulting to girls who, in his opinion, were "as virtuous as one could find in any religious community in any town in the entire country." The editor mockingly responded:

> In the future, if anyone speaks irreverently of our female citizens, we must say: "These young people are as virtuous as the pious girls one finds in the convents of the good Sisters of Providence or in the community of the Sisters of the Sacred Name of Jesus. The cloistered nuns of the Precious Blood [and] the Carmelites . . . are not more devout than they." Mr. Simpson, who has made a detailed study of these questions, has said this is the case, and no one has been found to contradict him.

Nowhere were concerns about the moral threat factory work posed to girls and women more clearly articulated than in the annual reports of the province's female factory inspectors. They shared the attitudes and priorities of officials in many other domestic and international jurisdictions. Louise Provencher certainly made physical and moral cleanliness the focus of her campaign for improved working conditions. In her 1900 report she provided a detailed summary of her concept of the ideal work environment:

> Workshops, for instance, in which the women are alone employed and under the control of a leading woman with all the authority of a foreman, but without abusing it as a man often does to the ruin of the young girls, factories, where the workwomen have a dressing room to take off and put on their outer garments in privacy, where the water closets are absolutely separated, isolated, and hidden away as prescribed by propriety and modesty, where they [female workers] have at their disposal pure, fresh drinking water, and where they have a clean and comfortable room to take their mid-day meal.

Provencher repeatedly expressed her conviction that the segregation of the sexes in the workplace was essential to protect women's morals. Not only should women have their own workrooms and work in silence under the supervision of female overseers, they should also have different starting and leaving times than male workers. The provision of separate toilets for women was not sufficient to satisfy her standards for, as she had complained in 1898, they were often placed "in a mixed workroom and without the slightest screen, or again, the key is hung up in a place where every person who takes it is inevitably viewed by the workmen." She longed for the passage of more explicitly worded legislation that would allow her to impose her own, more stringent interpretation as to what constituted separate toilet facilities for women.

This inspector's sense of propriety also led her to complain about the calendars and illustrations certain bosses hung in their premises that were of "questionable taste" and "forced one to lower one's eyes." The depth of her commitment to preserving the morals of young working class women extended beyond the confines of the factory, as she fretted openly in her 1904 report about how workers passed their time off the job. Citing the case of a "very young" worker she encountered on the tramway who was avidly reading Alphonse de Lamartine's 1836 romantic verse novel, *Jocelyne*, she worried that this young woman might pass along the book, a sure cause of "moral ruin," to her workmates, and mused on how employers might be prevailed upon to put an end to such behaviour.

Louisa King authored, in the same year, one of the most explicit statements of the women factory inspectors' patronizing attitudes toward the women workers who fell under their jurisdiction. "Like bounteous dew falling noiselessly on thirsty plants and revivifying them," she wrote, "like the sun's rays that spread joy and life wherever they shine, thus does the inspectress fulfil her mission. Quietly, without ostentation, she adds to the comfort and safety of the women under her charge." Yet interestingly, King had no qualms whatsoever about the moral state of her charges. On several occasions, she stated unequivocally that "young women are much less exposed [to moral corruption] in the factories than the public appears to believe." She nonetheless continued to share Provencher's commitment to obtaining separate water closets, different starting and finishing times for women and men workers, improved lighting of passages, and separate workrooms for women. Amélie Lemieux, the relatively new inspector for the Quebec area, when commenting on the moral state of the workingwomen in her jurisdiction on the eve of World War I, did so in a manner similar to that of King. "The work-woman in a factory," she wrote, "is not more exposed there than elsewhere. All that is needed is to watch her strictly and protect her by giving her the means of making herself respected."

The women factory inspectors' focus on protecting the morals of young women working in industrial settings has made them an easy target for criticism and even ridicule. While it is easy to decry their lack of attention to the low wages and to workplace dangers caused by employer indifference, it must also be recognized that the ideological and administrative structures within which they worked prevented them from being more proactive on these matters. Given the weak controls the Quebec government placed on employers, the difficulty of enforcing the loose regulations that did exist, and the ongoing, widespread public concern about women's morality, it would have been surprising for the overworked and poorly paid women inspectors to have effected wide-ranging reforms. Insight into their situation can be found in Louisa King's appeal to the minister of public works and labour that he increase the women inspectors' salaries to more accurately reflect their workloads and level of responsibility. In 1913, for example, King recorded 315 inspections and Clémentine Clément, Louise Provencher's successor, 350.

To their credit, the women inspectors consistently stressed the need for better ventilation and improved hygiene in workrooms in an age when tuberculosis was a major health threat. In several cases, they were able to obtain improvements in conditions that women workers brought to their attention. Furthermore, practical reasons prompted them to call for the replacement of foremen by women overseers in departments that were staffed predominantly by girls and women. While it is impossible to document the extent of sexual harassment during this early period, clearly it existed, but most men did not consider it a serious problem. A concrete example of both the problem and men's reaction to it was contained in *La Presse*'s coverage of the Magog hearings of the royal commission enquiry in August 1908. The reporter noted, "Mr. Paquette asked the witness [M. Champagne] if he wasn't driven from the factory because he mistreated an old maid in his department who refused to marry him. (General hilarity)."

But what of the women workers themselves? To what extent did they share the concerns and priorities of those who liked to cast themselves in the role of their advocates and protectors? Few references to workers' actual complaints can be found in the factory inspectors' reports. One exception was a list of grievances contained in Inspector Clémentine Clément's 1908 report that had been formulated by women workers at the Hochelaga mill. They included a claim that shuttle fillers were still being exposed to the "kiss of death" as a result of inhaling cotton fibres when they sucked the thread into the shuttle. Given that the automatic shuttle had been available since the mid-1890s and that Dominion Textile prided itself on its modern machinery, it is surprising that this major health issue continued to be a problem. Other complaints the Hochelaga workers registered included dirty toilets,

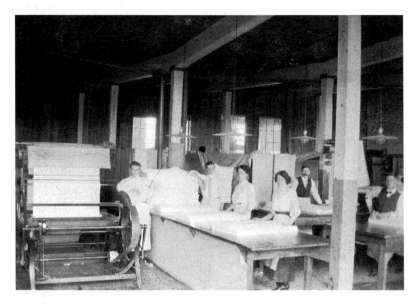

Wabasso Workers, Trois-Rivières, circa 1914. These workers appear to be employees of the folding room where the fabric was folded prior to packaging. (McCord Museum, M2011.64.2.2.173.2.)

smelly spittoons, and the provision of only one drinking cup for an entire department to use. In 1911, Inspector Clément was still raising the issue of bobbins used in the cotton industry that might cause consumption among the female workers. Overall, the inspectors interpreted the gradual increase in the number of complaints, particularly of signed ones, as an indication of a mounting confidence in them and their work.

During the war years, the only official recording of grievances specifically raised by female workers themselves occurred once again in Clément's reports. In her estimation, cotton workers were a "category of persons who particularly required her surveillance and protection," a judgment predicated on the "incessant number" of complaints she received. The workers' concerns focused mainly on the lack of ventilation, the high levels of humidity in the mills, and employers' increased use of overtime permits. Only by making repeated visits and several investigations, the inspector claimed, was she able to avert serious labour disruptions.

By contrast, Louisa King's wartime reports underlined the general satisfaction of the workers she visited, a situation she attributed to greatly improved wages and to the women's no-nonsense attitude in dealing with male co-workers who might wish to impugn their virtue. In her 1918-19 report based on more than 450 inspections, King enthusiastically affirmed:

> From the perspective of hygiene, the large factories of our city leave nothing to be desired. More than ever this year I have been struck by the healthy appearance and the good humour to be seen on the faces of the great majority of the female employees. To my often posed question, 'Do you have any complaints?' they nearly always reply 'Oh no! Madame' – 'So you are in a good mood?' – 'Oh yes! Madame, always' – and their smiling faces attest to the veracity of their words.

Women interviewed in Valleyfield and Magog who were working in the mills prior to 1919 expressed opinions about their working conditions that were much more akin to Clément's reports than King's. The heat and humidity introduced into the weave rooms to ensure the evenness of the weave were difficult to bear, particularly during the hot summer months. The only remedy attempted by the company—spraying ice water on the wooden floors when the temperatures soared—undoubtedly did little to alleviate the discomfort of the workers while creating yet another hazard in the form of slippery floors. Women who had been weavers stated that it was the deafening noise of the looms that was the most difficult to endure. Several described how they were able to communicate only by means of hand signals and how they eventually suffered hearing loss as a result of their work. Other complaints focused on the choking dust—*la wheeze*—created by the cotton waste that swirled through many parts of the mill. When "Léa" began to cough up blood due to irritation caused by the dust, her family doctor advised her to seek other employment.

The misuse of power by some foremen who chose to bestow favours on certain workers while punishing others was another common source of discontent. During this time period, the cotton mills had no human resources departments and no personnel officers. Workers were both hired and fired by the foremen of the various departments. The foreman's personality and actions played, therefore, a crucial role in determining the physical and psychological conditions under which a woman worked. In 1906, Magog mill workers drafted a petition containing a specific complaint about the brutal behaviour of the card room foreman who was accused of striking the young women under his authority, insulting them, and blaspheming at the slightest thing. For Florida, injustices arising from the fact that the foremen did the hiring and often played favourites constituted a serious problem. As noted earlier, foremen could impose fines for any work or behaviours they personally considered unacceptable. In fact, the power imbalance between men overseers and women workers was manifested in a variety of ways. For example, Agathe reported that the women in her department had to hide their lunches, or the foreman would eat them just to make the women angry. Given the reproduction of patriarchal social relations within the mill and the resulting imbalance in male-female power relations, the problem of abusive foremen would be an ongoing one for women workers.

CHAPTER THREE

Fighting Back: Workplace Activism

Appearing before the Royal Commission on the Relations of Labor and Capital in 1888, John A. Rose, a cigar manufacturer from London, Ontario, explained his preference for women workers by declaring, "Women do not go on strike and do not get drunk." While acknowledging that they were paid substantially less than men, he nevertheless claimed that even if women were to receive the same rates of pay as men, he would still prefer to hire them. Not only were they much less partial to strong drink than men, but also they were cleaner, less "abusive," and did not join unions, the real source of the workingman's problems in Mr. Rose's considered opinion.

This view of girls and women as a cheap, sober, and docile source of labour was pervasive in late nineteenth-century accounts. While employers valued women workers for these ascribed attributes, male labour leaders largely resented them for precisely the same qualities. Union organizers characterized women factory workers as a form of unfair competition, especially to skilled male workers, and as a serious impediment to the establishment of an effective labour movement. In reality, prevailing gender stereotypes and biases motivated the exclusionary practices of the skilled crafts unions as much as rational economic concerns. Labour groups frequently justified excluding women from their ranks by claiming that female workers could not be organized since they were young, temporary employees lacking a long-term commitment to paid labour. Consequently, they believed, women did not develop the same sense of workplace solidarity as men. It was hardly surprising, then, that in 1898 Canada's Trades and Labour Congress officially declared itself in favour of abolishing all forms of female industrial labour.

It would be misleading to suggest, however, that only men viewed women workers as obstacles to the betterment of the workingman's situation. In her pioneering study, *The Conditions of Female Labour in Ontario,* published in 1892, Jean Thomson Scott concluded that women did not remain long in the workforce and so they were not interested in the benefit and pension schemes that unions were struggling to implement. "Moreover," she wrote, "there does not exist that 'class spirit' among women in employments that is necessary to organized progress; and men with reason complain that it is difficult to operate plans of any sort which require unselfish action among large bodies of women." Scott did soften her harsh indictment of women workers somewhat, pointing out that where women and men performed the same work and were represented by unions demanding equal pay for equal work, the women were eventually forced out of their positions. As a result women knew "in such cases that it is not to their individual advantage to belong to the unions."

In addition to stressing working women's youth and the brevity of their employment histories, more recent accounts of Victorian and Edwardian women workers have underscored other impediments to their engagement with unions. They include the low-skilled nature of women's jobs that made them easily replaceable, the segregated nature of the workplace that made it difficult for women workers to develop a sense of common cause with men, and an all-pervasive gender ideology that characterized women as unassertive, subservient, and irrational. Even speaking up at a union meeting was considered "unladylike" in many quarters. Given the many real obstacles to women workers' activism, it is important to analyze the extent to which the particular demographic characteristics, social and cultural milieus, and workplace actions of girls and women toiling in the Quebec cotton industry led them to conform to or deviate from these low expectations for workplace engagement.

French-Canadian, Catholic, Daughter, Wife:
Women's Intersecting Identities

In a number of their demographic characteristics, the Quebec cotton workers seem to have closely resembled the female industrial workforce of this period. They entered the industry at a young age, and only a minority continued to work outside the home once they were married. Among the fourteen women interviewed in Valleyfield and Magog born between 1895 and 1904, most were between twelve and sixteen when they started working in the mills. Overwhelmingly, they were recruited into the industry through their family connections and worked in the same complexes as their relatives.

Family needs remained paramount in the lives of these young women after they entered paid employment. In most cases, they continued to live at home and to hand over all or nearly all of their wages to their parents. This situation was considered completely normal, and interviewees remembered with pride the contributions they were able to make to the family economy. As Véronique recalled, "I gave all my salary [to my parents]. They gave us a few cents for our purchases. It gave me pleasure to give them my pay." Similarly, "Clémence" reported that she was "happy to help my parents, because they were good to me. I gave them my pay—that didn't cause any problems." In Agathe's home, payday involved the ritual of children putting their wage envelopes under their father's plate. Only one woman, Marie-Berthe, suggested that surrendering one's pay was a manifestation of imposed dependency, but, even for her, the benefits outweighed the disadvantages. "I was well fed and lodged," she said. In an age when there were no universal social security programs such as health insurance, unemployment insurance, or pensions, it was essential in working class families that as many members as possible make a financial contribution. Each wage, however meagre, helped tip the balance away from grinding poverty and indebtedness toward self-sufficiency and a modicum of stability in the family's financial condition.

Once young women reached marrying age and became engaged, they usually concluded some new financial arrangement with their parents. Instead of handing over their entire wages, they paid a set sum for room and board while a significant portion of their earnings went toward their trousseaus. As several interviewees explained, money was scarce, and they needed to help their prospective husbands in whatever way they could to establish their new household. In many instances, they had to look no farther than the workplace to find a marriage partner. Over half of the ten women who wed accepted proposals from men who were also employed in the cotton industry. Often it was a family member or a friend who worked in the mill who was responsible for bringing the couple together.

For women who remained single and continued to live at home, the timing of the conversion from contributing all of one's wages to the family to paying only part in the form of room and board varied considerably. In the case of Desneiges, the change came when she turned twenty-one, seven years after she first started working. For Philomène, it occurred only when she reached the age of twenty-five, although she, too, had started to work when she was fourteen, and, as in the case of Desneiges, several other family members also worked in the mills. Sometimes unwed daughters continued to contribute their entire earnings for many years. As Florida recalled, "I gave my salary to my parents until they died. We owed a lot to our parents. I felt dependent on my parents, but I was proud to work."

Among interviewees who married, the average age at which they wed was twenty-three, and the median length of time they spent in the mills before they left to establish their own households was nine years. This was a considerably longer period of time for young women to work for pay than most of the secondary literature dealing with women and work suggests. Due to a lack of alternative forms of employment for young working class women in the smaller textile centres, the turnover rates among women mill workers does not appear to have been high. Some women did continue to work in the industry for a short time after marriage in order to put their new household on a firmer financial footing. This was the situation for five of eight women interviewed who began working before 1919. Only Hortense, however, pursued employment after becoming a mother. Following the birth of her first child, she worked for an additional six months before giving birth again and retiring from the workplace to devote herself to a family that would eventually include twelve children. On the other hand, married women who did not bear children continued their employment for several decades. Ursule, who remained childless, ended up working for Montreal Cotton for forty-seven years. Her employment longevity resembled that of other women in her cohort who remained single. On average they worked in the mills for forty-two years, with Florida and Desneiges each recording just over a half century of work. Such workers could hardly be categorized as temporary.

For the most part, girls and women were concentrated in certain departments where they formed the majority of the workers, such as the drawing-in, ring spinning, inspecting, and folding rooms. Even when men and women worked in the same departments, they often worked on opposite sides of the room and did not eat together at midday. Nonetheless, the cotton industry provided greater opportunity than many other enterprises for women and men to interact, for example, in the card and weave rooms. During the late nineteenth and early twentieth centuries, weavers accounted for the largest single group of employees, and they were the group most likely to initiate work stoppages. Since most women workers had male relatives working in the mills, they would have found it natural to make common cause with them. These strong family ties, however, could potentially act as a curb rather than a stimulus to women workers' workplace activism. When work stoppages occurred that involved a number or all of a mill's departments, the entire family's income was jeopardized.

Living within the family home, as well as prevailing social norms, did prevent young women from engaging in the type of social and leisure activities outside the workplace identified as important to the development of working-class consciousness. After work, men might congregate in taverns, participate in mutual aid associations, or join unions where they existed. By contrast, after completing a ten-to-twelve-hour shift at the mill, young women returned home to face a variety of domestic responsibilities. They were expected to help with chores such as preparing meals, doing dishes, cleaning, minding younger siblings, doing laundry, and mending. As Rachel vividly recalled, "When we finished work at six in the evening, we weren't interested in running around." In Gabrielle's case, it was her strict parents who kept her and her siblings from straying too far from home once their factory shift was over.

In a society in which the Roman Catholic Church played a dominant role, what little time girls and women managed to retain after putting in their hours at the mill and at home was spent in religious observances. Without exception, all of the women interviewed went to mass each Sunday and on required feast days. Several also attended mass on the first Friday of every month and vespers on Sunday evenings. During special periods such as Lent, *le mois de Marie* ("the month of Mary," May), and *le mois du rosaire* ("the month of the rosary," October), they attended church even more frequently. When they had to work on religious feast days, they went to mass as early as 5:30 a.m. so that their employment would not interfere with the fulfillment of their religious duties.

Associational life was also directly linked to the church, whose official position was to oppose any voluntary groups outside its control. Girls were encouraged to join the Enfants de Marie (Children of Mary), originally created in France in 1837. Grouping girls at the parish level from the time of their first communions, its objective was to reinforce girls' piety by having them emulate the essential qualities of the Virgin Mary, namely purity, humility, obedience, and charity. For married women, the Dames de Sainte-Anne (Ladies of Saint Anne) was one of the most common parish groups. Designed to encourage religious and charitable works, its members supported the local church through their volunteer and fundraising activities. These were the two organizations that the majority of women interviewed identified as groups to which they had belonged. Nevertheless, just over a third of them stated that they had not belonged to any organization and cited their lack of free time as the cause for their non-participation.

Opportunities for women employees in Quebec to be involved in groups outside the workplace that recognized them as paid workers were virtually non-existent before 1920. One association in

Montreal did specifically focus on industrial workers—L'Association professionnelle des employées de manufactures (Professional Association of Women Manufacturing Employees.) It was organized under the auspices of the Fédération nationale Saint-Jean-Baptiste (National Federation of Saint John the Baptist), a predominantly middle class, French-Canadian Catholic women's reform movement, founded in 1907. Among the many national and charitable causes the FNSJB took up was improving the physical, intellectual, and moral state of young employed women.

To help working class girls better their situation, to keep them from falling prey to "socialistic" union organizers, and to assist them in preparing for their ultimate roles as wives and mothers, the FNSJB launched separate organizations for various categories of female workers such as teachers, office workers, shop girls, domestic servants, and factory workers. The workers' group proved to be one of the most active, with over 471 members by May 1907. Many of its members listed the Hochelaga cotton mill as their place of employment. Objectives set by the manufacturing employees' association included getting factory owners to observe Catholic holidays, securing the physical separation of women and men workers, having the former supervised by women overseers, and ensuring that the names of women factory inspectors were prominently displayed in the workplace. On behalf of the Hochelaga textile workers, the association also lobbied mill management to correct the poor artificial lighting in its establishment.

Given the young age at which women typically began working in the mills, most of their informal social networks involved other cotton workers. As adolescents, they chummed with other girls, usually from their own departments. There were few diversions in the smaller textile towns, and the small amounts of pocket money they had at their disposal imposed yet more restrictions on the types of activities they could pursue. Most women in Magog and Valleyfield recalled that they took pleasure in simple amusements such as playing cards, holding house parties on Saturday night, strolling around town, swimming and picnicking in the summer, and tobogganing in the winter. Such activities provided an opportunity to deepen workplace relationships and to build up a sense of camaraderie. Some mentioned that others who did not work in the mill looked down on them as "factory girls" and did not want to associate with them.

The women workers' French-Canadian, Catholic, and gender identities supposedly predisposed them to be a docile workforce. Certainly the pronouncements of the male Catholic hierarchy about the roles of girls and women offered little encouragement for them to consider themselves as wage earners in their own rights. In a pastoral letter decrying the pursuit of luxury and pleasure published in the local newspaper in March 1917, Bishop Émard of the Diocese of Valleyfield stressed how important it was for working class wives to help the family exercise frugality. Each home should be a domestic science school where the mother taught her daughters how to cook and to keep house appropriately. The one slight nod in the direction of recognizing young women as paid workers came in the form of an admonition about saving. All children who earned wages and who were allowed to keep a portion of them should have a savings account that "would grow gradually with little weekly economies and protect against external temptations."

Monsignor Émard's linking of girls and women with domestic life was a formulation widely enunciated in Quebec society. An article signed "Gertrude," published in *Le Progrès de Valleyfield* the same year as Émard's pastoral letter, contained a message very similar to his. Addressed specifically to workers' wives, it harangued them about the virtues they needed to help their husbands stretch their earnings. The author recommended that they always "carry a smile on their lips" so that sons and husbands would not stray from home, and that they forego expensive silk dresses in favour of printed calico to help the family budget. This article did acknowledge, however, that working class girls could be involved in paid employment. Such girls were to help their parents to the extent they were able and to conduct themselves modestly. All women, whether they were working daughters, wives, or mothers, were told to "accept your lot with courage, carry your daily cross, love your family, try to put a few pennies aside for bad times. In this way you will be as happy as one can be on this earth in the worker's humble state."

Press coverage relating to women mill hands also reveals the great degree of ambivalence that male editors and journalists felt about them. Members of the press clearly had difficulty reconciling their idealized concepts of womanhood with the reality of working class girls and women who toiled for their daily bread. Commentaries ranged widely, from the negative and disdainful to the affirmative and supportive, but underlying all was a profound unease about how to deal with these female subjects. In the case of factory workers, class and gender seemed to be in conflict, rather than mutually reinforcing as was the case for middle class women. By seeking employment outside the home, women followed the dictates of their working class status, but by doing so, they clearly violated the norms established for their gender.

Only a few progressive women journalists, such as Montrealer Éva Circé-Côté, endorsed the principle that women had a right to seek paid employment, while pitying the hard lot of those working in factories. On the few occasions when they did mention women workers specifically, male journalists might focus as much on the women's appearance and behaviour as they did on specific workplace issues. In its coverage of the March 1908 walkout by hundreds of Hochelaga and Saint-Anne workers, the pro-labour *La Presse* included several drawings of the strikers attending union meetings. Of seven such drawings, five had women strikers as their subject and represented them as attractive and stylish young women interested in amusing themselves during the course of the strike. One drawing of five well-dressed strikers carried the caption, "A group of pretty workers joyously discusses the situation. They are not worried about the results of the strike." Another showed a woman standing on a chair so that she could catch a better view of the singers and dancers performing on the stage of the hall where union members were meeting. Other depictions included a woman knitting, "a joyous past-time" according to the accompanying caption, a group of women playing cards, and a woman reading *La Presse*, which is declared to be the "stylish" newspaper for women textile workers. The combined effect of the drawings was to create a general image of well-being and even frivolity among the women on strike, yet the text of the accompanying articles suggested that some had endured physical and emotional abuse at the hands of harsh, unjust foremen.

Strikes and Other Work Actions, 1880-1900

Girls and women often walked off the job to protest working conditions in the cotton industry. Initially they did so spontaneously, since the industry was not unionized. Women weavers, for example, instigated the first recorded strike in Quebec's cotton industry when they took action at the Hochelaga mill on April 14, 1880. Approximately one hundred left their looms to protest increases in their work hours and in the amount of yardage they were expected to produce, increases required by the new English plant manager, William James Whitehead. By the next day, nearly all four hundred employees had walked off the job to demand shorter hours and a wage increase of 15 percent. Not only did the women strikers outnumber the men by a ratio of two-to-one, but they also took the defiant step of using a lawyer to state their grievances rather than follow the advice of their parish priest and the mayor, both of whom advised them to return to work. Furthermore, the women signed an agreement to pay a ten-dollar fine if any of them returned to work before an acceptable settlement was achieved.

Management responded by keeping the existing hours of work with the sole concessions of delaying the morning start time by fifteen minutes and lengthening the dinner hour from thirty to forty-five minutes. It also threatened to close the mill for six months if the strikers did not return to their machines. The work stoppage dragged on for just over two weeks, by which time the strikers' larders were bare. With the exception of the strike leaders, whom the company refused to take back, and some workers who had already left Montreal to find better working conditions in American mills, the strikers returned to their jobs on May 1. While they did not succeed in getting a wage increase, the strikers did manage to reduce the amount of unpaid overtime they were expected to perform.

There are several more instances of female workers—especially spinners and weavers—playing an active role in protesting working conditions during the 1880s and the 1890s. They were prominent in work stoppages in Valleyfield (1880 and 1885), Saint-Henri (1882, 1891, and 1899), and Hochelaga (1893). In the 1882 strike at the Merchants mill in Saint-Henri, the catalyst was the replacement of daily wage rates by piece rates. Many weavers left for the United States where they readily found employment at higher rates, and so the company found it necessary to recruit British weavers to replace them.

On October 6, 1891, more than two hundred women in the weave room at the same mill walked off the job in what *La Presse* described as *"La Grève des femmes"* (Women's Strike). They were protesting the firing and replacing of their foremen with Americans. In particular, the women were incensed by the firing of a man named Duplessis, identified as the only remaining French Canadian in the mill with the status of overseer. Some of the weavers alleged that he lost his job because he was not as hard on them as management wished and was not imposing enough fines. The women complained that a reduction in the quality of the cotton yarn they were weaving made it more likely they would make mistakes and be fined. The strikers paraded through the main streets of Saint-Henri and by the following day had gained new supporters, including the twenty men in their department who had continued to work the previous day. Of the resulting four hundred protesters, three-quarters were women. Responding to a letter from municipal officials asking them to consider the workers' grievances, company officials reprimanded the council for its intervention, closed the mill, and threatened to move it out of Saint-Henri unless the strikers returned to work. They also stated that they made personnel decisions without consideration of nationality and pointed out that only forty of their five hundred employees were English.

Unlike the women strikers in Hochelaga a decade earlier, the Saint-Henri workers agreed to have the mayor, the parish priest, and a local doctor negotiate a settlement with the company on their behalf. Their demands included a reduction in fines, a maximum workweek of sixty hours, and a guarantee that no strikers would be fired. In the face of the company's threats to move the mill, civic officials advised the workers to drop their condition that Duplessis be reinstated. At a meeting with company officials, the appointed delegation received only platitudes regarding the fining system and working hours but was assured that no strikers would be fired. On this basis, the priest appeared on the mill's balcony and exhorted the assembled strikers to return to work that afternoon. As the *La Presse* reporter noted, "So ended the remarkable Saint-Henri strike."

Women who led a strike at Saint Anne's mill in Hochelaga in September 1893 were also protesting the replacement of a popular French-Canadian foreman by an English one. They described their new overseer as unjust and quick to impose fines and fire workers. In this case, some fifty women visited a local lawyer's office and asked him to draw up a list of their complaints.

In the summer of 1898, it was women weavers at Montreal Cotton in Valleyfield who went on strike to protest management's decision to impose an extra half day of unpaid overtime work. The stoppage affected a total of six hundred workers. An account in the August issue of the *Canadian Journal of Fabrics* tells how the company backed down and accepted the workers' commitment to increase production during regular hours. In May of the following year, seven or eight young women precipitated yet another walkout at the Merchants mill in Saint-Henri in an effort to obtain a 10 percent wage increase. Their action cost them their jobs. According to *La Presse*, other "girls" rallied to their cause and refused to return to work until the company awarded them the increase in wages demanded and rehired all the strikers. The dispute was quickly resolved when the two parties agreed on a 6.5 percent increase.

Examples of militancy among women workers extended well into the first decade of the twentieth century. A new element was the rise of the first significant industrial union movement, the Chevaliers du travail, the Quebec wing of the Knights of Labor. Established in 1869 in Philadelphia, the Knights had established a presence in Quebec by 1882. It was the first labour organization to be condemned by Quebec's bishops on the grounds that it was a secular, Masonic-like, foreign entity. Although its presence had

FIGHTING BACK: WORKPLACE ACTIVISM   103

waned greatly throughout Canada by the end of the 1880s, the first evidence of its entry into the Quebec cotton industry dates from 1898 when some Dominion Textile workers in Montreal established a local. Additional evidence of the Knights' activities in the Quebec industry over the next few years remains fragmentary. It is apparent nonetheless that this organization, dedicated to organizing all workers, regardless of skill level, race, ethnicity, or gender, was attempting to make its influence felt.

In a letter written to Bishop Émard in 1900, Louis Simpson complained that the Knights were once again attempting to set up locals in Valleyfield, as they had on three or four occasions during the previous decade. Simpson credited their lack of success to Émard's clergy, who "have prevented their establishment." He warned the bishop that a local councillor was reportedly assisting the Knights in their endeavours and reminded him that "It would be very deplorable if this association were to be established in Valleyfield, as the working men of Valleyfield are far safer in Your Lordship's hands than they could be in the hands of such a society." Despite their exemplary devotion to the church and the clergy's hostility toward unions, women mill hands were not immune to the Knights' overtures. The practice of admitting women into its ranks and the existing activism of girls and women in the cotton textile industry must have assured the Knights of a certain measure of support among women workers. Indeed, the Knights represented a particularly useful form of unionism for the large cotton-mill labour force, since its members included men and women, French and English, and multiple skill levels.

In February 1900, women mill hands in Valleyfield, perhaps supported by the Knights, organized what came to be known as *la Grève des jeunes filles* (the young women's strike). The dispute erupted over the decision of the superintendent, Fred Lacey, to use women learners in the spooling department of one of the mills, thereby reducing the amount of work available to the experienced spoolers. The latter, thirty-seven in number, walked off the job to protest this practice. The strikers were also protesting the introduction of new machinery and accompanying pay schedules that they maintained were lowering their earnings.

What is particularly notable about the strikers is their youth and resolve. Florina Lalonde, identified by the correspondent for *La Presse* as one of the leaders, was only fourteen years old but had already worked in the Valleyfield mill for three years. Referring to the company manager's offer to provide different rates of increases according to the type of cotton yarn spooled, she impressed upon the newspaper's reporter that "we will not work under those conditions and not one of the spoolers will do so, and those who would dare present themselves at work for those prices would be mistreated by us." They would only agree to return to work if all the spoolers enjoyed an increase of 10 cents per hundred pounds of yarn spooled. In the face of their intransigence, company manager Louis Simpson ordered the mills closed and effectively locked out the other employees.

Simpson sent a detailed account of his problems with the spoolers to Bishop Émard, asserting that the alterations in machinery he had ordered would result in improved rather than reduced wages for them. He also complained that they were not working as hard as they could and asked Émard to use his influence to get them "to do their best." After a further investigation of the spoolers' complaints, management did agree to stop using learners and to correct the piece rates paid for spooling certain counts of yarn. Simpson, believing that he had reached an agreement with the disgruntled workers, reopened the mills. The young women, however, refused to accept the proposed remedy. Simpson described his ensuing confrontation with some of the spoolers in the following manner:

> I reached the mill office at 8:30 a.m., having already learned that there was trouble. I found the office full of girls. In the outside office were the four bad girls who have raised the whole trouble, and I was told that upon the person of Bertha Lecompte were found two bludgeons, which had evidently been cut out of green wood the day before, and which she had brought into the mill in order to use to assault somebody.

He was incensed that the local chief of police refused to imprison the girls, but the police did load the leaders into police vans and drive them home.

Upon learning of this latest development, the weavers, unhappy with their own wage scales, walked out to support the spoolers

In July 1900, 400 unskilled workers walked off the job at Dominion Textile's Magog mill, to protest the harsh treatment meted out by foremen and a change in the company's pay day. The strikers brought operations to a standstill by cutting off the water supply to the mill. In response, the company asked local authorities to summon the militia from Sherbrooke to protect its property. After persisting for eight days, the strikers won a 10 percent wage increase, but the pay day was not changed. (Photo Société d'histoire de Magog and Serge Gaudreau, *Au fil du temps: Histoire de l'industrie du textile à Magog*, 1883-1993 (1995).)

and were subsequently joined by all of the French-Canadian workers. The strikers held a mass meeting at the town hall during which they directed the town's clerk to draw up a list of their grievances. By this time tensions had mounted between the English-speaking and French-speaking workers, since the former did not want to join the strike. The riot act was read to disperse the crowds and the mills were shut down. The strike lasted a fortnight, during which considerable damage was done to the company's new Empire mill. In the end, the spoolers won a 10 percent general increase, and for some types of work, the increase amounted to as much as 35 percent.

Public reaction to the strike was mixed. This was one of the few occasions when the editor of *Le Progrès de Valleyfield* was highly critical of strikers. In a long editorial published on February 9, 1900, he lambasted the strike as "a real waste, an insane undertaking. It had no element of legitimacy." While acknowledging that low wages were a problem and that workers were having increasing difficulty making ends meet as the cost of living increased, the editor referred specifically only to the problems of young male workers. No doubt the spectacle of a handful of young women setting off a walkout that brought the town's most important enterprise to a standstill was a disquieting one. The unpleasant confrontation between French and English workers, the forced idling of employees who wished to continue working, and the damage to private property sustained during the strike also coloured the editor's view. The town's merchants were also unhappy to see business plummet for two weeks, and even some local male trade unionists condemned the spoolers' actions.

One month after *la Grève des jeunes filles*, and perhaps emboldened by the gains the Valleyfield strikers had made, workers at the Montmorency mill created a Knights local. The *Canadian Journal of Fabrics* reported that by July 1900 the Knights had recruited 540 members, nearly the entire mill workforce. In response to the Knights' recruitment efforts, the company closed the mill and demanded that all workers sign pledges renouncing membership in any union before they could be rehired. The company also retaliated against the strikers by bringing in many new families, mostly from the Lac-Saint-Jean area, to take their place. The conflict dragged on for two months. Since the Knights had no resources to aid the workers during the work stoppage other than moneys donated by supportive labour organizations in Quebec City, many of the experienced workers left Montmorency to locate work in the United States. The rest returned to work.

Back in Valleyfield, labour peace continued to prove elusive as well. In July 1900, there was another massive walkout by the French-Canadian mill hands. Once again, ethnic tensions played a key role, since the French-speaking employees struck to protest the assignment of a set of looms previously operated by a French-Canadian woman weaver to an English woman named Jones. This time the strike lasted only two days, but as in the earlier work stoppage, the company reported a significant amount of damage to the Empire mill. It was after this strike, according to Simpson, that some workers organized a local of the Knights of Labor.

Even more damage was incurred in October 1900 when construction workers who were building the new Gault mill in Valleyfield went on strike for higher wages. The Knights of Labor were involved, and soon some three thousand cotton workers walked out in support of the construction workers. Once again, the company's entire operations were brought to a halt, this time for eight days for an estimated twenty-one thousand lost working days. Company property was extensively damaged, and the militia was called out to restore order. In this confrontation, the mule spinners played a key role. On October 29, a payday for cotton workers, nearly all mill hands with the exception of the mule spinners returned to work in the early hours of the morning. The mule spinners refused to do so until the militia was recalled.

The following day, William Lyon Mackenzie King, the federal deputy minister of labour appointed to arbitrate the dispute, reported to *La Presse* that the mill workers were back on the job and the troops were preparing to leave Valleyfield. His self-congratulatory description of the situation expressed his belief that the workers were satisfied with the resolution of the difficulties with the company, despite the fact that some mill hands had been fired. King appears to have accepted the company's explanations that the dismissals were not strike-related, that only the young girls from one department were let go, and they could apply for jobs in other parts of the mill.

Union Involvement

In 1902, the Quebec government passed a conciliation and arbitration act providing a mechanism to avert such unsettling and costly strikes. This legislation was designed to regulate relations between capital and labour through the agency of an agreed-upon third party and to provide a framework to settle disputes without resorting to massive work stoppages. Yet strikes continued to recur regularly in the cotton industry, and frequently women workers were actively involved. An example of young women's willingness to strike to try to maintain some control over the pace of work occurred in February 1903 at the Merchants mill in Saint-Henri. *La Presse* reported that the majority of the seventy-five who started the protest were young women. They were objecting to the introduction of new machinery that, while more efficient, increased spinners' workload.

Evidence amassed for Mackenzie King's commission showed thirty-four more strikes and lockouts occurred in Quebec's cotton mills between April 1906 and June 1908. Seventeen took place in Montreal mills, seven in Magog, five in Valleyfield, and five at Montmorency Falls. Although mule spinners most frequently initiated the work stoppages during this period, spoolers, spinners, and weavers were also instrumental in bringing production to a halt. In at least five cases, it was clearly women who took the lead, as was the case in three strikes at the Montmorency mill. Between August and October 1907, spooler tenders there walked off the job on three separate occasions to protest their piecework rates. In the first instance, twenty-six spoolers took part, while in the second incident thirty spoolers were joined by the entire ring-spinning department of a hundred hands who staged a one-day walkout. In October, only three spooler tenders were directly affected by a dispute over piece rates, but the entire department walked out for a day in a show of support.

As ring spinning increasingly replaced mule spinning, it became imperative for strike leaders to gain the support of the women ring spinners if production were to be brought to a halt. An excellent example of this necessity occurred in Valleyfield in 1908 when the mule spinners walked out but the weavers did not. A Montreal Cotton superintendent reported, "The mule spinners therefore began to work upon the feelings of the ring spinners, who on two or three occasions went out on strike for short periods." The large number of conflicts and lost work days, and the serious economic impact they inflicted, reflected the increased militancy of the cotton workers of both sexes, a militancy both fanned and controlled by the new industrial unions in the province of Quebec.

The specific gains the Knights of Labor had achieved for the cotton workers, though ephemeral, did constitute an influential model of industrial unionism that subsequent labour organizations imitated. The most important during this period was the Fédération des ouvriers du textile du Canada (FOTC; Federation of Textile Workers of Canada) formed in 1906. It grew out of an organizing drive among mule spinners at the Hochelaga mill in April that year conducted under the auspices of the International Spinners' Union, an affiliate of the United Textile Workers of America (UTWA). The movement spread first to other Hochelaga departments and then to the Saint-Henri and Saint Anne mills. Anxious to head off general strikes in all three mills, Dominion Textile management agreed to a 10 percent wage increase, and the strikers returned to work in early May.

In June 1906, Wilfrid Paquette, a Montreal striker, travelled to Magog to set up a UTWA local. Dominion Textile responded by ordering its workers to sign anti-union contracts. When some three hundred workers refused to do so, the company locked them out. Within a few days, over eight hundred employees from both the mill and print works walked out. In an impressive show of worker solidarity, the mule spinners employed at the company's three Montreal mills staged a sympathy strike. At the end of three weeks, the Magog workers not only regained their jobs and had their right to join a union recognized, but also won pay increases of between 12 and 14 percent.

Within three months, however, the newly created locals left the UTWA to form their own national federation. Language was their primary motivation, since the international organization, with headquarters in the United States, functioned entirely in English. By the fall of 1906, two-thirds of textile workers in Montreal had joined the new textile federation. It succeeded in organizing both woollen and cotton mill workers in Ontario as well as in Quebec. By 1907, twenty-four FOTC locals had formed across Quebec boasting a combined membership of over seven thousand members, with Wilfrid Paquette filling the role of president.

Like the Knights, and unlike the internationally affiliated unions of skilled workers such as those established by mule spinners, this new organization actively recruited women. Women reportedly accounted for two-thirds of the membership, and most were integrated into locals along with men. Some locals did restrict membership to skilled male workers, as was the case for the mule spinners, while in Valleyfield, girls and women formed their own local, Number Seven, Les Dames et Demoiselles de Valleyfield (Ladies and Young Ladies of Valleyfield). In both Magog and Valleyfield, English-speaking workers had separate locals.

The 1907 list of officers and executive committees of nineteen locals contained in *Le Fileur*, the union's official publication, reveals that women held executive positions in six, including in the separate women's local in Valleyfield. With the exception of this group and another representing silk workers in a Montreal mill, the only position women held was that of vice-president. This office, while granting the holder representation on the executive committee, was largely honorific since duties related to it were less central to running the local than those connected to the other executive positions.

According to contemporary newspaper accounts, large numbers of women turned up for union rallies, and some occasionally assumed a visible role in labour disputes initiated by the FOTC. In August 1907, for example, all Montreal Cotton workers "took a holiday" to lend support to a group of mule spinners who had walked off the job in a wage dispute with the company. Led by the union, the employees declared they would only return to work if the company agreed to a general 10 percent wage increase. Women and girls were highly visible participants in this protest, as they joined their male co-workers on the streets and in the meeting halls. At one mass meeting attended by over three thousand people, reporters noted that a relatively large number of women were in attendance. Two women—Clotilde Daoust and Pamela Laberge—sat on the nine-person strike committee. Although it was specifically the wages and working conditions of the mule

M.A. Lavigne, Local No. 4,
Fédération des ouvriers du textile du Canada (FOTC), Magog
This photo of Mlle Lavigne appeared in the Federation's official
publication, *Le Fileur* [The Spinner] along with photos of three men from
the same local. While their administrative positions were clearly
indicated, hers was not. At the time, the Magog local claimed that
it had 1000 members. (*Le Fileur*, I, no.8, (June 1907).)

Clementine Perron, Local No. 3,
Fédération des ouvriers du textile du Canada, Montreal
Mlle Perron is identified as a member of the administrative committee
for the FOTC local organized at the St. Anne Spinning Mill. However, her
actual role is not specified, nor does her name appear in the listing of the
members of the committee. (*Le Fileur*, I, no.8, (June 1907).)

spinners that had provoked the walkout, the conduct of certain overseers soon became a central issue as well. The union demanded that the company not only increase wages but also that it take measures to curtail favouritism. Given the importance of foremen's conduct for women workers, it is likely that this issue was an important rallying point for the women strikers. In fact, some voiced their grievances in public at a mass rally on August 15. As the journalist for *Le Progrès de Valleyfield* recorded, "Men, women and children complained unanimously and equally about all sorts of bad treatment." The strike lasted for two weeks and came to an end when the two parties agreed to arbitration.

The presence of the FOTC seemingly emboldened girls and women to take independent and collective action to assert control over the work process. In correspondence with Bishop Émard, Louis Simpson included a detailed report from a card room foreman compiled between August 1907 and April 1908. It contained several examples of women workers under his charge taking action on their own account. Some, such as Orise Leduc, Youvenne [sic] Monpetit, and Antoinette Seven, were away from their jobs without permission and were seen shopping or attending local fairs. Several other women refused to run certain machines or certain types of rovings. In one case, all the hands, led by Pamelia [sic] Laberge, ceased work and threatened to walk out unless a particular worker was assigned to a specific set of machines. The foreman was particularly upset by the behaviour of Rosie Chevigny, "one of the stubborn sort that will only do what she wants to." He accused her of falling asleep on the job, refusing to work to her full capacity, and walking off the job when he asked her to perform certain work. He also complained that she and at least nine other women he named were visiting the water closet and the sink at least three or four times every hour to avoid work. "They have the idea," he contended, "that belonging to the union, they can do as little as they like."

In several instances, the foreman noted that although he sent recalcitrant workers home, he took them back the next day. Far from being unskilled and disposable, these workers were experienced hands whose command of intricate, semi-skilled tasks

made it difficult to replace them without adversely affecting production. Additional complaints about the behaviour of young
female workers occur in correspondence between Louis Simpson
and Wilfrid Paquette. In one instance, Simpson reported that
eighty-six sides of spinning frame went unattended because "the
girls failed to report to work this morning and some more, it being
a fine day, stayed away this afternoon." Simpson attributed their
insubordination to the recent advance in wages the union had
negotiated with the company.

Gender-related issues cropped up on the union convention floor
as well as during walkouts. An early FOTC objective was to reduce
the length of the workweek. Many historians have argued that
union attempts to restrict the hours of work performed by women,
while making no demands for similar limits on the number of hours
worked by men, was motivated more by self-interest than by
humanitarianism or chivalry. Limiting women's hours made them
less competitive. Delegates attending the first FOTC general
assembly held in Montreal in December 1906 voted to set up a committee to study the length of the workweek in other industrialized
countries including England, France, Germany, and the United
States. In introducing the proposal, President Wilfrid Paquette
spoke only in general terms of the need to reduce the workweek in
the mills, and so it is possible that the union leadership intended
to secure shorter hours for all hands, not just for women.

At a large public meeting called by the FOTC in February 1908,
however, Secretary-Treasurer L.-A. Girard announced that the
leadership was committed to obtaining more humane working
conditions specifically for women and children. Subsequently, at
the third general convention, held in Valleyfield two months later,
a formal motion to reduce the workweek to fifty-five hours limited
the proposed reduction to children and women. The delegates,
several of whom were women, greeted the resolution with applause
and passed it unanimously. Given the excessively long hours in
the industry, it seems likely that most women would have approved
a reduction, particularly since they were rarely competing directly
against men for jobs in the mills. *Le Progrès de Valleyfield* noted,
"the applause [for the resolution] is easy to explain for at 4:30 a.m.

the cotton mill whistle in Valleyfield begins its series of thunder-
ing calls warning workers to get to work by 6:10 a.m."

The grouping together of women with children, and singling
them out for protective measures, was, of course, common practice throughout the industrialized world. The FOTC was simply
following established practice in this regard, and its efforts to
protect the morals of children and women also reflected prevailing social concepts. *Le Fileur* reported that at the April 1907 convention women and men delegates unanimously endorsed the
following resolution:

> This convention, considering the present precarious condition of
> women and children, both from a physical and moral perspective,
> moves: 1) That a permanent surveillance committee be appointed in
> each mill, with at least one member for each department, for the pur-
> pose of keeping a watch on, maintaining and encouraging sanitary and
> moral conditions in each mill. 2) That a monthly report be submitted
> by the committee and communicated to the executive council.

In essence, women's position in the union was fraught with
contradictions. On the one hand, their presence and active participation was encouraged, but, at the same time, their sex prevented them from being treated as true equals, as "brothers." The
confusion surrounding their status in the union is reflected in the
report of the general assembly held in 1906. Two women delegates
from Montreal were appointed to a five-person committee
charged with the important task of meeting the federal minister
of finance, William Fielding, to urge him to provide more protection for the Canadian textile industry. Yet, at the very same meeting, before he addressed the delegates, Alphonse Verville, member
of parliament for Hochelaga, excused himself for "speaking before
the ladies... and paid them a nice compliment." Judging from the
lists of delegates at each convention and the reports of the pro-
ceedings, women trade unionists were a minority and did not take
an active role in the discussions.

Despite its success in expanding its influence and securing
wage increases of up to 25 percent for mill workers between 1906
and 1908, the FOTC's fortunes soon suffered a serious reversal.
On March 2, 1908, some 1,200 Hochelaga mill workers voted

L'ASSEMBLEE D'HIER APRES-MIDI, A LA SALLE TREMBLAY.

Fédération des ouvriers du textile (FOTC)
Strike Meetings in Montreal, March 1908
In March 1908, workers at the Hochelaga and St. Anne mills in Montreal
went on strike under the direction of the FOTC to secure higher wages
and improved working conditions. The top illustration of a strikers'
meeting published in *La Presse* shows the large number of women
workers, wearing their "Sunday best," present at a strike meeting.
According to the accompanying report, women formed the vast majority
of the audience. A key demand for them was the dismissal of a foreman
named Venne who was accused of mistreating the women under
his control. Shown speaking to the audience is L.-A. Girard,
Secretary-General of the Fédération.

unanimously to strike in an attempt to have the start of their work
day changed from 6:15 to 7 a.m., the time at which most industrial
workers began, and to obtain a 20 percent wage increase. Another
major grievance was management's refusal to deal with workers'
complaints about mistreatment by certain overseers. This was an
important issue for women weavers in particular, and they called
for the outright dismissal of one reputedly abusive assistant foreman, Joseph Venne. The following day, some three hundred workers from the Saint Anne mill joined the strike.

According to *La Presse*'s report of a large workers' meeting held
on March 4, women workers, decked out in their Sunday finery,

La Presse's coverage of the strike the following day featured four more drawings of women workers. The captions illustrate the tendency at the time to trivialize the seriousness of the situation for the women on strike:

a) Group of women talking – "A group of pretty young workers discuss the situation. They are not worried about the outcome of the strike."

b) Woman standing on chair – "One must make every effort to see the singers and dancers on the stage, who are doing their best to entertain the others while waiting for developments."

c) Woman reading newspaper – "One must keep up to date on events, and *"La Presse"* is the newspaper 'a la mode' for the women textile workers."

d) Woman knitting – "The strike is not a waste of time for this brave worker. Her knitting provides her with a joyous pass-time."

e) Women playing cards – "The strikers are not bored during their hours of unemployment."

La Presse, March 4 and 5, 1908.

were front and centre and made up most of the audience. The following day, the union organized separate meetings for women and men in the afternoon and a combined meeting in the evening at the Collège de Hochelaga that attracted an estimated 1,500 workers. Several women spoke out in favour of Venne's dismissal and declared that the strikers should not return to work until he was fired. Significantly, Secretary-General Girard declared that the public would be critical if Venne were found guilty before he had an opportunity to defend himself. He proposed accepting the company's offer to investigate the charges against Venne once the workers returned to their jobs, but with the proviso that the accused be suspended until the investigation was complete. By returning to work under these conditions, Girard argued, the union would certainly come out "more powerful and more glorious, because people would see what noble and great goal it was pursuing: the protection of all workers, and especially women and children." The audience subsequently unanimously approved a motion endorsing Girard's plan of action.

Four days later, Paquette assured another mass meeting of strikers that the general manager's promises to undertake a full investigation of the complaints against Venne were sincere. If the complaints were founded, the manager would dismiss him. Paquette therefore proposed that the strike be terminated. This time, however, the "discontent that rose here and there in the room" indicates that union officials did not get unanimous approval for what was essentially a dismissal of a major grievance for the women. The women's disappointment must have been all the more keenly felt since some 1,500 workers at the Merchants mill had already voted to join the strike the next day if Dominion Textile did not satisfy the demands of the Hochelaga and Saint Anne workers. The abrupt end of the strike seemed to signal that the union leadership was more concerned about due process for the male overseer than about the interests of its women members.

Following the return to work, company officials did launch an immediate investigation into the allegations against Venne under the auspices of a Quebec government inspector. According to the resulting report, the charges against him "were not substantiated by any of the witnesses called," and the union failed to make any written charges against him. Consequently, the entire matter was dropped. However, the company did agree to increase the wage scales in some departments of the Hochelaga mill.

A month following what had been a disappointing result for women strikers, the FOTC adopted a resolution that strike action could only be taken if two-thirds of local members voted in favour and the federation's executive approved. The adoption of this procedure represented a concerted effort by the union's leadership to eliminate spontaneous work stoppages by the rank and file such as had occurred at Hochelaga. Increased conflict between President Paquette and Secretary-General Girard led the former to resign his position and the latter to set up a rival organization, L'Union amicale (Friendly Union), in April 1908. In contrast to the FOTC, the new group officially renounced the strike as a legitimate form of labour action and also admitted foremen into its ranks. Endorsed by the company, the Union amicale undertook an organizing drive at the Hochelaga mill. The same day the new union was formed, Dominion Textile announced a 10 percent general wage reduction in all its mills, to commence on May 4. In reaction, mule spinners in Hochelaga, Saint-Henri, and Valleyfield walked off the job the day the cut took effect. This wage loss was especially difficult to accept since there had been a great deal of downtime during the previous months.

The FOTC executive was split over whether to support the mule spinners' action. By mid-May, Paquette and his supporters had taken control of the executive and thrown their support behind a strike that now involved thousands of mill workers across Quebec and that had led both Dominion Textile and Montreal Cotton to close their production facilities. Concerned over the widespread nature of the labour unrest in one of the country's most important manufacturing sectors, in June 1908 the federal government created the royal commission headed by Mackenzie King to investigate its nature and causes. The textile companies refused any concessions, and the strike went on in most mills for four to five weeks. In the end, the strikers straggled back to work on the companies' terms and the general wage reduction remained in place. Moreover, according to Wilfrid Paquette's testimony before King's enquiry, hundreds of hands were not taken back, in retaliation for their actions. Those numbers included many women. Others, if they were kept on, were subject to reprisals. Delima Viau, a sixteen-year-old Valleyfield worker employed for three years before she testified before the royal commission, told *La Presse* that she had always been a member of the union. Following the May 1908 strike, the number of frames she was assigned was reduced from two to one, and she was told this drastic reduction in her means to earn her living was due to the fact that she had agreed to appear before the commission.

Given the depressed state of the cotton trade by 1908, mounting unemployment, and the hardship arising from lost wages during the prolonged unsuccessful strike, the FOTC's bargaining power was greatly reduced. To offset declining numbers, union dues rose dramatically from the initial rate of 5 cents a month to 23 cents a month. This dramatic increase was undoubtedly a major stumbling block for the lowest-paid workers, most of whom were women, to maintain membership in the union. The union did attempt to annul the 1908 general wage reduction the following year by supporting approximately nine hundred strikers in Magog who were demanding a 10 percent increase and an end to the blacklisting of union members, but that strike also failed. By June 1909, most of the union's locals had disbanded. Over the next three years, Paquette attempted to reorganize the FOTC and win back its membership, but it never recovered its former strength. In 1919, the UTWA absorbed the last two remaining locals.

Nearly all of the women interviewed in Valleyfield and Magog who began as mill workers before 1919 started to work after the FOTC had already disappeared as a force in the industry. The one exception was Léa, who laboured in the Magog mill from 1906 to 1909, first as a doffer and then as a ring spinner. She did not recall any union or strike activity occurring during that time period, although she did remember being laid off for a period of time. Léa's lack of knowledge about the FOTC seems surprising, given that the period of her employment coincided with that of greatest activity and highest visibility for the union. However, only two of the five strikes that took place in Magog between 1906 and 1908 involved all mill workers. The remainder were limited to groups of skilled men workers such as mule spinners, loom fixers, and specialized print room employees who walked off work for one or two days over grievances specific to their respective departments. In these cases, women such as Léa were not directly affected and might well have been unaware of those work stoppages.

Between 1909 and 1918, no large-scale organizing drives occurred among the province's textile workers. However, women mill hands continued to initiate their own work actions when they felt they were warranted. As reported in 1912 in *Strikes and Lockouts in Canada,* three hundred women left their machines at the Hochelaga mill in November 1911 to protest the dismissal of a foreman whom they wanted the company to retain. The strike lasted twelve days, and the women succeeded in having the foreman reinstated. Two years later, in March 1913, a group of thirty-seven women employed in the Montmorency mill walked off the job to support their demand for a wage increase. Their action resulted in over four hundred employees in other departments being absent from work for five days. In the end, the striking workers returned to their machines without gaining the wage increase and had to resort to arbitration to get management to take them back, as others had been brought in to replace them.

The UTWA, dedicated to organizing skilled men workers, did manage to attract some support at the local level and among certain groups of specialized workers. Its appeal grew during World War I as workers sought to hold their own against deteriorating working conditions and the devastating impact of spiraling inflation. In June 1918, some three thousand employees of the various Dominion Textile mills in Montreal went on strike under the auspices of the UTWA, and cotton workers in Montmorency and Magog soon joined them. As reported by the provincial ministry of public works and labour, their demands included: union recognition; a forty-four-hour workweek; a 50 percent wage increase; bonuses for overtime work, night shifts, and work on Sundays; the abolition of the fining system; continued payment for workers when production was stopped for reasons beyond the workers' control; and publication of the price lists for piece work.

The company refused to accede to any of the strikers' demands or to recognize the union on the grounds that, having its headquarters outside the country, the UTWA would jeopardize the ability of the company and its employees to act in their own best interests. Management also defended the continued use of fines, claiming that they were used only in the card rooms to penalize operators one cent for each bobbin of poor quality twist that subsequently had to be repaired by other workers. Dominion Textile did offer to increase wages by 10 percent, provided the strikers returned to work immediately. The strikers clung firmly to their list of demands, and the work stoppage dragged on for two months.

Not surprisingly, given the intransigence of the company and the high financial costs of such a prolonged strike for the workers, the strikers were finally forced to concede. They returned to work in August 1918 under conditions that had existed before they walked out. The company did promise to re-evaluate wage schedules within three months and to make an upward adjustment if its financial circumstances permitted. Over the next several months, various public officials urged the company to live up to its promise, but it was only in April 1920 that management formally replied to workers' demands. In a terse letter addressed to the government's industrial disputes arbitrator, General Manager F.G. Daniels claimed that, while there had been no general increment in wage rates, workers' wages had increased because the company had implemented a bonus system. The more workers produced, the more they earned. On the basis of some fragmentary and highly questionable data, he argued that wages had increased 35 percent during the previous year. This explanation more than satisfied the government's representative, who proudly proclaimed to his superiors that he had gained more for the workers in his negotiations with the company than the workers had been able to gain after an extremely costly two-month strike.

Issues such as the fine system and foremen's behaviour were of great significance for women workers and were often at the root of their militant actions. They engaged in numerous strategies to counteract managerial power and control, ranging from the individual and informal (slowing production by taking toilet breaks, helping companions with their work, taking unauthorized holidays) to the collective and formal (participating in work stoppages and strikes, joining a union). Initially, women resorted to spontaneous walkouts to try to address their problems, but with the arrival of unions such as the FOTC and the UTWA, their actions were increasingly subject to organizational control and the dictates of collective bargaining. In more than one instance, unions abandoned women workers' demands in favour of reaching an agreement with management. Gender parity within the labour movement was still a long way off.

PART 2
1919-1951

Dominion Textile, Magog
The Magog cotton mill and print works remained one of the largest
cotton manufacturing complexes in Canada. (BAnQ, 464-57.)

CHAPTER FOUR

DOMINATING THE CANADIAN
COTTON INDUSTRY

By 1919, the euphoria created by the Allied victory had given way to economic, social, and political turmoil as Canada contended with post-war recession, unprecedented waves of labour unrest, the Spanish influenza that left fifty thousand Canadians dead, and the increased alienation of Quebec as a result of the 1917 conscription crisis. Canadians would experience some of the most serious challenges in their country's history over the next two decades. The so-called "roaring twenties" started with a deep recession and slow economic growth. Despite a few years of unprecedented prosperity toward the end of the 1920s, the decade ended in a financial crisis of epic proportions. The Great Depression saw the country's economy plunge into uncharted territory, and its social fabric was severely tested as unemployment rates soared and bread lines grew. Then, at the end of the decade, just as Canadians started to enjoy improved economic conditions, World War II broke out, and the country was once again stretched to the limit to fulfill its obligations as a principal combatant. The ensuing period of uncertain post-war adjustment was fortunately short and was followed by a prolonged economic boom. Another international conflict, however, was just around the corner. In 1950, Canadian soldiers were once again playing a substantial role, this time in Korea, in a three-year conflict that would claim over five hundred of their lives.

All of these events directly affected the fortunes of the Canadian cotton industry, increasingly concentrated in Quebec. This dominance resulted from the unrivalled ascent of Dominion Textile as not only the largest cotton manufacturer in Canada but also one of the largest in North America. During years of prosperity in the 1920s, the Quebec manufacturers expanded operations by adding to their physical plants, installing more modern machinery, and continuing to actively recruit labour. When the Depression resulted in a decline in demand for their products and posed a serious threat to their financial well-being, the companies did not stop their investments in new machinery. Rather they sought to weather the economic downturn by calling for increased tariffs, reducing the number of workers on their payrolls, and relying on technological innovations to reduce costs. Only when unprecedented demand for their products occurred during the war did companies actively recruit more workers. Demand for experienced workers remained strong following the war due to pent-up civilian demand, but by the late 1940s, a renewed emphasis on improved production processes and more modern machinery resulted once again in the need for fewer workers.

Key to the ability of Quebec's cotton manufacturers to adjust to their oscillating fortunes were women, who acted as a readily accessible labour pool. During World War I, women workers, including married women, had played an important role in enabling companies to meet their production demands. Once the war was over, however, women with husbands capable of supporting them were let go. A decade later, even the right of single women to find employment in the province's mills was hotly contested, and women lost ground to men. When the companies faced critical labour shortages during World War II, once again they turned to women to solve this problem. By the end of the war, married women comprised a much larger proportion of the workforce than they had previously. While many were let go again when the post-war demand for cotton products fell, married women continued to represent an increasingly significant proportion of women in the industry's labour force.

The Tortuous Twenties

For Canadian cotton manufacturers, the reconstruction period immediately following World War I marked the beginning of a very uncertain future. Lucrative war contracts dried up even as wages and the cost of materials such as bleaches and dyes soared. Federal taxes, introduced as a temporary war measure in 1917, also represented a new draw on company revenues, one that would soon prove permanent. Renewed competition from abroad also threatened to undercut profits. Nonetheless, the *Annual Financial Review— Canadian* indicated that 1919 and 1920 were generally satisfactory years for the industry. After an initial slump in business resulting from the termination of hostilities in Europe, the companies were able to find new outlets, including Romanian orders organized by the federal government, and manufacturing operations were maintained at full capacity. In response to these favourable circumstances and mounting surpluses, the three dominant companies in Quebec—Dominion Textile, Montreal Cottons, and Wabasso—all raised the dividends paid on their common shares.

The trend toward concentration and specialization that had characterized the pre-war industry accelerated. By the 1930s, 70 percent of all cotton textile mills in Canada were located in Quebec. Dominion Textile's operations were located at eight plants, namely, Hochelaga, Merchants, Colonial, Saint Anne, Mount Royal, and Verdun, all of which were located in Montreal, as well as Montmorency and Magog. Each mill was assigned its own special line of products, with the Colonial branch serving as the dyeing centre for goods produced at the various factories, and Magog as the printing site. Dominion Textile was by far the largest of the primary cotton manufacturers. As its directors boasted in their seventeenth annual report issued in March 1922, "We have now in operation 530,000 spinning spindles, 17,000 twisting spindles, 11,023 looms and supply direct employment to upwards of 8,000 operatives." Another innovation was the elimination of external sales agents when the company expanded its own sales department to deal directly with the garment industry and the retail sector.

Montreal Cottons, Valleyfield
This inter-war period post card shows the impressive Montreal Cottons
site. In the 1920s, some 3500 workers made the daily trek into the mill.
(BAnQ, CP 037571 CON)

Shawinigan Cotton Mill, Shawinigan Falls
Built in 1910 by promoters who had established the Wabasso Cotton
Manufacturing Company three years earlier in nearby Trois-Rivières,
this mill operated until 1985. Initially, some of the women workers
resided in a boarding house operated by Dominican nuns.
(BAnQ , CP 021472 CON)

By this time, Montreal Cottons had been under the control of Dominion Textile for a decade, sharing the same board of directors, although it continued to retain its separate corporate status. In January 1921, the *Canadian Textile Journal* reported that the company provided employment to more than 3,500 persons in Valleyfield, a city boasting just over 9,000 inhabitants. Depressed conditions in the industry had led management there to impose a four-day workweek from January to September that year, but conditions improved to such an extent in 1922 that the company erected a four-storey addition to the mill and installed a new hydroelectric power system. Wabasso also expanded its operations in 1923 and added more modern equipment, including 150 new automatic looms. By the following year, it was providing work for over 2,500 people in Trois-Rivières, a city of some 33,000 inhabitants.

Dominion Textile's strong performance, as reflected in the $5 million surplus accumulated by that time, led to a corporate reorganization in 1923. To the 225,000 shares of new common stock, the company ascribed a book value of $15 million. In actual fact, only $2,500,000 of new capital had been added to the $1 million originally invested in 1905. The company's explanation for the prodigious increase in the stated worth of its common stock was the added value of its assets, appraised at over $10,450,000 in 1921. Some years later in his enquiry into the textile industry, Judge W.F.A. Turgeon severely criticized this method of accounting, pointing out that the 1920 appraisal was very suspect since it was conducted during a period of highly inflated values. "The real question," he mused, "is what amount of money can properly be said to have been 'invested' from the point of view of the adequacy of earnings?" Following this reorganization, Dominion Textile's president, Sir Charles Gordon, also assumed the presidency of Montreal Cottons.

Unfortunately, the years immediately following the financial reorganization of Dominion Textile were unsettled ones for Quebec cotton manufacturers. As reported in the *Canadian Textile Journal* in December 1923, less-than-rosy prospects led Dominion Textile to renege on a promise to Saint Lambert's city council to build a new mill in that community located on the south shore of the Saint Lawrence across from Montreal. Workers in communities with long-established mills also felt the impact of the industry's volatility. "Carmen," who started as a doffer in the card room in the Magog mill in 1921, reported that she and her brother left to go to work in the mills in Manchester, New Hampshire for three months in 1923 because they were unable to secure more than two days of work each week at Dominion Textile. While they enjoyed the higher American wages they were able to earn, a sister's illness forced them to return to Magog. In August 1924, citing a reduction in orders and competition from abroad, Dominion Textile closed all of its mills for two weeks, leaving approximately eight thousand employees without work. According to Clémentine, short time continued to be a feature of employment in the Magog mill throughout the late 1920s. As a spinner, she found that she was often sent home during the summers from 1926 to 1930.

Successive cotton-crop failures in the American south, slumping sales, and generally depressed conditions in the trade, particularly from March to September 1924, led to lower net profits. Not surprisingly, manufacturers blamed their problems on tariff reductions and stiff foreign competition. In at least one instance, a spokesperson for the Canadian textile industry linked the tariff directly to protecting the jobs of the some fifty thousand women employed in this economic sector. "It is of the greatest National importance that women industrial workers in Canada, and the sources of their employment, should be safeguarded." wrote Major Douglas Hallam in the *Canadian Textile Journal* in February 1925. He called upon all "who have at heart the welfare of women industrial workers in Canada, and the welfare of Canada as a nation" to lobby for an increase in duties on imported textiles. By the following year, corporate profits had improved substantially, with increased sales paving the way. Share prices in 1926 and 1927 also reflected renewed confidence in the industry. In March 1927, Wabasso issued 17,500 additional no par value shares at $60 each that were fully paid for by October of the same year. The following year, shareholders bought up another issue of 17,500 no par value shares for $80 a share.

The need for new capital resulted from the cotton companies' determination to introduce the latest in labour-saving machinery. Increased efficiency was their watchword, and their mentor was Frederick W. Taylor, the American engineer and father of "Taylorism," who published *The Principles of Scientific Management* in 1911. Many articles outlining the advantages of time and motion studies, the installation of new machinery, improved systems designs, and the bonus scheme for piece workers appeared in the pages of the *Canadian Textile Journal* throughout the decade. Beginning in 1928, Wabasso transformed its manufacturing system from one based on British technology to one that relied on American methods of cloth production. The other Quebec companies were also equipping their plants with new automatic machinery. Dominion Textile, for example, added twenty new print machines to its Magog operations that enabled it to "bleach, dye, print and finish any class of cotton, silk and artificial silk cloth up to 60 inches wide." It also expanded and introduced new machinery into its Merchants, Verdun, and Montmorency plants.

At the same time the companies were making major capital investments, conditions in the industry remained extremely volatile. Dramatic fluctuations in the price of raw cotton throughout 1927, declining sales, and strong competition from foreign producers combined to end the few years of prosperity they had enjoyed. In June 1928, Wabasso reported a decline in profits compared to the previous year, and one year later, a net loss of over $87,000. The company halted payment of dividends on common stocks, and they would not be reinstated for another decade.

Between September 1927 and March 1928, Dominion Textile's plants ran at between 50 and 75 percent capacity. General Manager F.G. Daniels told a *Canadian Textile Journal* reporter in May 1928 that about one-third of the workers had been laid off. Company officials put part of the blame for their difficulties on the federal government, since it had reduced protection for cotton products under the general tariff by between 2.5 and 7.5 percent. Still, at the same time that Dominion Textile was cutting back production and sacking workers, it launched a new issue of forty-five thousand no par value common shares at $75 a share.

The resulting $3,375,000 was used to help finance the acquisition of two American-owned tire fabric plants, one in Drummondville and the other in Sherbrooke. By 1929, Montreal Cottons was also in difficulty, and its profits declined to an unprecedented post-war low of just over $55,000. Daniels, who had succeeded Sir Charles Gordon as president of Dominion Textile in 1928, took over as president of Montreal Cottons as well. Consequently, as the economic crisis of the 1930s set in, Dominion Textile had a virtual stranglehold on the Canadian primary cotton industry.

While company officials were transforming their physical plants in significant ways during the 1920s, they continued to rely on the French-Canadian working class to turn investments into profits. Indeed, patterns related to how, why, and when young women found their ways into the province's cotton mills changed remarkably little in the 1920s. Most young French-Canadian women continued to seek employment there due to a lack of attractive alternative employment opportunities, and because they had relatives who were already working in the mills. Family recruitment remained the textile companies' preferred method of obtaining workers, with Dominion Textile's Frank Daniels outlining its various advantages in terms very similar to those used by manufacturers in previous decades. As reported in the provincial ministry of labour's 1919 annual report, he contended:

> We believe that our system of employment is very suitable for this country, given that it provides young workers with the opportunity to learn and to grow with the development of the industry itself, and at the same time, it permits an entire family, from the father to the child of fourteen years, to find work in the same factory, where the child will, in a certain measure, be under more direct supervision of his parents.

There was one example at this time of a Catholic order offering boarding-house accommodation to single young women. In 1919, the Franciscan order in Trois-Rivières set up La Maison Sainte-Claire with a capacity to house forty female textile workers.

Among interviewees who started working between 1919 and 1929, 60 percent migrated with their families from the countryside to the textile centres, and 80 percent had family members who also worked in the mills. Some of their families were offered company housing as an additional incentive for them to move. "Stéphanie" entered the mill alongside three of her sisters and a brother in 1921 when a Dominion Textile agent convinced her father to move his large family from Saint-Côme, in the Beauce, to Magog. Similarly, "Alphonsine" became a mill worker when a recruiter talked her father into selling his farm near Wotton, some fifty kilometres north of Sherbrooke, and moving his family to Magog. They secured company housing, and seven members started working for the company. In Carmen's case, it was one of her brothers who first went to Magog to check out employment opportunities there. Subsequently, her entire family left Saint-Victor, in the Beauce region, for Magog, and seven family members went to work in the mills on the very same day. In 1929, "Andrée" and her family migrated from Saint-Louis-du-Ha!Ha!, a village located fifty kilometres southeast of Rivière-du-Loup, to Magog. Her mother, who was American, had previously worked as a weaver in New Hampshire. Soon eight family members were employed either in the cotton mill or in the print works. In contrast to these examples, "Zoé's" experience was quite singular. She left Sainte-Luce-sur-Mer in the lower Saint Lawrence region on her own for Magog, where she had some acquaintants. She rented a room and earned extra money by taking in laundry during the first year she worked at Dominion Textile.

While continuing to rely primarily on Quebec families for its labour needs, Dominion Textile also maintained its efforts to recruit experienced women factory workers from England. According to the 1921 census, 6 percent of Quebec's women cotton workers were British-born. The company used a British hiring campaign to add women to the workforce at its new Verdun operation, but the results proved less than satisfactory. According to one company source, the women who signed on were too militant and rough for the company's liking. This experience, compounded by the elimination of the need to recruit workers actively during the Depression, led to a reduction of women mill workers born in Britain, so that by 1941 they accounted for less than 2 percent of all women working in Quebec cotton mills.

With several family members working for one company, it was common for them to work in the same departments. Three of Alphonsine's sisters started in the weave room with her, three of Stéphanie's sisters were spinners, while three of Clémentine's sisters worked in the card room. Uncles and cousins also continued to play an important role in helping young people both find employment and secure better positions within the mill. Notable for their absence in recruitment stories were employed mothers. As "Régina" succinctly stated, "They didn't take married women in those days." The few married women who worked in the industry during the 1920s were mostly widows or, more rarely, those separated from their husbands. While the companies had actively courted married women to offset wartime labour shortages, they were no longer interested in this group once war industries closed down and droves of single women and men sought employment in the mills.

In families struggling to survive, girls continued to be sent as early as possible into waged labour or to be kept at home to help with housework and childcare. Although provincial educational reforms in 1922 had extended the primary school system from four to six years, with optional seventh and eighth years of study in agriculture, commerce, and industry for boys and domestic science for girls, education was not compulsory and there were still school fees to pay. Among the interviewees who began working in the 1920s, 60 percent started in the mills before their fourteenth birthdays, and 80 percent had begun before the age of seventeen. As a result, nearly half had only four years of schooling or less, and fewer than one in five had more than six years.

In every case, the women who began working in the 1920s cited economic necessity and the lack of other job opportunities as reasons for entering the mills. "There was nothing else," explained "Emma" from Valleyfield. "The boss met us and talked to my father. We were a family of twenty children." "Suzanne's" situation was strikingly similar, for she had sixteen siblings and a widowed mother reliant on her children's wages. Only one woman interviewed who started working in the 1920s indicated that she chose to become a cotton worker for personal rather than eco-

Card Room, Mount Royal Spinning Mill, 1929
This interior shot depicts the cavernous nature of mill departments
and the large numbers of machines they typically contained.
The carding machines produced a single strip of cotton (sliver) that
was fed into the narrow cans located at the front of each machine. The
large straps connecting the machines to overhead pulleys and a common
power source are another striking feature. Workers identified breaking
straps that could fly across the room as an ongoing workplace worry.
(LAC, PA800636.)

nomic reasons. "Louisette" went to work at Montreal Cottons
when she turned eighteen, despite her mother's objections and
her family's relative comfort, because she wanted to earn some
money. She had no close relatives working in the mill, in contrast
to nearly all of her workmates.

In many areas of cotton cloth production, girls and women
retained a strong presence during the 1920s. Women interviewed
who worked during that decade maintained that more women than
men were employed in the grey mills and that occupational segregation according to sex continued to be a significant feature of
mill life. According to them, women comprised the overwhelming

majority of workers in the spinning, spooling, warping, bobbin preparation, weaving, and inspection departments. Several commented that there were either no men or only a single man in their own department. Women who worked in card rooms, however, reported that they worked alongside men. In the Magog print works, the numbers of men and women employed were more evenly balanced, but for the most part, jobs were assigned according to the sex of the worker. Women were employed as sewing machine operators, pantographers, folders, and sample makers. Men, by contrast, held jobs as slashers, dyers, and calenders (operators of glazing and smoothing machines). There also continued to be more English-speaking women employed in the print works than in the grey mill, where working conditions were more difficult and where few English-speaking women were to be found.

Even when women and men did the same job such as spinning, women worked on the day shift while men worked at night when conditions in the industry necessitated the addition of a second shift. Women who were questioned also pointed out that men and women did not normally eat together even when they worked in the same department. The youth of the women in the Quebec cotton textile workforce compared to the men also continued to be striking. In 1931, nearly 73 percent were under twenty-five, compared to just 43 percent of men. By contrast, fewer than one in ten women workers was older than thirty-five, while more than one in three men fell into this age category.

Dealing with the Great Depression

It was the smallest of the three major firms that continued to feel fortune's reversal most acutely in the wake of the financial collapse of October 1929. Although Wabasso reported a smaller net loss in 1930 than the previous year, it was still over $50,000. Montreal Cottons also had a difficult year. Sales declined from more than $3.5 million the year before to just over $1 million, and the company declared a manufacturing loss of over $300,000. Only the giant Dominion Textile was able to escape the turbulent years of 1929 and 1930 relatively unscathed. While its mills oper-

Wabasso Cotton Company, Trois-Rivières, circa 1930
Construction of the original mill began in 1907. The company,
specializing in fine white cotton goods, took its name from the Ojibway
word for a snow-white rabbit. Its well-known white rabbit logo featured
prominently on the packaging of its sheets and other household goods.
Substantial additions and improvements to the mill in the 1920s resulted
in the impressive building featured in this photo. The mill closed in 1985.
(McCord Museum, MP-0000.25.600.)

ated at only 50 percent capacity during the latter months of 1928
and the first six months of 1929, they functioned at 80 percent
capacity in the six months leading up to 1930. The company maintained sales at a healthy level by adopting an aggressive policy of
accepting all contracts, no matter the price.

The industry's reaction to increasingly difficult economic circumstances was entirely predictable: it clamoured for increased
protection through tariff regulation. During the 1930 federal election campaign, Conservative leader R. B. Bennett promised to
"use tariffs to blast a way into the markets that have been closed."
In September that year, his newly elected government raised rates
under both intermediate and general tariffs. The Turgeon Commission subsequently documented examples of the very significant increases that took effect as a result of those revisions. For
example, import duties on a common type of American flannelette
jumped 50 percent between 1931 and 1932.

Such favourable government action appears to have alleviated somewhat the cotton manufacturers' problems. At the beginning of 1931, the *Canadian Textile Journal* declared, "the immediate situation for Canadian Textile manufacturing is the most favourable in many years.... As a result of recent tariff revisions, Canadian mills are now in a position to supply a larger share of the domestic market." In their financial report for the year ending in June 1931, Wabasso's directors attributed part of their success in obtaining profits of just over $3,600 to the recent tariff revisions. Observers also credited an expansion of Dominion Textile's operations to the beneficial effects of tariff increases. The company increased activities at its Magog plant in July 1931, and, during the first three months of the following year, production there increased by 25 percent. Magog was now the fifth-largest cotton manufacturing operation in North America, with the day shift alone producing over one million yards of finished cloth each week.

Any gratitude the cotton manufacturers felt for increased protection was short-lived, particularly after Great Britain abandoned the gold standard in September 1931. Although it was expected that this move would result in higher costs for raw cotton for British manufacturers, the prices of their finished products did not increase proportionately. At the same time, Canadian manufacturers had to purchase cotton with their own depreciated currency so that, according to their account, the real margin of protection they enjoyed was at one of the lowest levels ever. To add insult to injury, the Canadian government proceeded to reduce some duties as part of the 1932 Ottawa Agreement on tariffs. Specific duties for cotton goods established in 1930 were reduced by one-third, and certain fine quality fabrics of British origin were now to be admitted duty-free.

It was precisely these revisions that the companies blamed for their worsening economic performance. At the end of June 1932, Wabasso claimed its greatest loss ever of nearly $300,000, and Montreal Cottons failed to record a profit. According to the annual report of the latter company, the plant had not functioned at even half of its normal capacity, and the board took the decision to suspend payment of common stock dividends. "Conditions," the *Annual Financial Review–Canadian* proclaimed in 1933, "have never been so difficult in the cotton manufacturing business in Canada as they are today." Even the dominant Dominion Textile experienced nearly a 60 percent decline in net profits between December 1931 and December 1933. Although sales did improve in 1934, unstable conditions persisted, and the industry continued to rail against foreign competition.

The Quebec cotton companies sought to counteract the negative economic conditions by aggressively modernizing their facilities in order to reduce their per-unit costs. All invested large sums of money in new machinery and reorganized production so that productivity was greatly enhanced. In 1932, while it declared a net loss of over $280,000, Wabasso announced capital expenditures of nearly $190,000 "principally for the purchase of machinery," with a stated purpose of increasing output. In one Valleyfield weave room, technological changes resulted in a three-fold increase in each experienced weaver's output. In 1935, Dominion Textile expanded facilities at its Sherbrooke branch, installing more than one thousand looms and seventy-seven thousand spindles devoted to cotton-goods production.

Indeed, it was the drive for lower overhead costs that led Blair Gordon, managing director of Dominion Textile and son of former company president Sir Charles Gordon, to announce a major change in the company's operations. When the city of Montreal, desperate for additional sources of revenue in the depths of the Depression, sought to increase taxes on the Saint Anne plant, the company responded by closing its operations there in 1934 and relocating the equipment to mills in other parts of the province. The company also closed its Verdun plant and moved its rayon production to Sherbrooke in 1935. As Gordon explained to the *Canadian Textile Journal* in May 1935, "With the highly competitive situation which exists today between domestic and imported goods, it is absolutely impossible to absorb any additional manufacturing costs occasioned by further taxation.... Our only recourse is to concentrate operations in quarters where there is the least threat of further additions to the present cost of manufacture."

The following year, testifying before the Turgeon Commission, Gordon outlined both the extent of the company's operations and how each plant had its own specialized operations. In Montreal the Hochelaga mill produced grey cloth and the Merchants mill turned out wide grey sheeting and yarns. Their products were sent to either the Colonial bleachery in Montreal or to the Magog dye and print works for finishing. The Mount Royal mill in Montreal produced narrow grey cloths that were left in their unfinished state for use in manufacturing or in households. By this time, the Verdun mill was the general machine shop, and the Saint Anne mill, a warehouse. The Magog mill produced a variety of grey cotton fabrics that were subsequently bleached, dyed, or printed in the adjacent print works. The Sherbrooke facility, originally set up to produce tire fabrics, had been converted into a cotton and rayon fabric facility, with the grey cloth being sent to Magog for finishing. Looms for the Sherbrooke cotton division had been shipped from the company's Verdun and Hochelaga operations. The company retained its Drummondville plant for the production of various types of cords used in the manufacture of tires.

By 1936, Dominion Textile also effectively owned its main "competitor," Montreal Cottons. Although the latter continued as a separately incorporated company, Dominion Textile had acquired ownership of just over 50 percent of the common stock. Since Montreal Cottons comprised both a grey mill and a finishing facility for bleaching and dyeing, its products included plain dyed or bleached goods for the tailoring, furniture, and draperies trades, as well as a variety of dress goods and yarns. In addition, Valleyfield was also producing some rayon goods. Orders for materials that required printing were shipped to Magog for completion since Montreal Cottons did not have its own printing facility.

Tariffs on textiles underwent significant changes in 1936. The previous year Mackenzie King's Liberal government had replaced Bennett's protectionist Conservative administration. Given the prime minister's background in industrial relations, pro-labour leanings, and distaste for "tariff-coddled manufacturers," textile manufacturers had their work cut out for them to maintain their

Warp Room, Dominion Textile Verdun Mill, 1929
This photo reveals a number of features related to the warping process
and the mill environment. In this large room, thread from many rows
of spools are being fed onto large rollers (warp beams) to form
continuous warp threads for weaving. The overhead power belts
connected to each spooling frame are also clearly visible.
(Library and Archives Canada, PA800616.)

competitive advantage. King was also incensed when he learned
that workers in some mills had found notes in their pay envelopes
encouraging them to vote Conservative in the 1935 election. When
the King government did act on tariffs, it ordered further reductions covering several cotton products. But it was not only British
manufacturers who were able to secure lower duties. As a result
of a trade agreement concluded between Canada and the United
States, values for the purpose of establishing duties on American
cotton fabrics were abolished as of January 1, 1936. The overall
effect of these additional tariff alterations was an augmentation
of imported cotton goods. The Turgeon Commission's final report
showed increases in the number of pounds of various cotton yarns

and fabrics imported between 1934 and 1937 ranging from 4 percent to as high as 77.5 percent.

Despite the industry's many challenges, both the Royal Commission on Price Spreads, created in 1934 and headed by H. H. Stevens, and the Turgeon Commission, concluded that it weathered the Depression far better than most other sectors of the economy. According to Turgeon's *Report*, domestic producers' share of the Canadian market increased from 65 percent in 1929 to 77 percent by 1933 as a result of the upward tariff revisions. Although imports increased as a result of the revival of trade and tariff reductions in 1936, Canadian manufacturers' products still accounted for 71 percent of cotton goods consumption in that year. Moreover, in comparison to wholesale prices for cotton fabrics in the United States and the United Kingdom, those in Canada remained higher. The Stevens Commission *Report* concluded:

> The textile industry is the favourite child of the tariff, it was the first to receive additional consideration when the depression descended upon us. Excessive duties were imposed on textiles entering the country in order to assure the Canadian market to the Canadian manufacturer. . . . Imports of cotton fabrics were reduced by 50 000 000 yards — but the Canadian manufacturers did not supply the deficiency. They reduced their own production by approximately 20 per cent. . . . Perhaps they could not produce the goods at a price our people could pay but other people could, and had it not been for the tariff, would have sold us textile fabrics at prices more within our reach than the prices asked by Canadian manufacturers.

The textile industry responded by arguing that it had saved many communities from the dire effects of the prolonged economic downturn. In September 1936 the *Canadian Textile Journal* proclaimed, "Textile labour in the primary manufacturing branches of the industry has met and conquered the depression years with fortitude and contentment, and there are literally scores of textile manufacturing communities in this country where the ravages of the depression have scarcely been felt." Indeed, by the end of 1936 the cotton companies were reporting improved results. In its review of the 1936-37 fiscal year, Dominion Textile pointed out that, for the first time in three years, the amount needed to meet dividend payments had been entirely earned. In addition, another expansion of the grey mill and printing facilities in Magog and an increase in the number of employees province-wide from approximately 6,000 to 7,000 suggested a renewal of confidence and growth. Montreal Cottons also reported a much better financial position and made improvements to its plant in Valleyfield. It had increased its workforce to 2,800 employees. For its part, Wabasso was able to pay dividends on its stock in 1937 for the first time since 1928, and the number of workers exceeded 2,000. Rising stock prices in the industry also reflected increased investor confidence by 1937.

A massive strike among Quebec's cotton workers, however, brought the industry to a standstill for four weeks in August of that year and resulted in yet another decline in production. Short-time operations were common once again, and all three companies reported subsequent declines in net profits. Montreal Cottons' annual report for 1937 stated that yearly earnings were scarcely sufficient to cover the required dividends. Over the next two years net profits for all three companies failed to reach their 1937 levels and, once again, the companies blamed the federal government's tariff policies. They also cited high labour costs as the other main contributor to the industry's problems. Dominion Textile officials in 1938 claimed that the cost of labour involved in the transformation of one pound of raw cotton into one pound of manufactured goods was greater than the total of all other manufacturing costs. They warned government and workers that if domestic markets were not assured and if employees pressed too hard for wage increases, the size of the workforce might have to be reduced. This was a very real threat considering the technological enhancements that mill managers had continued to introduce, even at the nadir of the Depression.

The case of Sherbrooke illustrates the power of a company such as Dominion Textile to influence the local employment situation. Although that city was less dependent on a single employer than were smaller mill towns, in March 1939, municipal officials there requested a special meeting with Blair Gordon to draw attention to the need to generate more work in their community. This request had been prompted by the appearance of a workers' delegation to city council that pointed out that some two hundred Dominion Textile workers were working only a few days each fortnight. A subsequent meeting with company officials demonstrated both the urgency of the situation and the stature of the company. Held in Quebec government offices in Montreal, it was attended not only by municipal politicians but also by the local member of the Quebec legislature and the federal member of parliament for the Sherbrooke constituency. Despite the considerable pressure that was brought to bear on him, Gordon remained noncommittal.

One of the critical issues motivating the federal investigations into the state of the Canadian textile industry in the 1930s was the extent to which it maintained employment during the Depression. In return for tariff protection, government officials expected textile producers to do all in their power to shield their workers from the devastating effects of unemployment. According to the Royal Commission on Price Spreads, however, the volume of employment between 1930 and 1934 in the primary cotton industry declined 6 percent despite an increase in the volume of production. The principal reason given was the implementation of technological innovations that resulted in a reduced need for labour. In 1935, Montreal Cottons claimed a total of 2,476 workers, fewer than the 2,722 it reportedly employed in 1902. Nonetheless, the local newspaper estimated that some 7,500 individuals among Valleyfield's almost 14,000 inhabitants were dependent on cotton workers' wages.

Judge Turgeon reported two years later that between 1929 and 1937 employment in the cotton yarns and cloth sector was the most adversely affected of all branches of the primary textile industry. The number of workers reached its lowest level in 1933, the depth of the Depression. Even with the return of more favourable conditions in the latter part of the decade, employment figures remained low. Moreover, raw data regarding the total number of employees could be very misleading because they did not necessarily represent the number of full-time workers. Nor did the declared number of individuals necessarily work fifty-two weeks each year. In fact, it is clear from the testimony presented before the Turgeon Commission that many did not.

Competition for jobs was fierce and led to deeply felt resentment toward outsiders taking mill jobs, even if the "strangers" lived only a short distance away in neighbouring municipalities. The *Progrès de Valleyfield* reported in June 1934 that civic officials in that town passed a resolution requesting that Montreal Cottons hire only local residents, a proposal the company endorsed by proclaiming that it would restrict its hires to individuals who had resided in the town for at least six months. Given the decreased demand for workers and the desire of townspeople to protect remaining jobs for their own citizens, recruiting campaigns that featured so prominently in earlier decades were no longer needed. Only one of sixteen women interviewed who started working in the Magog and Valleyfield mills in the 1930s reported that she had moved from the countryside to find employment. All of the others already lived in the community in which they went to work. Some other corporate practices with regard to maintaining and, to some degree, controlling mill workforces did persist. In the mid-1930s, for example, Montreal Cottons was renting some two hundred cottages to its workers. The company also continued to operate its 235-acre farm, winning provincial prizes for its herd of over a hundred purebred Holsteins and Ayrshires. The milk processed at the company-owned dairy and sold in MOCO [acronym for Montreal Cottons] bottles was another daily reminder of Montreal Cottons' pervasive presence in Valleyfield.

Reduced employment opportunities meant that women interviewed in this group were also older when they entered mill employment than their counterparts of the 1920s had been. Only one was under fourteen, and only 40 percent were under sixteen. They also had more education, with 40 percent reporting that they had nine years or more. Only two women had attended school for less than six years. In 1929, the Quebec government had extended the school system once again to include an eleventh year. It seems that some working class girls were staying in school longer since jobs were not readily available. "Léda" attended convent school in Thetford Mines until she was eighteen and then

Left: Montreal Cottons Advertisement
This ad, featuring the well-known MOCO trademark, celebrated the
diamond jubilee of the local Valleyfield newspaper. The company had
marked its own 60th anniversary in 1934. It boasted that Montreal
Cottons was one of the largest textile operations in Canada and the oldest
cotton factory to still be operating under the same company name.
(*Le Progrès de Valleyfield*, December 30, 1937.)

Right: MOCO Milk Bottle. Montreal Cottons continued to operate its
own dairy, using milk produced by the award-winning herd of dairy
cattle stabled on its 225-acre farm. The milk was distributed in bottles
bearing the company name. The farm operations and dairy closed in
1948 following the acquisition of Montreal Cottons by Dominion Textile.
https://laiteriesduquebec.com/dairies/cotton.htm.

taught for eight years. However, she earned only $250 a year teaching during the 1930s, and so jumped at the chance to become a clerk at the Magog mill in 1939 when a friend of her brother-in-law brought the position to her attention.

The Turgeon Commission identified two significant employment trends, namely a decline in the proportion of the workforce composed of women, and the replacement of skilled workers by unskilled operatives as more automatic machinery was introduced. Evidence amassed during this enquiry shows that the proportion of girls and women among Canadian cotton workers fell from 46 percent in 1920 to 36 percent by 1935. Three possible reasons were advanced for this reduction: the pervasive bias against women's employment during the Depression, the replacement of women by men as a result of minimum-wage legislation that initially applied only to women, and an increased emphasis on finishing processes that typically employed more men.

It is not difficult to identify various obstacles to women's employment. According to "Adèle," married women were let go at the Magog premises during the 1930s and a new night shift composed entirely of men spinners was created. Many of them had been moved from Dominion Textile's Sherbrooke mill. A married woman who testified before Judge Turgeon, Josephine Fortin, testified that she was let go from her position as a weaver in 1936 because her husband had a job. Still, women's representation in the cotton goods industry was 10 percent higher in 1934 than it was in Canadian manufacturing in general. It was also a younger workforce, with more than one in three women wage earners under the age of twenty, compared to just over one in four women in domestic manufacturing as a whole. Among the many exhibits that were introduced at the Turgeon hearings, one from February 1936 outlined the age distribution of workers for Dominion Textile, Montreal Cottons, and Wabasso. The proportion of women workers under twenty-five ranged from 55 percent at Dominion Textile and Wabasso to 66 percent at Montreal Cottons. By contrast, only one-third of men workers at both Dominion Textile and Montreal Cottons and just under one-half of those employed by Wabasso fell into the same age category.

Minimum-wage legislation, ironically designed to protect women, had a well-documented deleterious effect on women's employment. One poignant example was the petition to the Quebec Minimum Wage Board submitted on behalf of a group of young women employed at Montreal Cottons:

> We, the undersigned, being employees of the above-mentioned manufacturer [Montreal Cottons], as battery hands, receive a lower salary for this type of work than the salary required by the Minimum Wage Board for our length of experience. Nonetheless we wish to continue our present work under the same conditions, until there are openings for higher paying work which requires more skill, and by the present, we abandon our right to a higher salary, as required by our length of experience at our present work.

Two of the battery hands, Thérèse Leblanc and Alice Leduc, testified that their foreman, Jack Hill, had used an interpreter to instruct all the battery hands in the Louise mill weaving room in Valleyfield to sign the document. When they asked Hill what would happen if they did not sign, he told them that if they were not satisfied with their jobs, they could look for another one elsewhere. One employee refused to sign, and she was let go. For its part, the provincial minimum wage commission readily acceded to the companies' requests to continue to employ women workers at wages below the legislated minimum so that they would not dismiss the women.

Women had to worry not only about being replaced by other, less experienced women workers, but also faced keen competition from men, especially young unskilled men. In his report, H.H. Stevens recommended "minimum wage laws for men. Otherwise the practice, so often illustrated in the evidence, will continue of substituting men and boys for women at wages below the legal rate that must be paid the latter." The accuracy of Stevens' analysis was illustrated when Blair Gordon testified before the Turgeon Commission that "you are limited by the Quebec minimum wage law to a certain number of females in the lowest paid group . . . you cannot have more than 10% of all your females earning wages in that low group . . . if it was a question that having more girls in that group would put us over the 10%, we would naturally use boys instead."

The technological changes identified by the Turgeon Commission also played a role in the changing patterns of women's employment in the Quebec industry. As already noted, the companies continued to make substantial capital investments throughout the Depression and to increase their productive capacity. In an interview published in the *Canadian Textile Journal* in March 1932, H. F. Mills, general superintendent of cotton manufacturing for Dominion Textile, claimed that more technical changes were made following World War I than during the previous twenty-five years. More specifically, he mentioned "one-process picking, two-process drawing, long drafting on speeder frames and spinning frames, high speed spooling, winding and warping, hot air drying of yarn during slashing instead of cylinder drying, [and] the high speed automatic loom." He further underlined the importance of changes in work processes that had put cotton mill workers in entirely new circumstances. "In the weave rooms of our mills some of our weavers are operating up to 100 looms without any hardship. In spinning, card room speeder processes, and on carding engines the number of machines or spindles attended per operative has been increased by 50 per cent or more. For instance deliveries of draw frames have been stepped up from 24 to 96 per operative." These changes, Mills contended, resulted in "the elimination of the weaker labour," but had not resulted in any labour unrest, presumably because the employees understood that changes were necessary in order for the company to meet "severe competition."

The introduction of new machinery in carding, spinning, and weave rooms worked to the disadvantage of women since it greatly reduced the numbers of workers needed to produce ever-greater quantities of grey goods. At the same time, the work that experienced female spinners and weavers performed could be transferred to less experienced male workers as a result of technical improvements to the machinery. Fully automatic looms required less intervention and therefore less skill. Leonard Marsh, the well-known Montreal social worker, pointed out in his 1935 study of employment trends:

Increased mechanization means that the complicated tasks formerly performed by skilled workers are continually broken down and simplified until the task approaches the routine. The skilled operative is replaced by the 'machine minder.' Mechanization, immensely increased output and large-scale operation have all proceeded together.

The overall result was that there were fewer opportunities for women to find employment in the cotton industry, and the jobs available to them were increasingly of an unskilled nature. An analysis of the Quebec cotton industry produced in December 1937 reported that women made up 36 percent of the entire cotton mill workforce at that time, compared to 39 percent in 1931. These trends in women's employment can be further documented by census data for 1931 and 1941. Over the intervening decade the number of women workers increased by only 21 percent whereas the number of men grew by 59 percent. Furthermore, among women production workers employed in 1931, approximately half were either spinners or weavers. Ten years later, only 42 percent were spinners, twisters, or weavers. By contrast, the proportion of spinners who were men rose from just over one-third in 1931 to one-half by 1941, and the proportion of weavers who were men increased from just over one-half to over two-thirds. Women had clearly lost considerable ground in terms of both the relative number and quality of jobs they were offered.

Wartime Conditions

Although the Depression was now behind them, the first few months of 1939 did not augur well for the cotton manufacturers. At the end of March, officials for Dominion Textile reported a decline of 18 percent in the volume of sales compared to the previous year and the necessary disposal of several product lines at unsatisfactory prices. Once again, they blamed the federal government's failure to provide adequate tariff protection and workers' higher wages for this unsatisfactory state of affairs. For Dominion Textile shareholders, earnings per common share ($3.38) fell to the lowest level recorded since 1933, when they had reached an unprecedented low of $1.80. Management accordingly announced that it would limit capital investments in new machinery to necessary replacements.

The eruption of hostilities in Europe in September 1939 was to alter the fortunes of the cotton companies in ways that the directors and management of Dominion Textile could not possibly have imagined six months earlier. With Canada's entry into the war on September 10, demand for cotton goods soared almost immediately. Canadian mills began to transform thousands of pounds of cotton yarn into khaki, canvas, camouflage cloth, airplane fabric, and fuses for explosives for the Canadian armed forces, and into a myriad of cotton products that other war industries required. In its annual report ending in December 1939, Montreal Cottons highlighted a significant upturn in activity, substantially higher profits, the creation of a number of special reserve funds, and a 10 percent increase in workers' wages. At the same time, it was quick to point out that dividends had not been increased and that shareholders with common stock were continuing to earn only 2 percent on their investments.

The year 1939 also ushered in significant changes in the administration of Montreal Cottons, following the death of Sir Charles Gordon in July. He had held, often simultaneously, the key positions of Dominion Textile managing director, president, and chairman of the board since 1905 and similar posts with Montreal Cottons since 1906. His son, G. Blair Gordon, who had been named managing director of both Montreal Cottons and Dominion Textile in 1934, now became president of both companies. A graduate of McGill with a degree in electrical engineering, the younger Gordon enjoyed recounting how he had worked his way up the ranks at Dominion Textile. Employed as an assistant adjuster at the age of twenty-three, he worked a regular shift from 7 a.m. until 6 p.m., cleaning and adjusting machines for 41 cents an hour. In addition to emphasizing his "lowly" beginnings with the company on the mill floor, Gordon also liked to stress that he personally held less than 1 percent of the company's common shares and that no shareholder controlled more than 5 percent.

Gordon astutely arranged for the direct purchase of one million bales of raw cotton from the government of Brazil following the declaration of war. That was enough raw material to keep all of the province's cotton mills functioning for a full year. As the war progressed, however, and overseas raw cotton became too dangerous to ship, the Canadian plants had to rely on American cotton that was commanding significantly higher prices.

Following the German occupation of Belgium and the Netherlands and the subsequent fall of France in the spring of 1940, Canada found itself as Britain's main ally and involved in a total war effort. It would be yet another year and a half before the Americans would enter the fray. Consequently, the Canadian textile industry experienced the full impact of a rapid ramping-up of wartime production. A report in the *Canadian Textile Journal* published in April 1942 indicated that Montreal Cottons had increased its cotton cloth production by 34 percent compared to the amount it had manufactured in 1938. Dominion Textile similarly reported substantial increases in output, particularly of heavier types of cloth needed for war purposes. To meet the military and civilian demand, management put the old Saint Anne plant in Montreal back into production and sold the Verdun plant, closed since 1935, to the federal government. Altogether Dominion Textile produced more than 25 million yards of cotton drill cloth for the Canadian armed forces by war's end. Both companies also manufactured significantly greater quantities of rayon, a fabric derived from cellulose. The induction of women into the armed forces stimulated the demand for rayon since large quantities of this material were used in the manufacture of their uniforms.

Competition within the tender system for textile war contracts was extremely limited. Since external supplies from the United Kingdom and Japan were no longer available, domestic companies had guaranteed sales for all they could produce. Only four companies—Dominion Textile; its subsidiary Montreal Cottons; Wabasso; and Canadian Cottons, with mills in Ontario and New Brunswick—had the capacity to produce the drill cottons and cotton shirting the department of munitions and supplies required. Most frequently, Dominion Textile and Montreal Cottons submitted the lowest bids, whereas Wabasso, operating at capacity prior to the outbreak of war, was not so anxious to secure government orders. Consequently, it was primarily the first two companies that benefited from defence orders.

In December 1941 the cotton manufacturers struck a voluntary agreement with the Wartime Prices and Trade Board to regulate prices. It was the first industry to be so regulated, and provided the model that was applied to other industrial sectors. The terms of this agreement set prices for all consumer goods on the basis of 1940 manufacturers' prices. In return, the cotton manufacturers received a subsidy from the Commodity Prices Stabilization Corporation to offset increases in the price of raw cotton, since it was not subject to price control. To get the subsidy, textile earnings could not exceed 116.67 percent of standard profits. In an attempt to forestall the extensive war profiteering that had occurred during World War I, the federal government also introduced excess-profits legislation in 1940 that imposed a minimum corporate tax rate of 30 percent.

Given the heavily regulated economic framework in which they functioned, the cotton companies continually complained that the federal government was the primary beneficiary of the substantial earnings generated by the unprecedented levels of production. The Dominion Textile directors' report for 1942 claimed "the apportionment of income between shareholders and the Government is in the ratio of 1 for the shareholders to 5.384 for the Government." While there is no doubt that corporate income and excess-profit taxes did drain off a great deal of the company's gross profits, net profits and net earnings per common share showed a very substantial improvement over 1939 levels. By March 1945, net earnings had nearly tripled. Although Dominion Textile maintained its dividends at the usual rates, various reserves grew significantly. The contingency reserve, for example, increased by 344.5 percent. By 1945, the corporation also had a deferred surplus, representing the refundable portion of excess profits tax, of over $565,000.

Despite its healthy financial position and the national focus on winning the war, however, Dominion Textile and its subsidiaries continued to dispute municipal assessments. In 1941, for example, Montreal Cottons initiated court action against the municipality of Valleyfield in an effort to have the $3.7 million assessment of its properties reduced by $1.9 million, an action that it ultimately lost. The textile companies also persisted in contesting matters such as the payment of water taxes and public use of company-owned bridges within the municipalities in which they were located.

When Canada entered the war, the Depression was at an end. Its effects, however, were still being felt, especially by the significant number of unemployed people, estimated to be around 900,000. Nevertheless, this surplus pool of labour was soon depleted. Between September 1939 and February 1940, Montreal Cottons alone added an additional 500 employees to its workforce. By mid-1940, the cotton companies were struggling to find enough workers to fill all three shifts. The 1941 federal census indicated that Valleyfield's population was slightly more than 17,000 inhabitants and that Montreal Cottons was by far the largest employer. Of the 2,431 men recorded as engaged in manufacturing occupations, more than half were already working in the textile industry. For women, dependence on mill employment was even more pronounced. Those who worked in textiles represented 94 percent of all women engaged in manufacturing and 50 percent of all female wage earners.

To alleviate the chronic labour shortage and mobilize Canadian labour as effectively as possible, the federal government created the National Selective Service (NSS) in March 1942. Two months later, it turned its attention to the mobilization of women and created the Women's Division to oversee the recruitment of women into a wide range of settings, including primary and secondary war industries, the service sector, agriculture, and the newly created women's divisions of the armed forces. Although 65 percent of the Canadian cotton industry's production was destined for war orders or essential use, the federal government did not designate the textile industry as "essential" but rather as "restricted." This designation meant that workers could leave the industry without much difficulty. The *Canadian Textile Journal* reported in May 1942 that "both volume and quality of production have suffered in spite of employment of new labour and action by the industry to train such labour as rapidly as possible." In the face of ongoing labour shortages, the industry lobbied the federal department of labour and the NSS to help keep workers in the industry. The minister of labour, Humphrey Mitchell, responded by sending telegrams to textile workers indicating that the government did consider textiles to be an essential war industry.

Even before the establishment of the NSS Women's Division, Canadian women were entering the workplace, albeit slowly at first. Only twenty thousand women joined the ranks of wage earners during the first year of the war, but the following year, another one hundred thousand did so. The 1941 census showed that urban women residing in Quebec recorded the highest rate of gainful employment at 29 percent, compared to 27 percent for urban women at the national level. Analysts attributed this fact to the huge presence of the textile industry in Quebec and to the fact that working class women in that province were seeking to make up for the economic hardships they had endured during the previous decade. Close to six thousand women were reportedly working in the Quebec cotton industry.

The first stage in the federal government's efforts to attract even more women to paid employment involved the national registration of all women between the ages of twenty and twenty-four. Although both single and married women in this age group had to register, it was hoped that a sufficiently large pool of single young women would be created so that married women would remain at home. The NSS Women's Division undertook a massive publicity campaign to encourage single women to enter the workforce, and initiated mobility programs to relocate them from the Maritimes and Prairies to work in central Canadian factories. From June to October 1942 alone, an additional 238,000 women joined the paid workforce so that by the latter date, an estimated 1.2 million women were earning wages—nearly double the number recorded in June 1939. Of these, nearly one-third were employed in manufacturing, and in Quebec, women accounted for 56 percent of all textile workers.

Montreal Cottons War Bond Announcement, 1941
The company placed this ad in the local newspaper to draw attention to
the fact that its workers were actively supporting the war effort by
purchasing war bonds. As the ad points out, the 3205 workers were
buying bonds worth $68,000 each year. Tellingly, there are no women
clearly visible in the drawing of the workers. One former woman
employee told the author that she used the proceeds from her bonds after
the war to purchase a fur coat. (*Le Progrès de Valleyfield*, March 27, 1941.)

Most of the readily available single women had already joined
the labour force by 1943, so the NSS turned its attention to the
recruitment of married women, particularly those residing in
urban areas. As more mobile workers abandoned low-paying positions in traditionally female industrial and service sectors for
higher-paying jobs in war-related industries, the government
agency called on housewives to take on part-time work.
Nonetheless, the labour shortage continued to be a serious concern, and so the government's recruitment plans expanded to
include the full-time employment of married women as well.

Specific encouragement came in the form of changes to the federal income tax act. Starting in July 1942, married women were considered to be full dependents, regardless of how much they earned. In addition, Ottawa introduced the Dominion-Provincial Wartime Day Nurseries Agreement to share equally with the provinces the cost of establishing daycare services for children between the ages of two and six years whose mothers were employed primarily in war industries. Only two provinces— Ontario and Quebec—actually implemented the program, with a total of six nurseries established in Quebec, all in Montreal. Some war industries also created special evening shifts so that married women could more readily combine paid work with their domestic responsibilities.

For Quebec's textile manufacturers, accessing reserve pools of women workers became increasingly important. Once again, the numbers of workers recruited from rural communities and smaller municipalities increased. Over 20 percent of the twenty-nine women interviewed in Magog and Valleyfield who began working in the 1940s reported that this had been their experience, and 80 percent of them had relatives who also worked in the mills. Originally from Lac-Mégantic, "Reine" went to work at Dominion Textile in Magog in 1942 along with her father and two sisters. Several of her aunts and uncles were already employed there, and it was they who encouraged her family to join them. The same year "Huguette" followed her father, her brother, an aunt, and three uncles into the Magog operation. By this time, however, employment procedures were more formal than they had been previously, and it was no longer as simple as presenting oneself at the factory gate. There was now a personnel department to which one had to apply for a position. Dominion Textile employed some 1,400 more women in 1943 than in 1939, while the number of male operatives had grown by only 1,000. Women replaced men on the day shifts so that the mills could continue to operate at night by using male workers. According to the company's annual report for 1943, "women make up a little under 40 percent of our working force and this condition is not subject to much change without offending very influential opinion."

Women sought employment in the mills in the 1940s for many of the same reasons as earlier generations. Most cited their lack of a high school education and resulting limited occupational choices. "It was the only place where you could go to work at that time unless you were well educated," explained "Aline." "If you didn't have training as a nurse, teacher, or secretary, it was the only place. We were very happy to go to work there." A number of the interviewees had worked at other jobs before going into the mills, mostly in domestic service. The poor pay and working conditions associated with this type of work made millwork an attractive option. "Estelle" was most emphatic in representing her entry into the Magog mill in 1942 as a step up: "Goodness me! I was very happy because I increased my wages. I had been working hard in private homes for $1 to $3 per week." Similar reasoning led "Évangeline" and her sister "Elmire" to seek mill employment in 1947. "I didn't earn enough in private homes," explained Elmire, "only $2.50 to $4.00 a week, and that for seven days of work a week." "Hélène" also considered herself fortunate to find a job in the mill a year later: "I was fed up with washing dishes in the Union Hotel. I wanted to work in the textile plant because it paid better."

What was new in the women's accounts of when and why they went to work was that nearly all made their own decisions. They emphasized their own desires more than family necessity to explain their leaving school and starting to make their own money. "Like all young girls," explained "Agnès," "I wanted to go to work. I was fed up to my back teeth with school. I wanted to have money." The fact that it was difficult for women to obtain positions in the industry before the onset of the labour shortage meant that many were older when they first entered the cotton mills. Among the twenty-seven women interviewed who started their employment there in the 1940s, only two were under sixteen. Although they were older, schooling levels for individuals in this group had not increased. Nearly half had six years of education or less, and only one in five had completed nine years or more. They had been out trying to earn a living rather than extending their education.

The oral testimony of women workers also underlines the very noticeable increase in the numbers of women in various departments of the Valleyfield and Magog mills during the war years. Huguette reported that when she began working in the card room in the Gault mill in Valleyfield in November 1942, there were at least four women to every man employed in that area. "Rita," a Magog mill hand who started in 1940, estimated that women comprised approximately half of the workforce at that time. Similarly, "Estelle" noted that there were more women, both single and married, working in the Magog cotton mill during the war. When "Collette" began as a cloth inspector in the same mill in 1939, there were no married women in her department. However, as the war progressed, their numbers grew. According to "Zépherina," at the beginning of the war, Dominion Textile was still firing married women, especially those who were pregnant. However, after 1942, it started to retain married women. She attributed this situation not only to the need for more hands, but also to the *"course aux mariages"* [race to get married] that took place in Quebec as many young Quebecers sought to avoid the compulsory military mobilization of single young men by embracing matrimony. As the shortage of experienced hands became more acute, manufacturers had to reverse their previous policy of letting married women go.

With mill machinery running day and night, it became difficult to arrange repairs and even more difficult to obtain needed parts and new machines. Major replacements of machinery and other plant improvements would have to wait until the conclusion of hostilities in 1945. Dominion Textile's production fell 15 percent by 1943 as a result of the wear on the machinery and the growing dependence on inexperienced workers. Still, by this time, Canadian cotton manufacturers had produced enough military products to fill a train seventy miles long. The next year, Dominion Textile's production fell yet again as a result of a reduction in personnel from 11,000 in 1943 to 9,500 in 1944. This dramatic decrease was due to the large numbers of employees leaving for military service or to take advantage of higher wages in direct war industries such as munitions factories. Company records show

Weave Room, Magog, circa 1940
Marie-Ange Breton stands proudly at one of her looms. She was able to
move from battery hand to weaver as a result of the manpower shortage
created by the war. (Courtesy of Marie-Ange Breton.)

that over 1,000 of them served in the Canadian armed forces during the course of the war.

Dominion Textile's labour shortages were representative of those experienced across the entire Canadian primary textile industry; it was operating with some 150,000 workers instead of the 165,000 industry analysts claimed were needed. Even as production demands were declining towards the end of the war, evidence indicates that at least one company was making a concerted effort to retain married women. One wife who had previously worked at Montreal Cottons received a company letter, dated May 21, 1945 and personally signed by the general manager, W.G.E. Aird, inviting her to return to work. The letter underscored the pressing need for experienced workers to help the company meet post-war civilian demand for textiles in war-torn Europe and Canada.

Overall, not only were there more women in Quebec's mills, but in some instances they were also being assigned to jobs previously reserved for men. Emma, who started as a doffer in Valleyfield's Old Mill in 1924 and then became a spinner, retrained as a machinist during the war. She was given the task of cutting and gluing straps used on compressors that pumped water into the mill. As the war progressed women also took over more physically demanding work that had previously been assigned to men. Zoé worked in the folding room of the Magog print works, handling heavy bolts containing three to four hundred yards of cloth and operating a folding machine that involved using a foot pedal to raise a heavy wooden table on which the cloth was spread. "When I started there [in the folding room]," she explained, "it was all girls, and some women, because it was wartime." Agnès also worked in a non-traditional role for female employees, operating a machine in the finishing room. Moreover, some women also worked on the night shift, which had previously been prohibited. "Guylaine," who married in 1939, reported working from 6 p.m. to 5 a.m. during the war years. It is impossible to ascertain the exact degree to which women assumed exclusively "male" jobs during the war, but it was a minority of women who did so.

It should be noted that some women lost their jobs during the war. This was the case for more highly skilled women who had been working in the engraving section of the Magog print works. Since the production of textiles for military purposes rather than civilian goods became the priority, employees who had been engaged in the finishing of high-end print materials had considerably less work. "Claire," who worked as an engraver, reported that a number of people in her department were laid off during the war. She told her foreman, "If you can't find me a job, I'm going to Montreal." Two days later, he found her another position in the folding department. "Henriette" also indicated that she left her job in the engraving room in 1942 and stayed home until 1958 because they closed that department during the war.

Readjusting to Peacetime

During the hostilities, the domestic textile industry's foreign competition was essentially eliminated, and by war's end Dominion Textile had consolidated its position as the undisputed leader in its sector. As president and managing director of the largest cotton manufacturing conglomerate in Canada, Blair Gordon pushed forward an agenda of greater integration, efficiency, and attendant sweeping technological changes. In addition to its seven grey mills, two converting plants, and controlling interest in Montreal Cottons, the corporation boasted three fully owned subsidiaries. Its American subsidiary, the Howard Cotton Company, purchased raw cotton directly from southern producers, while Industrial Specialty Manufacturing in Valleyfield produced wooden items such as spools and bobbins. Its third subsidiary, Drummondville Cotton, produced tire cord, as well as nets, lines, and ropes for the commercial fishing industry.

Dominion Textile expanded the scope of its operations yet again in October 1945 when it entered an agreement with Burlington Mills Corporation of South Carolina, the largest American producer of rayon product, to form Dominion Burlington Mills Ltd. Each partner owned half of the new subsidiary. The production and sale of all rayon goods was subsequently transferred to the new company's plants in Montreal and Sherbrooke. With its accumulated surplus of over $5 million and average earnings of just short of $10 per common share, investors considered Dominion Textile an attractive investment. The price of a common share had risen from $81 in 1943 to $120 in 1946. The House of Commons Committee on Prices (1948) reported that Dominion Textile's capitalization was more than two-and-a-half times greater than that of its two largest domestic competitors, Wabasso and Canadian Coloured Cottons.

The Quebec cotton industry was healthy in 1945 and 1946 due to a combination of factors, including the significant backlog of civilian orders for cotton goods, a post-war housing boom that strengthened demand for household cotton products, generally stable prices for raw cotton, expansion into new textile products such as rayon, and advantageous tariffs. The return to peacetime conditions was nonetheless a complex transitional period during which the federal government's wartime price controls and sub- sidy program remained in place. Dominion Textile officials declared that over 85 percent of the company's production for 1945-46 sold at fixed rates averaging less than 80 percent of regu- lar selling prices. For most of the following year, the price control/ subsidization program continued, but the Wartime Prices and Trade Board did raise the ceiling on cotton goods prices and the Commodity Prices Stabilization Corporation increased the sub- sidy on raw cotton. Still, it was a difficult period of adjustment as cotton manufacturers were confronted by a combination of rising costs for raw materials and labour, and sales of goods at prices often below the cost of manufacturing.

When net profits showed a marked decline in March 1947, Dominion Textile's management blamed the continuation of price controls as well as the work stoppages in its Montreal mills and the prolonged strike at Montreal Cottons the previous year. Nonetheless, it reported nearly $1.8 million in surplus and reserve funds. On September 15, 1947 all price controls officially came to an end in Canada, and both Dominion Textile and Montreal Cottons issued new price lists the following month. However, with rising competition from artificial fibres such as rayon and nylon, cotton manufacturers were not in a very good position to demand much higher prices. Their sales situation was made somewhat more secure in November 1947 when the federal government imposed restrictions on imported cotton goods. At year's end, Dominion Textile reported an increase of $1 million in net profits, and the return on shareholders' equity was just over 10 percent.

This financial success led to a reorganization of capital and yet another important transformation of the Quebec cotton industry. Dominion Textile's shareholders ratified a plan at the end of November 1947 to provide nine new common shares for each existing common share. This swap was done to provide greater marketability of investors' holdings, since each common share had been trading at $120. The long-standing relationship between Dominion Textile and Montreal Cottons became even closer. In February 1948, Dominion Textile issued a formal takeover bid to Montreal Cottons common stock shareholders, offering them a straight share-for-share exchange for their stocks. By the end of the year, the manufacturing giant controlled its subsidiary's equity, but it took another five years to redeem all of the preferred shares. Despite the takeover, Montreal Cottons continued to retain its corporate identity and to issue separate financial statements. Dominion Textile also acquired a substantial interest in the Caldwell linen mills located in Iroquois, Ontario and majority control of Flax Industries in Drummondville, a company devoted to the production of linen yarn.

The year after Dominion Textile took over Montreal Cottons proved to be truly outstanding from a financial standpoint. Net profits soared to $5 million. Wabasso, Dominion Textile's remaining rival in Quebec, also showed impressive results in the immediate post-war era. Its common stock prices in 1946 were triple what they had been immediately prior to the war. In 1948, management reorganized that company's capital by providing for a five-for-one common stock split. The following year each new share earned a dividend of 90 cents, and then $1.00 in each of the ensuing two years.

Starting in 1946, as machinery became more readily available, Dominion Textile began to undertake significant physical changes to its plants, improvements that had been postponed during the war years. A continuing shortage of skilled and semi-skilled labour, rising wages, and the spectre of renewed foreign competition motivated extensive capital investments designed to substantially increase output per individual worker. Management replaced remaining old British equipment with new American machinery, including state-of-the-art, high-speed looms and new twisting machines. Clémence recalled being trained on a twisting device by an American woman who had been sent to Valleyfield to demonstrate how the new machinery worked.

Further reflecting its healthy bottom lines, Dominion Textile invested over $11 million in improvements in its facilities between 1946 and 1948. It enlarged its Valleyfield operation and added a new two-storey building to its Magog mill to ensure that a large supply of grey cloth could be kept on hand for the print works. A further consolidation of the company's operations took place with the closure of the Colonial branch in Montreal and the transfer of all bleaching, dyeing, and printing processes to Magog. Dominion Textile also constructed a major addition to its Saint Anne yarn mill and modernized its Mount Royal plant. By 1950, however, the company began to reduce significantly its expenditures on fixed assets. According to its report to stockholders the following year, it had ". . . been forced to take a breathing spell, although the need for a continuing programme is still imperative to maintain our competitive position." This proclamation notwithstanding, it also completed an imposing new head office on Sherbrooke Street West in Montreal in 1951.

The decision to reduce capital expenditures was no doubt influenced in part by the poorer year-end results reported for 1949. Earnings per common share fell to $1.15 from the $2.03 recorded in the previous year. A recession that had begun in the United States in the spring of 1949 had a dampening effect on domestic sales. By June, one of Dominion Textile's publications declared the situation to be "alarming" as the stockpile of unsold goods grew. At its Magog plant alone, workers were turning out a million yards of cotton goods per week, and so management put a stop to supplementary work on Saturdays. True to its habit, the company laid the blame for the deteriorating state of affairs squarely at the feet of the federal government for its failure to provide adequate protection from foreign competitors. In an attempt to help the United Kingdom in its post-war recovery, the federal government had abolished import duties on British cotton piece goods in May 1948. As a signatory to the General Agreement on Tariffs and Trade (GATT) signed the previous year, Ottawa had also reduced the tariff on goods from other nations, including those from the United States and East Asia. In the case of cottons, import duties fell from approximately 22 percent in 1947 to 19 percent three years later.

American competitors had the advantage of low labour costs, by now the single most important cost of production, since their mill workers were mostly non-unionized and earned significantly lower wages than their Quebec counterparts. Due to their much larger domestic market, they could also benefit from economies of scale resulting from much larger runs of specific products. In the end, the abolition of import duties on British goods did little to benefit a waning Lancashire industry that continued to rely on old technologies and inefficient organizational structures, but it did allow American companies to dump some of their oversupply into the Canadian market. Although dividends on Dominion Textile's common shares declined from 85 cents per share in 1948–49 to 70 cents a year later, net earnings per common share were still above those recorded in March 1948.

Rather than investing more heavily in its marketing and sales efforts during these unsettled times, Dominion Textile continued to rely on manipulating the costs of production to achieve profitability. It used the time-honoured mechanisms of reduced hours and layoffs to lower production and to cut costs. Not surprisingly, it was the same married women they had been so happy to recruit during the war who were the first to be let go. Federal government records indicate that in November 1947, women accounted for approximately only 32 percent of Dominion Textile's workforce at its Magog, Montmorency, Sherbrooke, and Drummondville operations, rather than the 40–50 percent they had represented during the war. Huguette asserted that "After the war, they sacked the married women." Similarly, "Marcelle" noted, "Every time

Women Folding and Packaging Cloth
This photo, likely taken in the 1940s, appeared in a Dominion Textile
publication explaining the various stages involved in manufacturing
cotton cloth. One of the final processes was preparing the cloth for
shipping. While the women perform their tasks, a foreman keeps close
watch. *L'Usage du coton est universel: voici comment on le fabrique...*
(Montréal: La Cie Dominion Textile Limitée, c. 1950.)

there was a layoff, they kicked out the married women first. Later
[when conditions improved], they would seek them out again. In
the 1950s there was always prejudice against married women,
even on the part of the union." Woman workers who had been
performing work during the war traditionally done by men were
reassigned to "women's" work. Agnès, who had worked in the finishing room, reported that as a result of the men returning, she
was transferred to the folding room and shortly after to the grey
room, where she was assigned to operate a sewing machine. Zoé
also noted that once the war was over, whenever a woman co-
worker married or left her job in the folding room, management
replaced her with a man. Only she and one other woman remained,
she claimed, because they were able to outperform the men.

The industry's downturn in the late 1940s proved to be short-
lived. Canadian participation in the Korean War beginning in July
1950 created a resurgence in defence orders that increased both
cotton manufacturing production and profits. Dominion Textile

Wrapping Cloth at Dominion Textile, Magog
As this photo indicates, packaging cloth for shipment
in the mid-twentieth century cotton industry was women's work.
There is one man in the background, possibly a foreman.
(Courtesy of former Magog employee, Marie-Ange Giguère.)

raised its prices on finished goods by over 18 percent in the last six months of 1950. Net profits jumped by over $2 million between 1950 and 1951, and earnings per common share rose significantly, to $1.94 from $1.15. The company increased its dividends to 90 cents per share while engaging in a concerted public relations exercise to put its $5 million of profits—equivalent to $45.6 million in 2017—into perspective. Dominion Textile, as its publicists liked to point out, was owned by many small shareholders, none of whom owned more than two-thirds of 1 percent of the common stock. Furthermore, women outnumbered men among the stockholders—3,180 compared to 2,225. Numerous religious, educational, charitable organizations and life-insurance companies were also identified as stockowners. The company's annual report in 1951 went to great lengths to provide data showing that increases in stockholders' dividends were not keeping pace with the cost of living, whereas workers' hourly wage rates, it contended, generally were:

> In contrast to the monetary difficulties of the Company and to the declining returns by way of dividends and real purchasing power to its shareholders, it is gratifying to note that another large group of persons, also vitally interested in the Company, have fared rather better. The wage earners in our plants, through greater earnings per hour, have been well protected against the rising cost of living.

Despite the fact that the company was doing very well, it decried the federal government's excessive corporate income taxes and insufficient tariff protection yet again. These would remain constant themes throughout the next decade as Canadian cotton textile producers entered a period of increased volatility as a result of intensified international competition and consumer attraction to new synthetic fibres.

The 1951 census shows that women accounted for 32 percent of wage earners employed in cotton yarn and woven goods manufacturing in Quebec. Interestingly, the level of women's participation in different textile centres varied considerably. In Trois-Rivières, women accounted for just over half of the cotton-industry labour force, while in Valleyfield they represented only one-third and in Magog, only one-quarter. What had changed noticeably from previous decades was the age composition and marital status of the industry's women workers, since 37 percent of the women were at least twenty-five years old and 17 percent were married. The significant increase in the presence of married women reflected the same demographic trend occurring within the entire female workforce in Quebec, with 17 percent of its members wedded. An extant list of employees working on the second shift at Montreal Cottons on August 29, 1951 is also quite revealing about the nature of women's mill employment in the early 1950s. Of the 854 workers on the list, 28 percent were women, and 54 percent of them were married. The high proportion of married women on this shift supports the oral testimony of women interviewed who reported that working the afternoon shift from 3 to 11 p.m. made it possible for them to more readily combine their domestic duties with paid employment.

This list of employees also provides a glimpse of both the continuation and permeability of the industry's gender dynamics. Those departments and jobs that had been traditionally male preserves such as mercerizing, slashing, calendering, dyeing, and maintenance continued to be so. Other departments such as carding, spinning, and weaving had workers of both sexes, but on this particular shift, men outnumbered women in most of these areas. Perhaps even more surprisingly, departments that had been almost exclusively composed of women workers in the past, such as spooling, twisting, and drawing-in, had either few or no women. Among thirty-seven separate departments, women formed a majority of the workers on this shift in only three: one small spinning room, the cloth room, and the sales yarn room.

The proportion of women and men workers was quite possibly different on the first shift, as it was most certainly for the third shift, which employed only men. However, two conclusions seem to be in order. A significantly higher percentage of women workers were married than in previous generations, despite the continuing strong societal bias against their employment. In addition, men were increasingly moving into jobs that had been women's preserves in the past. This change most likely stemmed from the installation of newer, more automated machinery that required less close attention and manual dexterity. With minimum wage legislation that applied to both women and men, managers no longer had a monetary incentive to prefer women workers for jobs that could be performed by either sex. Overall, girls and women had lost their predominant role in the industry's workforce.

CHAPTER FIVE

New Technologies, Old Problems: Working Conditions and Wages

Aimé Geoffrion admitted it—working conditions in Dominion Textile's mills could sometimes be unpleasant. As the company's legal counsel appearing before the Royal Commission on the Textile Industry in 1937, he conceded that excessive heat and humidity were issues in some departments, while swirling fibres and high noise levels were common in others. However, he portrayed these negative conditions as "unpleasant" only to those unaccustomed to them and implied that, for experienced labourers, they were perhaps inconvenient but certainly not a threat to their health and well-being.

Other industry representatives also portrayed Quebec's cotton mills in the interwar period as safe and progressive workplaces. In February 1922, a writer for *The Canadian Textile Journal* contrasted the unenviable lot of mill workers from times past with their contemporary situation. "Today," he boldly concluded, "the mill worker receives better pay and works amid a better environment than does the worker in a store or office." In the same vein, an editorial published in December 1926 asserted, "It is a pleasure today . . . to see the clean, healthy atmosphere in which the workers are carrying on their manifold tasks," and queried, "What other industry can do so much for the thousands of women who are happily employed in Canadian textile mills?"

In addition to praising improvements in the mill environment, textile spokesmen claimed that their industry was a leader in employee welfare work, including the provision of attractive recreational facilities such as covered curling rinks, bowling greens, softball diamonds, lawn-tennis courts, and billiard tables. A *Canadian Textile Journal* article from January 1921 described the Montreal Cottons club facilities as offering "something for the taste and enjoyment of everybody," provided they paid a monthly membership fee of 25 cents. The housing the company rented to some of its workers also garnered an enthusiastic endorsement for being "model dwellings . . . and delightfully picturesque."

Provincial factory inspectors' reports for the 1920s and 1930s also suggest that there was steady and substantial improvement in the working environment for factory workers. Women factory inspectors, in particular, frequently referred to the general amelioration in conditions under which women laboured. Mesdames Bérard, Massicotte, and Lemieux, the three women factory inspectors appointed in the early 1930s, recorded few complaints, and they had a familiar ring: more attention was needed to ensure hygienic, well-lit toilet areas, and cleaner workroom floors and windows. Thanks to their various interventions, they claimed, women workers were never better treated nor enjoyed such secure and healthy conditions.

In contrast to these positive assessments pointing to continuous improvements in working conditions, evidence presented at the two federal inquiries launched during the interwar period provided damning indictments of conditions in Quebec's cotton mills. Workers' sworn testimony focused on many ongoing issues including poor sanitation, respiratory problems, high heat and humidity, production speed-ups, reduced wages, and mistreatment at the hands of foremen. Their words, reported extensively in major newspapers across the nation, helped galvanize public opinion in their favour. Compared to textile workers in other parts of Canada, those in Quebec experienced some of the worst working conditions. This reality drew attention once again to the conflicting interests of the English-Canadian business elite and the French-Canadian working class.

By the early 1950s, Quebec's cotton workers had experienced many improvements in their working conditions. They included a reduced workweek, paid statutory holidays and vacations, premiums for overtime work, safer working environments, and the extension of corporate welfare schemes. Wages rose significantly between 1939 and 1952, but so did the cost of living. Increased production levels per worker and the significant technological changes introduced to achieve those upward trends resulted in more speed-ups and more pressure on workers. Favouritism and sexual harassment also remained serious problems for women workers. As a result, they continued to confront many of the workplace issues that previous generations had experienced.

Child Labour

Child labour was one problem that both supporters and critics of the Quebec cotton industry agreed had not been resolved at the end of World War I. "It is estimated that at the present time," wrote one contributor to the *Canadian Textile Journal* in February 1919, "under the existing non-compulsory laws, over 90,000 children in the Province of Quebec are not in attendance at school." The new provincial Industrial Establishments Act of 1919 continued to require the testing of all boys and girls between the ages of fourteen and sixteen to verify if they could read and write. Workers in this age group who were incapable of reading or writing were required to attend night school in order to receive official permission to continue working for wages. A new provision prohibited employers from hiring girls or boys under sixteen unless they presented an official ministry of public works and labour certificate indicating whether they could read and write and whether they were attending night school. To reduce the incidence of underage children using older siblings' documentation to obtain employment, the ministry designed its new certificate to include information about the age and physical characteristics of the child in question. Failure to verify young workers' status before hiring them could result in a fine for the employer.

It took some time, however, for the authorities to put into place the testing and the remedial night school courses, and the application of the law remained uneven, varying according to geographical location. Testing was first undertaken in Montreal, where it was much easier to establish night schools for those who needed them. According to Deputy Minister of Labour Louis Guyon, authorities would continue to take into account the needs of poor families and widows who relied on their children's wages for support and, in some cases, would issue special permits for illiterate adolescents to work even if they were not attending night school. However, as he expressed in his 1918-19 report, he continued to have no sympathy for the majority of parents who chose the factory over the school for their children:

> What are we to think about a father who sends his ten-year-old son into the cotton mill to see him come home the next day with one arm amputated? We have had four cases of this nature during the course of the year. What can we say about parents who alter baptismal records in order to get the child into the mill two or three years before the legal age for his entry? Inspector Robert [Montreal district] turned up six such cases in the same industry. Finally, what are we to think say about the numerous trickeries? John, who shows up at the factory with the baptismal certificate of his brother who is two years older than he? We would never finish if we were to try to enumerate all of the abuses which are drawn to our attention every day.

Guyon laid the blame for the ongoing problem of child labour squarely on the shoulders of illiterate and selfish parents and contended that most of the offences committed by employers occurred in small and medium-sized industries. This conclusion would suggest that the cotton industry, composed of large-scale enterprises, was no longer a significant employer of child labour. However, as his previous statement indicates, there were still numerous cases of underage workers in this industry. Indeed, the reports of other factory inspectors and the oral testimony of former workers in Valleyfield and Magog clearly reveal that young adolescents continued to find employment in the province's cotton mills.

The presence of children in industry was particularly noticeable in the immediate post-war period, with inspectors attributing this phenomenon to a variety of causes including labour shortages, the high cost of living that motivated working class families to send underage children into the workforce, and lazy fathers who exploited their own children. Inspector Alfred Robert remarked that cotton mills in Montreal required continuous surveillance in 1919 due to their large numbers of underage employees, many of whom were in frail condition. He admitted, however, that it was difficult to end the practice abruptly. In cases where a family was dependent upon a child's wages, he would arrange to have the underage worker moved to a safer, less physically demanding job within another department.

Testing and registering young workers between the ages of fourteen and sixteen for literacy proved a challenging, time-consuming task for the ten men and three women comprising the inspection service. The work commenced in March 1920 and by the end of June, nearly seven thousand adolescents had been tested in the city of Montreal, with just over half assigned to attend compulsory night school beginning the following October. The inspectors estimated that there were as many as twelve thousand workers in the target age category in that city alone. Other areas of the province where examinations of young workers took place included Quebec City, Valleyfield, Trois-Rivières, Shawinigan, and Montmorency, the latter four being centres with significant textile operations.

While the lack of literacy skills among adolescent workers was clearly a major issue, the inspectors' individual reports during the 1920s were optimistic that the number of employees who were underage was declining. Madame Lemieux of the Quebec office reported in 1921 that she had found only two girls and one boy who were not of the required age to work, and credited the decrease in infractions to the new, stricter legislation. Similarly, R.H. Gooley's report of the same year suggested that the problem of child labour was well in hand in the Eastern Townships. By June 1925, inspectors had tested over twenty-two thousand adolescents between the ages of fourteen and sixteen, and two years later Guyon triumphantly announced, "the legend of the child between ten and twelve years of age in industry is finished."

Interviews with former textile workers, however, indicate that the factory inspectors were overly sanguine in their pronouncements about the eradication of child labour. Although it was rarer in the 1920s to find underage girls entering the mills, six of the thirty women interviewed who were born between 1905 and 1914 began working in the cotton industry before their fourteenth birthdays. All six were hired before 1927 and were well aware that they were breaking the law. For "Renée," economic hardship dictated her early entry into Montreal Cottons since her father had died, leaving behind five children. She quit school at the age of thirteen in 1923 and went to work to help her brother support the family. Similar circumstances led "Luzina" to the Magog mill in 1923, when she was only twelve, to help her widowed mother support her seven children. She reported that no one asked for proof of age. Three years later, a similar scenario played out yet again when thirteen-year-old Suzanne began working to assist her widowed mother and sixteen siblings. Although economic circumstances were not quite as desperate for Stéphanie and her family, her wages were needed, and so she began working in 1921, some four months before her fourteenth birthday. When company officials initially asked for her baptismal certificate, she replied that she had not yet received it. Only after she reached the legal starting age did she produce it for them.

The efficacy of legislation requiring workers between the ages of fourteen and sixteen to attend night school remained highly questionable. The further one got from Montreal and Quebec City, the more difficult it was to enforce this provision, since many of the smaller centres did not offer night school courses. As a result, inspectors limited their efforts in outlying areas to verifying the ages of workers. Where night school did exist, government reports show that the young students frequently skipped classes and went only as often as needed to get the required signature attesting to their registration. Even if they did attend, it is hard to imagine how much learning they could accomplish after a demanding ten-hour workday.

The difficult economic conditions of the 1930s, rather than legislation and enforcement, solved the persistent problem of

child labour in the mills. In 1931, only 3 percent of male mill workers and 4 percent of female workers were sixteen or younger. With
paid work in short supply throughout the 1930s and the resulting
pool of unemployed adults willing to work for low wages, manufacturers did not need to resort to child labour. W. G. Aird indicated before the Turgeon Commission that he gave firm orders to
his foremen not to hire anyone under sixteen after his arrival as
the new manager of Montreal Cottons in August 1932. The 1941
Census of Canada reported that only ten boys and four girls under
fifteen were working in the Quebec cotton industry. While these
numbers might have reflected an underreporting of the phenomenon of child labour, they certainly indicate that the numbers of
young adolescents in mills had fallen dramatically.

As the demand for workers to support the war effort grew, however, significant numbers of girls and youths under sixteen once
again found their way into the cotton industry. The chief factory
inspector's report for 1941-42 indicated that there had been a dramatic increase in age and schooling certificates his staff had issued
to children between the ages of fourteen and sixteen, compared
to the previous year. In fact, the number had exploded from 1,667
to 9,238, with several hundreds of these young people working in
cotton mills. Between them, Dominion Textile and Montreal
Cottons employed 38 girls and 71 boys aged fourteen and fifteen
and another 243 girls and 257 boys who were sixteen to eighteen.
The labour shortages developing in industry and the rising cost
of living were clearly motivating larger numbers of young people
to enter the workforce.

In 1943, the Liberal government, headed by Adélard Godbout,
passed the first compulsory school legislation in the province. The
law provided for free elementary education and required children
between the ages of six and fourteen to attend school during regular
school terms. Since attendance was compulsory and free, working
class families had an incentive to keep their children in school for
at least eight years. Adolescents aged fourteen to sixteen could nonetheless still take on full-time paid employment, provided they could
satisfy labour inspectors that they could read and write. Otherwise,
the law continued to require them to attend night school.

Among the fourteen women interviewed who were born between 1925 and 1934 and who began working between 1939 and 1951, two started before they turned sixteen. Aline entered one of the Valleyfield spinning rooms in 1942 when she was fifteen, the same age at which "Laure" began working as a spinner at Montreal Cottons in 1948. As late as 1951, 159 girls and 121 boys under sixteen were employed in Quebec's cotton industry. They represented respectively 2 percent of all female workers and fewer than 1 percent of all male workers.

Hours

The fifty-five-hour workweek for girls, boys, and women had been in effect in Quebec's textile industry since 1912 and would remain an industry standard until the late 1930s. This characteristic placed Quebec on the same footing as China, India, and Japan; most other industrialized countries had already reduced the workweek in textile mills to forty-eight hours or less. Moreover, it appears that the practice of requiring or encouraging workers to work during their mandated meal breaks continued to exist in some mills. Two Magog mill hands wrote to provincial officials in 1921 asking if Dominion Textile had the right to oblige its employees to run their machines over the noon hour.

Despite the fifty-five-hour designation for their industry, adolescents and women employed in cotton mills, like their men coworkers, experienced considerable variation in the number of hours they actually worked each week. Mills regularly resorted to overtime since the 1912 legislation had not removed the provision for supplementary hours contained in the original provincial factory act of 1885. Textile manufacturers could still seek permits to have adolescent and women workers work as late as 9 p.m. from Monday to Friday, for a total of seventy-two hours per week. Such permits could be issued for up to six weeks per year.

The yearly factory inspectors' reports indicate both the cotton industry's frequent requests for extended hours during the 1920s and the inspectors' growing reluctance to grant them. Louis Guyon wrote that the department of labour was not in favour of the extension of hours for any workers, including men, given that the increased workload posed a threat to workers' health. The special provision during World War I that had allowed manufacturers to employ women at night had been withdrawn at war's end, but Inspector Robert reported that he had to visit cotton and woollen mills at night in 1919 and 1920 in order to stop continued infractions. During the same period he received thirty-four requests for extended hours of work for women and children, but granted only eight. He specifically singled out requests from the cotton industry as not being justified and refused them on the grounds that the workers wanted shorter, not longer, hours.

The space given over to factory inspectors' accounts in the annual report of the department of public works and labour was greatly reduced beginning in 1926, and tables of statistics increasingly replaced their individual narratives. This change makes it harder to decipher what was transpiring in the cotton industry after this date. In 1927, the consolidated annual report did reveal that Dominion Textile had secured permits for supplementary hours at its Montreal, Magog, and Sherbrooke mills. Guyon reported in 1930 that his department granted thirty-two overtime permits the previous year, mostly to textile mills located in smaller centres. The next year, with fifteen overtime permits, the textile industry also registered the largest number of any industry. No information was provided about the number of requests that had been refused. In 1931-32, the number of permits provided to the textile industry in the Montreal district was reduced to two. However, a total of thirty-seven were granted to textile manufacturers and one clothing factory in the Eastern Townships.

Workers' own testimony reveals that the workweek frequently surpassed the fifty-five-hour limit during the 1920s. Several women reported that they were usually on the job well before the official 7 a.m. starting time. Alphonsine, a Magog weave room employee, stated that she had to be at work by at least 6:30 a.m. in order to clean her machines before starting them up, and on Saturday, she was busy cleaning by 5:30 a.m. "Flore" also remembered the long days: "I worked hard, we didn't stop. We got up at

5:30 a.m. in order to start work at 7 a.m. and then we finished at 6 p.m. We had one hour to eat. There were times we worked three evenings a week until 9 p.m. and Saturday afternoons until 5 p.m." "Marie," a Valleyfield mill worker in the 1920s, also recalled working three times a week until 9 p.m. on a regular basis.

For Zoé, being on the job early was in part a personal decision. "They only gave us ten minutes to oil our machines—that wasn't a lot of time. My friend and I arrived, oiled our machines, took down the numbers for the kinds of cotton that we would be running that day, and made up our work slips ... When 7 a.m. arrived, the machine was oiled and we were ready to run." Since workers were paid by the piece, it was of utmost importance to spend the extra time before the daily shift began to ensure that their machines were in top working order. When Clémentine started work as a doffer in 1926, she often worked more than sixty hours a week. "At that time," she stated, "we reported to work early each day and Saturday mornings to clean the machines, because we weren't to clean them while they were running. We started cleaning around 5:15 or 5:20 a.m. The foreman passed by and inspected. Then we started working at 7 a.m. We weren't paid for cleaning." Other workers, such as Adèle and "Théodora," reported that they enhanced their earnings by "cheating" and working through their lunch hours.

Production schedules in the mills continued to vary significantly, depending upon the season of the year and the state of the industry. While workers often found themselves working extremely long hours, they could also find themselves with shortened workweeks or no work. Depressed conditions in the industry led Montreal Cottons, for example, to introduce a four-day workweek from January 1921 to September of the same year. In August the following year, Dominion Textile closed all of its mills for two weeks, leaving some eight thousand employees without work. *Le Progrès de Valleyfield* reported that this action was the result of decreased tariffs leading to increased foreign competition, and production outstripping demand. With the onset of the Great Depression, reduced hours became an all-too-common occurrence. By 1929, Clémentine had graduated from doffing to a sewing job in the Magog print works,

At The Time Punch Clock, Magog, 1950s
One of the familiar routines for cotton mill workers was punching
their time cards at the start and end of their shifts. Here a group of
women workers congregate around the clock to record their times.
(Courtesy of Anita Vachon, former Magog mill employee.)

but was laid off annually for several months over the next four years
because there was not enough cotton cloth to process.

The variability in hours that workers experienced during the
Depression years created stress for them and their dependents.
Shortened hours and resulting imposed "holidays" had a devastating impact on biweekly wage packets, according to testimony
given before the Turgeon Commission. Paulette Cabana, a nineteen-year-old Sherbrooke doffer, worked only one day during the
first week of March 1936. At other times in the 1930s, workers
were expected to work longer hours than normal, and some complained that they were sometimes required to work overtime during the first few days of the week, only to be sent home on Thursday
afternoon. They were also unhappy that they were required to

work on Good Friday since no provincial law prohibited it. One worker's lengthy anonymous letter of complaint to the minister of labour in 1935 claimed that Dominion Textile kept a stranglehold on its employees in Magog by running the mill there for three days a week for five or six months and then operating night and day for the next six months by bringing in outsiders. In this way, the local workers could not become too independent. Management representatives responded that such unevenness in hours of work was simply a normal function of an industry that was dependent upon seasonal orders.

It was also clear from the Turgeon Commission hearings that workers frequently did not take the one-hour dinner break required by provincial law. Since so many workers earned their salaries on a piece-rate basis, they either did not take the entire hour or ate their food on the job to save time. One report dealing with the Montmorency mill noted that only 10 percent of workers left the mill to go home for their main meal at noon. When factory inspectors for the area suggested that the company provide a dining facility, the manager objected on the grounds that there was no space and that the odours in the mill made it impracticable to consider creating an on-site eating area. Despite the bad air and dusty conditions in many departments, workers continued to eat their main meals there. Mill managers, at least in some locations, were much better served. In Valleyfield, managers, including at least some of the foremen, ate in the dining room of the company's institute. "Adelima" commented that her foreman was never in the workroom at noon because he "was off having a beer in the bosses' club." Some workers also claimed that when they were required to work until 9 p.m., they did not have a supper break but rather ate their evening meal while standing up and working.

A reduction in cotton workers' regular hours came only in 1937 on the heels of a province-wide strike against Dominion Textile led by the Catholic trade union movement. As part of collective agreement signed in December 1937, a fifty-hour workweek was implemented for both women and men workers. Despite the apparent attractiveness of reduced hours, significant numbers of the union's rank and file were deeply concerned that a shorter workweek would mean lower wages even though they had also won pay increases. Consequently, union leaders hastened to the various mills to explain that overall wages would not suffer. They argued that the number of hours employees worked each week would vary less since the company would be obliged to carry production forward if it could not be finished in the prescribed workweek.

Cotton textile manufacturing was in a precarious state for most of 1939 with significant seasonal fluctuations remaining a standard feature. Workers continued to experience alternating periods of short time and overtime as their departments either lacked work or were inundated by rush orders. With the move into full wartime production and the resulting shortage of workers, the mills began to rely on longer hours and the addition of a third shift to ensure that the highest levels of production were maintained. The provisions of provincial ministerial decree no. 1257, issued on March 15, 1940, allowed munitions industries and other industries filling Department of National Defence war contracts to apply for permits to prolong hours of work or to adjust shift times for up to six months at a stretch for adolescent girls, women, and boys under eighteen. Between April 1941 and March 1942, Quebec cotton mills requested a total of forty supplementary hours permits. The provincial ministry of labour approved twenty-nine for Dominion Textile's various mills and eleven for Montreal Cottons. Wabasso requested none since it was not directly involved in war contracts. According to the ministry, altogether the permits covered 281 girls and 328 boys under the age of eighteen and 3,043 women.

A number of women employed during the war pointed out that they generally worked from 7 a.m. until 6 p.m. from Monday until Friday, with a half day on some Saturdays. "Florentine" recalled going to work on Saturday mornings, much as previous generations of workers had done, to clean her machines so that they would be in good working order for the following Monday. "Josette," a battery hand in the Magog mill, reported that she was required to work until 6 p.m. on Saturdays throughout the war years. With fifty-five hours or more of weekly employment, women textile workers were among the 42 percent of women industrial workers in Quebec who toiled more than fifty hours. The 1941 revised act covering health and safety in Quebec's industrial and commercial establishments continued to permit the use of overtime permits for up to six weeks, although the number of hours worked each week could not exceed sixty-five hours.

The long workdays in most cases were made more gruelling by the lack of regularly scheduled breaks. "Isabelle," a day-shift employee in a Valleyfield spooling room, indicated that there were no coffee breaks in her department, but a one-hour meal break was provided at noon. This lack of rest breaks was endemic to the industry. A survey of working conditions in textile mills, carried out by the Primary Textiles Institute and published in *The Canadian Textile Journal* in December 1943, indicated that only about one-third of Canadian mills offered two rest breaks per shift, while hot drinks and snacks were available to workers in an even smaller number of establishments.

The war presented women with an opportunity to work at night, since provincial legislation also ended the ban on nighttime employment of adult women and boys between the ages of sixteen and eighteen in industries filling war contracts. However, girls under eighteen and boys under sixteen were still not allowed to work night shifts. On the night shift, women routinely worked from 6 p.m. until 5 a.m. Despite the strong opposition to women's nighttime work expressed in many official quarters, some women were not averse to working night shift. When "Bernadette" was hired for one of Montreal Cottons' spinning rooms in 1945, she worked nights. "I preferred that because it allowed me to sleep in late in the morning," she stated. Reine also worked the night shift as a spinner after she was hired in Magog in 1942. "Everybody recognized us," she commented, "because we were pale, we didn't have time to see the sun."

The provincial government rescinded its legislation permitting the use of women on night shifts in March 1946. Some of the cotton mills, however, including the one in Magog, were already using a three-shift system that made it possible for women to work on the second shift from 3 p.m. to 11 p.m. When Hélène was hired in

Drawing-In
During the Second World War, the National Film Board took a series
of photos of Dominion Textile's operations. This photo shows a young
woman, identified as Hélène Lalonde, working at the delicate task of
threading warp threads from the warp beam located behind her through
the loom heddles. Note the second set of hands visible in the photo as
another woman works from the other side to form the loom harness.
(LAC, PA160566.)

1948 to work in the spooling room, she was put on this shift, much
to her delight. "I liked it, it was restful. Working on the day shift
was more tiring." For some women, however, shift work was difficult, especially when they alternated shifts. "I worked the first
and the second shifts," said "Janine," who was already a mother
with four children when she started working for Dominion Textile
in Magog in 1947. "It was hard." The difficulties that shift work
could engender led at least two women to quit their jobs. Marcelle,
who had started working in 1937, found it too difficult to alternate
shifts after the three-shift system was introduced, so she quit for
five years. Aline, who worked on and off for Montreal Cottons
starting in 1942, quit in 1955 because management wanted her to

work the second shift. "I told them that I wasn't interested in meeting my husband only in bed. My husband worked from seven until three. So they closed my file."

In Valleyfield, post-war contracts struck between Montreal Cottons and the UTWA provided for only two shifts, a day shift running from 6 a.m. to 6 p.m. and a night shift from 6 p.m. to 6 a.m. Workweeks for day-shift employees were limited to forty-five hours, while men working the night shift routinely put in fifty hours. Nonetheless, provincial officials continued to issue permits to extend the working hours of adolescents and women beyond what the factory legislation normally allowed. In June 1947, for example, Dominion Textile received permits covering four of its Montreal mills, the Magog mill and print works, and the Sherbrooke mill. Wabasso also succeeded in obtaining permission the same month and again in February 1948 to extend its hours of operation in Trois-Rivières. Just over five thousand girls and women were affected.

Data collected in October 1949 and published in the *Labour Gazette* the following year indicate that the average number of hours worked per week continued to be longer for Quebec cotton mill workers than for their counterparts elsewhere in Canada. Just over 40 percent of them put in more than forty-five hours a week compared to only 20 percent of cotton workers in the Maritimes and 17 percent of those in Ontario. This report provided ammunition for unions in their subsequent bargaining with Quebec manufacturers. The 1950 contract signed between the United Textile Workers of America and Montreal Cottons brought in a shorter workweek. Although it was now only forty hours a week for most employees, a continuous shift of eight hours meant that designated lunch or coffee breaks were eliminated. Workers were expected to eat or drink on the job as best they could, depending on their workloads and their foremen's indulgence. Employees on the first and second shifts also continued to work every second Saturday, but now they were paid for this supplementary work on an overtime basis. Similarly, workers in Dominion Textile operations in Magog, Montmorency, Sherbrooke, and Drummondville covered by collective agreements negotiated by the Fédération nationale catholique du textile (FNCT; National Catholic Textile Federation) had achieved a standard workweek of forty hours by 1950.

Working Conditions

Not only did the hours worked by mill employees routinely exceed the standard workweek common in other manufacturing sectors, but also the jobs they performed in most departments continued to be physically demanding. Within a year of starting work in the Magog spinning room in 1926, Clémentine began to suffer hearing loss and serious nosebleeds as a result of breathing in cotton fibres. She also had recurring nightmares about her machines plugging up that made her feel she was working both day and night. Instructed by her doctor to get more rest, she hired a teenage boy to go in on Friday and Saturday mornings to clean her machines so that she did not have to get up so early. While Marie reported that she encountered no serious problems during the time she worked as a spooler for Montreal Cottons, she admitted that the work was hard and that, at one point during the 1920s, she quit work for a year and a half because she was exhausted.

Despite the much-vaunted improvements to the mills, most workers still found the excessive heat, high humidity, swirling lint, and deafening noise difficult to bear. "It was dirty work," commented Régina. "There was lint everywhere, it even stuck to our eyelids. I didn't like that." In the weave rooms, humidity rates were routinely kept between 65 and 75 percent and the temperature between 80°F and 90°F (27°C and 33°C). With temperatures sometimes reaching as high as 103°F (39.5°C), it is small wonder that a number of workers complained about constantly being drenched in perspiration. Flore vividly summarized the situation: "We left [the mill] each day with completely white hair....When I arrived home, I wrung out my clothing, winter and summer. I ask myself how it is that we are still alive. At any rate, I firmly believe that I lost a good deal of my health there." A factory inspector, who followed up on workers' complaints about conditions at Montreal Cottons in January 1936, found their concerns were justified. In the absence of change rooms, workers had to hang their out door clothes on workroom walls where they absorbed high levels of both moisture and dust. He ordered the company to build some cloakrooms and to take other measures to reduce the level of humidity, but as of the end of May 1936, the company had taken no action.

In departments where individual machines were still connected to a central power source, the huge overhead straps, pulleys, and belts remained a danger. "I was frightened one time," said Adèle. "A piece of iron from one of the straps fell just in front of one of my frames." Workers judged to have been injured due to their own negligence or who had injured themselves repeatedly were laid off for two weeks. Fortunately, with the improvement in machinery during the 1930s, there appear to have been fewer serious accidents. Women factory inspectors continued to stress the necessity for women workers to bear primary responsibility for safety by reminding them to wear their hair pinned up or under a cap to avoid being scalped.

Technological changes introduced into the industry during the interwar period that may have made the work safer ironically led to an overall deterioration in the work environment for many mill hands. Several women commented on the changes in their own individual work and in the general atmosphere in their workrooms. "When I first started [1924], I had one side [of a spinning frame] to mind," explained Adèle. "Toward the end [1934], I had eight. I was always running. Over the years, there were more tasks to do—disentangle the waste, untangle the feed yarn. In the beginning, we didn't have to do that and we could sit down, but that didn't last too long." Similarly, "Francine" reported that the number of frame sides she was assigned increased from four to nine during the ten years she spent in the spinning department after 1928. Stéphanie also found that the working environment changed significantly and that the foremen became more severe, prohibiting the workers from chatting. According to Régina, when she first started working in 1928, the employees had fun—they sang and sometimes hid for fun under the spinning frames, but that carefree atmosphere soon vanished.

Magog Weavers
Marie-Ange Breton, on the left, is shown with a co-worker in the weave
room at the Magog mill. Mlle Breton started as a battery hand in 1932 at
the age of fourteen, loading the magazines of automatic looms with
bobbins of thread. She became a weaver in 1939 and retired in 1979.
(Courtesy of Marie-Ange Breton.)

Time-and-motion studies became a familiar tool of management to increase production levels and thereby reduce labour costs. Luzina remembered the various attempts to change the speed at which spinning frames operated and the resulting difficulties: "Each time they changed the speed, the yarn broke—that caused a lot of problems for the spinners." Clémentine's memory of the time-and-motion studies proved even more graphic:

> They kept a check on us—it was serious. The 'checker' made a little stroke each time I wiped my glasses, noted the time I took to go to the washroom. . . . When I arrived home in the evening, I cried because it was so nerve-racking. Those guys were tiresome and serious. One time I asked one why they were doing that. It was for [identifying] the time one lost on the job, that was serious. They really got on my nerves with that—it lasted three months.

Pressures associated with piecework mounted as management increasingly introduced the bonus system for many categories of women workers. Using the most experienced hands working under ideal conditions as their experimental subjects, time-study experts established the amount of work a given class of workers should be able to produce during their regular shifts. Workers who generated more than the set amount were paid a bonus. Signs indicating production results for each employee were prominently posted in workrooms, thereby creating an intensely competitive and stressful atmosphere.

Women who began their working lives doffing as young girls in the early 1920s often remembered it as a somewhat carefree and easy kind of work. By the end of the decade, however, the increased pressure on spinners to augment production meant more pressure for the doffers as well. "There was no one to instruct you how to doff," explained Francine, who began as a doffer in 1928. "The [new] girls were crying. The other doffers and the spinners would get angry at the doffers who were just learning if they made mistakes." When Adelima started working for Montreal Cottons in 1938, she was reduced to tears because she could not make the production quotas set for her. She reported that many women cried at that time because they were so exhausted.

At least one manager shared the women workers' perceptions of increased pressure on the job. In an interview conducted in 1932 for the *Canadian Textile Journal*, a former superintendent commented about the changes he had witnessed over the years:

> Times were different then. There was none of this efficiency business, nor changing counts on the same frame twice a day. . . . Things ran so smoothly that we managed to leave the mill for two or three hours in the afternoon several times a week. There is a river quite close to the mill and many years ago the fishing was good. . . . We often went down to the river in the afternoon and put in some time fishing. But all that is finished. Today we are up against entirely different conditions. Industry has been completely reorganized.

Working conditions deteriorated even more in the 1930s as manufacturers sought to reduce labour costs by investing significantly in capital equipment and new technologies. Modern machines replaced workers in many instances. Flore, for example, explained how she lost her job as a spooler in the early 1930s when management at the Magog mill decided to install automatic spoolers. This one change allowed the company to reduce the number of women spoolers from seventy to only ten. In other departments, work was further broken down, with the least-skilled elements, such as cleaning, assigned to lower-paid learners. In this way experienced mill hands could focus on the more skilled tasks and thus increase their output. With the installation of looms with automatic shuttle filling devices, a new category of worker—the battery hand—was introduced. This employee, usually a young woman, was assigned the task of inserting full bobbins into the magazine-like cylinder that attached to the loom and fed the bobbins into the shuttle as required.

General Manager Aird of Montreal Cottons reported that the number of weavers at the Valleyfield mill declined from 514 in 1929 to 263 in 1935. A letter signed by "The Workers of Valleyfield," sent to Aird in 1935 and contained in the Turgeon Commission's evidence, pointed out several other examples of drastic reductions in the numbers of skilled workers and the resulting surfeit of work for those who remained. In one spinning room the number of operatives went from fifteen to four but production quotas were not adjusted. The letter further alleged that while the fifteen workers had previously made on average $38.00 every two weeks, the four remaining were earning only $22.00 each. Two cleaners had been added, but each of them had to clean 3,540 spindles daily. In the Louise mill weave room, where previously twenty-four weavers were working, now only four "were doing six times the amount of work for more or less the same salary." Other grievances in the letter included the excessive heat that had caused at least three employees to faint on the job when workroom temperatures rose to 90°F in the month of January and they were forbidden to open the windows; foremen insisting that employees begin work before the official starting time; and managers requiring workers to stay until 9 p.m. one night, only to send them home early the next day.

This letter became a focal point for claims and counterclaims regarding workloads during the commission's hearings. Legal counsel for the textile companies aggressively cross-examined witnesses who testified about greatly increased workloads and pushed hard to have them admit that, although the number of machines they were obliged to mind had increased, they were no longer responsible for as many specific tasks. The company lawyers argued that by having other employees perform such unskilled work as supplying the machines with material, cleaning, sweeping, and carrying away the processed product, the work was either no more strenuous than it had been in the past or was actually less onerous. They had also clearly hand-picked a certain number of long-time, highly experienced employees, dubbed "star" performers by the commission's counsel, to give evidence that their situation had actually improved as a result of the workload changes.

The sworn statements of the vast majority of workers, however, demonstrate that most found their workload had increased for the worse. Laurette Bouthillier, a Sherbrooke spinner, testified that she was minding twelve machines as opposed to the six she had operated when she first began working in 1928. Marguerite Caya, a twenty-one-year-old worker at the same mill, explained how she had to look after twelve machines in the drawing room, two of which were located at some distance from the others. Her

Women Weavers, Montreal Cottons, 1942
As this photo demonstrates, weave rooms typically contained many rows
of closely-spaced, noisy looms. The constant din resulted in workers
having to use hand signals to communicate. For long-time weave room
employees, hearing loss was a significant occupational hazard.
(Library and Archives Canada, e000760678.)

work included pushing trucks loaded with four or five cans of cotton about 150 feet every hour during her shift, cleaning her
machines, and making sure that they continued to run. When
asked about management's expectations regarding daily production, she replied that the assistant foreman made it clear that if
she were not capable of running her machines, they would be given
to someone else.

Doffers' work included pushing large wooden or iron carts laden
with full spools of yarn considerable distances. One twenty-two-
year-old woman shared that the work was "quite strenuous."
Cleaners' work was equally stressful. Teenager Georgette Paquin
removed cotton waste from 1,440 iron and copper rollers with her

bare hands for ten hours each day and then cleaned the spindles with a brush for half a day on Saturday. The assignment of extra machines to workers meant that they had to work at a faster physical pace, and most reported that they walked or stood all day long since there was neither time nor a place to sit down. When the quality of the cotton she was processing was good and the work went well, another worker reported that she had time to go and get a drink, but if the cotton was of poor quality, then there was no time to do even that.

A loom fixer at Montreal Cottons reported that weavers in his department had seen an augmentation in the numbers of looms they each attended from twelve in 1931 to twenty-four by 1933 and forty-four by 1936. One weaver stated that she had run as many as seventy looms and that she was always overworked and going beyond her strength as a woman. Another Sherbrooke weaver succinctly described the existing situation: "It is not permitted to sit down, because we have to watch over our work. If we sit down, it is because we are tired, and that is not permitted." Any opportunity for social interaction was greatly reduced. "We shouldn't talk, laugh, have fun" explained "Hermione." "It was hard. We didn't have the right to do anything." Luzina concurred: "They didn't allow the employees to talk even when the work was going well. . . . We weren't allowed to stop for two minutes. It was very hard."

Working conditions in Quebec's mills during the 1940s remained far from ideal. The demands of war-related production and a shortage of hands translated into increased workloads and difficult conditions for mill employees. Even following significant capital investments to modernize facilities following the war, studies conducted by Laval University researchers in 1946 and 1949 revealed that high levels of heat, humidity, noise, and dust continued to take a toll on workers' physical health. In hot, humid departments, workers were unable to sustain their maximum effort for their entire shift. While industry spokesmen trumpeted the wonderful improvements in ventilation and in industrial hygiene effected during the 1940s, the Laval reports found that management remained woefully unconcerned about workers' well-being. There were still no locker rooms and so workers continued to hang their outdoor clothing in close quarters in work-rooms where it collected dust and possibly helped transmit infectious diseases. The studies also indicated that medical exam-inations of some five hundred workers at the Montmorency and the Drummondville plants showed that 43 percent were under normal weight and that they showed abnormally high heart rates during rest times. The authors of the report blamed these indica-tors of poor health on the fatigue workers experienced as a result of too many hours of work without rest breaks.

The statements of Magog and Valleyfield workers who were in the mills during the 1940s corroborate these findings. They con-sistently identified the noise, dust, heat, and humidity as ongoing problems. High levels of noise remained a major issue for weavers, and both "Pierrette" and Josette reported that they became par-tially deaf as a result of their many years of work in weaving departments. Pierrette also blamed the arthritis that caused her to quit her job at the age of sixty-one on the high levels of humid-ity in the weave room. The heat in the spinning room where Reine worked "was nearly unbearable." "Jeannette," "Françoise," and "Célestine" additionally described the dirt and the cockroaches in the workrooms, the "wheeze" (cotton dust) that permeated the air, and the general unhygienic conditions under which they laboured.

Women interviewed also consistently observed a constant acceleration in the pace of work in the late 1940s and early 1950s. Rather than building more mills to meet high demands for cot-ton goods in the post-war period, companies sought to increase production in their existing facilities. "Ghislaine" emphasized the link between increased work levels over time and the estab-lishment of collective agreements. "With each contract that was signed, they (the bosses) removed people," she stated. Reine also noted that with the modernization of equipment came heavier workloads and more responsibility. Although most women work-ers were already paid on a piece-rate basis, this remuneration system became even more widespread. Several women linked the increased on-the-job stress to the conversion from hourly pay to piecework. "Eugénie," who sewed sheets in the Colonial

Cloth Inspection, Magog, 1950s
Women continued to comprise the majority of cloth inspectors,
as this photo shows, although men were also assigned to this work by
the 1950s. The work was safe and relatively clean, but required workers
to stand for hours on end and meticulously examine yard after yard
of material for any flaws. (BAnQ, 456-57.)

department in Magog, noted that, "Before, when we were paid
by the hour, it [work] was really a little paradise. We had time to
smoke, to go to the bathroom—paradise ended with the time
study." "Réjeanne," who started working as a sewing machine
operator in the Magog print works in 1947, also recalled that
initially she and her co-workers did not work excessively hard.
They even found time to play cards with the boss. However, as
time went on, plant modernization led to a decline in the number
of workers and an increase in workload for those who remained.
While wages improved, one had to work continuously. "We were
on our feet all day long," said "Éveline." "We didn't have the right
to sit down even if there wasn't any work."

The bonus system was applied primarily to semi-skilled workers such as spinners, weavers, and cloth inspectors. Only learners

Working in the Sample Room, Magog Print Works, 1950s
Women employees perform the task of cutting small samples
from bolts of cloth and pasting them in books used by
Dominion Textile sales personnel. (BAnQ, 459-57.)

and those in unskilled jobs such as doffers and cleaners continued to be paid exclusively on an hourly basis. "In the beginning," explained Aline, who began working in Valleyfield in 1942, "we worked less hard. After the bonus, then we worked harder." For her and other spinners in her department, the work intensified when the company took away the young boys who worked as doffers, and doffing became part of the spinner's responsibility. Magog cloth inspector Hélène commented; "I didn't like the bonus plan. They duped us with that, we lost out. I would have liked to have had a set salary." She and others pointed out that various factors, such as the speed and ability of loom fixers and machinists to repair faulty machines or the quality of the cotton on which one was working, were beyond the woman worker's ability to control, but they directly affected her ability to meet her assigned production target.

The demanding pace clearly exacted a physical and mental toll. Some women managed the stress by withdrawing periodically from their jobs and resting up until they had regained their strength. Such was the case for Josette who left her job for five months because she was exhausted. Françoise decided to quit her job for good in 1952, citing exhaustion as her main reason for doing so. Perhaps Laure captured best the pressures of the workplace: "In the end I quit because I couldn't do any more. There was too much speed, the boss was always on our backs, we always had to do more and more. It got on my nerves to see how things were going. We worked only for speed, and they were never satisfied with that speed." She continued to work for wages but sought out other places of employment where she felt less pressured.

Wages

The trend for textile workers, especially female hands, to have their wages more closely tied to production targets emerged in the 1920s. An article entitled "Piece Work or Day Pay" published in the *Canadian Textile Journal* in 1921 argued the case for installing various types of counting devices on machinery to monitor each worker's productivity. "In these times," the author wrote, "when our mills are so large, it is not possible for an overseer to watch and keep track of things as they once did." Weavers, he advised, should be paid by the pick [one pass of the shuttle] as recorded by their loom pick clocks instead of by the traditional method of paying them by a cut of cloth, and card room employees and mule spinners by the hank [a specified length of yarn] rather than by some other means. By the 1930s, piecework was also tied to the bonus-payment system.

Blair Gordon admitted before the Turgeon Commission that not many employees earned the bonus. That situation was hardly surprising, since the workers chosen by time-and-motion study experts to establish the base rate were the most experienced in their respective departments. They were also tested under ideal conditions where they did not have to wait for material to be delivered or for machinery repairs. Interviews with workers in

Valleyfield and Magog indicated that the bonus system increased competition among workers to be the most productive in their departments.

Women in Valleyfield and Magog who were working during the 1920s reported wages that ranged from as low as $10.45 fortnightly to as high as $40. Generally, new hands hired to strip yarn from bobbins or to doff earned between $10 and $18 every two weeks. Spinners indicated that their biweekly earnings could be as low as $12 and as high as $33, while weavers earned between $18 and $36. The considerable variation in earnings within each occupational category reflects differences in levels of experience, the number of machines tended, the type of cotton yarn worked, and the number of hours worked.

The Turgeon Commission was primarily concerned about the extent to which the textile companies shared the benefit of being a protected industry with their employees by paying reasonable wages during the Depression. Collecting data about Dominion Textile's average wages was a relatively straightforward process since the head office in Montreal set wages for all of the company's mills. Dominion Textile and the other cotton companies presented the commission with data relating to average weekly earnings for both hourly and piecework employees, based on two-week, 110-hour pay periods. Interpreting the wage data, however, and establishing whether workers were actually making a living wage were extremely complicated tasks.

As the commission's lawyers delved deeper, the complex, arbitrary, and exploitative nature of the wage schedules employed in the province's cotton mills became very clear. Irregularities in recording the hours that individual workers put in during a given week were rife. When the assistant foreman of the card room in Sherbrooke appeared as a witness on March 19, 1936, he submitted as evidence fortnightly time sheets that already contained hours for the week to come for some workers. This witness testified that it was not important what hours he entered for pieceworkers, and therefore he did not record them exactly. At least one worker kept track of his own hours, and several discrepancies existed between his record and that submitted by the assistant foreman. As the

Sherbrooke mill paymaster conceded, the columns of total hours that appeared on his pay sheets were suspect, and any attempt to establish hourly wage equivalents for pieceworkers was totally meaningless. Even more telling, an office clerk testified that the assistant foreman and the foreman would routinely reduce the number of hours recorded for any of the 131 pieceworkers in their department for the preceding two-week period if they felt they were too high. By doing so, the pieceworkers' wages, if translated into an hourly rate, would appear to be more reasonable.

Even if one worked the same number of hours each day, different rates of pay applied for each type of cotton worked, and those rates were never posted. Most pieceworkers who appeared before Judge Turgeon stated that they had no idea on what basis they were paid. Veteran weaver Josephine Fortin provided a typical response to the question of how she was paid: "I don't know, it should be based on production, we don't know if we have that, previously we knew how much a cut (roll of woven cloth) paid, that is to say, when I was a girl, I knew, that was about twelve years ago, today we don't know." When asked if she had made any attempt to find out how she was paid, she replied in the affirmative. Her efforts were unsuccessful, however, since the clerk she asked responded that it was forbidden to share this information. When pressed during cross-examination as to why she did not ask her own foreman to explain pay rates, she replied, "Because I knew that he wouldn't say, they claimed everywhere, in all departments that they didn't know, it was forbidden (to know), everyone said it."

Battery hand Yvonne Lacasse did not even know whether she was paid by the piece or on an hourly basis: "We take what they give us," she stated. When questioned further about whether there had ever been any discussion of what she would be paid, she replied, "They never said anything." Several other workers also testified that they were entirely reliant on the office clerk to read the measuring devices on their machines and to credit them with the quantities they produced each day. Weaver Anne-Marie Lemelin explained that her weekly wages for a full workweek could vary from $11 to $17, presumably as a result of different rates being paid for different types of cotton sheeting produced. Even had she known the prices paid for the various cuts of cloth, she could never have kept track of her earnings, given the frequent changes in material she was running. In addition, a night weaver worked on her machine, and if he did not also keep track, there was no use in her doing so. It was the total production of the loom that was used to calculate each of their wages. The better the night weaver, the better her wages, and similarly, the night weaver benefited from having an experienced and efficient operator on his looms during the daytime.

Dominion Textile's own data revealed that there was often a significant difference between the base rate of pay—the amount the company calculated the machine operator should earn—and the average rate of pay. In the case of the Sherbrooke mill weavers, their actual average weekly earnings were $15.01 compared to their base rate of $19.15. Blair Gordon blamed this difference on the new weaving techniques required when the mill was converted from tire fabric to cotton fabric production, even though that conversion had started to take place at least four years earlier. Another Sherbrooke official revealed that average rates were under the basic rates for a significant number of employees, but he had no explanation for the differences.

Workers' testimony before the Turgeon Commission further revealed that workers were often earning less than they had in 1929, despite the fact that they were now producing at least more than twice the quantity of goods they previously had. Dominion Textile had introduced a 10 percent general wage reduction in 1933 and only partially restored the cut with a 5 percent increase one year later. Weaver Fernande Hébert stated that her average salary in 1936 if she worked a full fifty-five hours was about the same as it had been in 1923—approximately $20 a week. In 1923, she ran twelve looms; in 1936, forty-four. She further reported that she was not always able to work to her full potential because she sometimes had to wait for a loom fixer before she could recommence her work. While the number of looms had increased significantly, there were fewer loom fixers than before.

One improvement for weavers at Montreal Cottons was the abolition of the system of fines for flawed work in the fall of 1934, after workers forwarded complaints about the excessive nature of the deductions to the local factory inspector. One witness testified that when he was working at Montreal Cottons in 1933, management posted a list of fines on the workroom wall, and the fines went as high as $1.25. By 1935, management was using other forms of discipline when an operator's work was judged to be of inferior quality. General Manager Aird explained that workers who produced bad work on two occasions were now warned, and if a third such incident occurred, they were given "a week's holiday." This was naturally a week without pay, and if, upon returning to work, they received two more warnings, they were laid off for three to four weeks. Such "holidays," he insisted, were not frequent.

By the time of the Turgeon enquiry, a minimum-wage law had been on the province's statute books since 1919, but the first regulations were issued only in 1927. The motivation for the legislation was ostensibly to protect women who were working in industrial and commercial establishments from the most blatant forms of monetary exploitation. The law applied only to women, since it was commonly believed that men did not need protecting. They could take advantage of unions, whereas women, considered for the most part to be temporary, unskilled workers, were considered unorganizable. In the social and economic turmoil of the immediate post-war period, legislators sold the idea of minimum wages for women workers to employers as a means of eliminating cutthroat competition from unscrupulous businessmen who used sweated labour in their operations.

The head of the Quebec minimum wage commission was Gustave Franq, a former vice-president of Canada's Trades and Labour Congress and founder of the progressive pro-union newspaper, *Le Monde ouvrier* (*Workers' World*). By 1930, the commission consisted of four men, although the enabling legislation had provided for the possibility of one woman member. Its mandate was to investigate rates of wages for women workers in industrial establishments and workshops attached to commercial establishments. The commissioners could hold hearings and summon individuals to appear before them to give oral testimony or to produce relevant written documentation. If they judged wages in a given industry to be too low, they could convene meetings to get advice on what the minimum wage should be for that industry. Half of the participants at those meetings were to be selected by employers and half by employees, with the commission appointing any other individuals they cared to include. The commissioners were free to accept, reject, or amend the advice the appointed panel put forward.

Once the commission fixed a minimum wage for an individual industry, it issued an order that normally became binding upon employers within sixty days, and the employer was obliged to post a copy in the work area in which women were employed. The end result was a complicated system, since the required minimum wage varied according to the type of industry, the area of the province in which it was located, and the level of experience of the workers it covered. Three geographical zones were initially identified: Montreal and its suburbs; Quebec City, Lévis, and other cities with populations of twenty-five thousand or more; and the rest of the province. Significantly, the legislation provided exemptions for girls under eighteen, apprentices, and women with reduced physical capacities, including the aged, so that employers could continue to pay them less than the required minimum. Employers who failed to comply with the legislation were fined a paltry hundred dollars or less. Order No. 5, issued in 1928, applied to the textile industry. None of the women interviewed in Valleyfield and Magog who worked in the 1930s were aware that such legislation existed.

The commission started by setting the minimum wage for experienced female workers in the industry at $12 per week in the Montreal area and $10 per week in other parts of Quebec. These amounts represented the lowest amount judged necessary for a single working woman to ensure her survival and made no provision whatsoever for supporting dependents, layoffs, ill health, or other emergencies. The minimum amount was arrived at following consultation with employers, union representatives, women workers, and social service clubs such as the largest women's organization in Quebec, the Fédération nationale Saint-Jean-Baptiste (National Federation of Saint John the Baptist.) The commission nonetheless opted for a lower amount than those recommended in the budgetary submissions they received from these groups. Even with such a low minimum, workers classified as apprentices were expected to live on even less. Those residing in Montreal were entitled to $7 weekly for the first six months of their employment, with an increase to at least $8 for the next six months. After two years they were entitled to $10 per week. Elsewhere in Quebec, the established rate for apprentices was $6 a week, with provision for an increase of $1 for each half year to a maximum requirement of $10.

The Quebec legislature did approve a number of amendments to strengthen its minimum wage legislation between 1930 and 1935. In 1930 the wage commission, having been given the right to regulate hours as well as wages, set the maximum number of hours per week to achieve the minimum wage in all industries at fifty-five. Another amendment in 1933 required employers to keep detailed records about their female workers, such as their ages and length of their workdays, as well as the wages they earned. By 1936, the minimum wage amounts were based on a forty-eight-hour work week. However, the unreliability of employers' recording of the hours actually worked by pieceworkers made it virtually impossible to know the equivalent hourly wage women were making.

Although minimum wage legislation was supposedly designed to protect women, it proved more harmful than helpful in a significant number of ways. The legislation and its implementation were both seriously flawed. Enforcement of the legislation initially fell to the already overburdened provincial factory inspectors, and even after the commission acquired its own inspectors, employers were rarely charged. When they were, penalties for violating the law were inconsequential. Fines for a first infraction ranged from a minimum of $50 to a maximum of $200, and for subsequent infractions, from $100 to $300. For a third offence within a twelve-month period, an employer, manager, or any director of a corporation, if convicted, was liable to a month in prison. Despite these potential penalties, charges against employers remained very rare.

Employers could readily avoid compliance by hiring young women under eighteen or by classifying or reclassifying employees as apprentices. Up to half of all workers in a given workplace when the legislation first came into effect could be classified as "inexperienced" if they had less than two years of experience. For the textile industry, a provision stipulated that only 80 percent of pieceworkers with six months or more experience had to receive the minimum wage. A 1934 amendment sought to keep employers from replacing workers with inexperienced ones once they had been employed for two years. The new provision specified that employers could declare only 10 percent of their female workers to be apprentices and 25 percent as semi-skilled, while 65 percent had to be classified as experienced. The mandated weekly minimum wages for each group in Montreal were $7, $10, and $12.50 respectively. For the rest of the province, where the vast majority of women textile workers were located, wages for the equivalent categories of workers were set at $6, $8, and $10. An unintended consequence of this new system was that employers were now free to assign workers to any of the three categories without consideration for how much actual work experience they had. Unfortunately, all too often the established minimum wage became the maximum wage that employers offered.

Despite the low prescribed wage amounts, the textile companies continued to find ways to evade the intended consequences of the law. Montreal Cottons, for example, petitioned the Minimum Wage Board at least twice between 1933 and 1935 for permission to pay certain of its female employees less than the minimum established for their industry. The rate the company paid its experienced battery hands was 15 cents an hour or $8.25 a day rather than the required amount of $9. General Manager Aird claimed that the company could not pay any more for that type of work and, rather than dismissing the employees in question, sought and secured exemptions from the Minimum Wage Board. When questioned what the company would have done if the board had denied the exemption, he admitted, "We would have complied, made the best of it, that is all."

The wage board's approval of Montreal Cotton's requests obviously surprised Judge Turgeon. As he pointed out, the legislation provided exemptions only for workers who could not carry a normal workload, such as the disabled and the aged. The commission's counsel delved further into the role of the Minimum Wage Commission and its inspectors during the course of the hearings. Gustave Franq explained in his testimony that granting exemptions under the initial legislation was necessary to keep experienced workers employed:

> She [the worker] achieved a certain experience in eighteen months and her pay started to rise, if she performed a minor operation she was fired and her place given to another.... A worker with 18 months of experience who had the right to a weekly salary of $10 in Montreal, if she lost her position, especially in the textile industry, could not work elsewhere, it was finished, it was impossible to find work because of the experience she had in a mill, whether it was in a cotton mill or a silk mill, she could not find a position, even in a knitting factory ... because it was covered by the same [wage] order.

In August 1935, the commissioners issued a new ordinance that allowed textile companies outside Montreal to keep up to 10 percent of all their female employees at the low level of 12.5 cents per hour, but after six months, those workers were entitled to an hourly wage of 17 cents. Montreal Cottons, however, continued to seek exemptions from the Minimum Wage Board so that it could keep paying the same workers 12.5 cents per hour. An anonymous letter sent by a Magog worker to the minister of labour alleged that Dominion Textile was forcing battery hands in that mill to sign forms renouncing their right to the minimum wage required by law. Moreover, the same battery hands were getting full-time work for only four or five months of the year.

The provision that allowed industry to pay no more than 10 percent of its female workforce at the lowest minimum wage level led manufacturers to replace young women by young men, who were not "protected" by minimum-wage requirements. A comparison of two pay periods for cotton workers at the Sherbrooke mill during 1934 and 1935 showed that while in 1934 four men and fourteen women earned between $7 and $8, in 1935, twenty-two men and only three women were at this level. Another document prepared for the Turgeon Commission revealed that in 1935 one out of every four men workers at the Montmorency mill was earning less than $10 per week. Blair Gordon openly acknowledged that Dominion Textile began to hire more young boys as doffers and battery hands in order to avoid raising wages.

Federal labour officials interestingly interpreted a 1934 amendment to Quebec's minimum-wage law that declared null "every agreement between an employer and employee fixing a lower wage than established by a decision of the [wage] commission" as covering men as well as women. A summary of provincial minimum wage legislation in effect across Canada in the *Labour Gazette* of January 1935 stated that, as a result of the amendment, "...males could not be employed in work ordinarily performed by females...at rates of wages less than the minimum for females." However, it is abundantly clear from the evidence garnered by the Turgeon Commission that, whatever the intention of the amendment, it did not stop the practice of companies employing young men at wages lower than those mandated for young women.

The textile industry prided itself on being an equal-pay-for-equal-work employer. In fact, however, the sexual division of labour in the mills meant that women and men frequently did not work at the same jobs, and even when they did, adult men still earned more on average. Men employed as spinners or weavers, for example, were often employed on the night shift and so earned a premium since the shift was one hour longer than the day shift. The most skilled and highest-paying jobs in the mills, such as those of mechanic and loom fixer, remained the exclusive preserve of men. In Montreal Cottons' spinning room in 1936, the rate of pay for second hands (assistant foremen) was 40–45 cents per hour while in the weave room section, loom fixers' pay rates ranged from 47–50 cents per hour. By contrast, even the highest-paying female occupations such as spinning and weaving had hourly rates of pay that did not exceed 36 cents. Pay rates for low-skill female occupations such as doffer, battery hand, and cleaner did not surpass 20 cents per hour. When asked about prevailing wages in his mills, Blair Gordon explained "the preponderance of pieceworkers are female, and that has a very direct bearing on the average wage of the pieceworkers because we know that on the average our females earn less than our males as a group." When asked why skilled women should not be paid similar wages to those paid to men, Gordon replied, "It isn't a question of relating it to men. These jobs are essentially female jobs."

Evidence provided by Montreal Cottons also underlined the difference between men's and women's average wages. While just over 40 percent of men earned less than 30 cents an hour, nearly 80 percent of women fell into this category. Women cotton workers' average hourly earnings in Quebec were also substantially lower than those earned in the same industry in other parts of Canada. Eighty percent of them earned less than 28 cents an hour compared to only 64 percent of their counterparts in Ontario and the Maritimes. In Quebec, women mill hands' average weekly wages of $11.80 earned them tenth place among women workers employed in thirty-five different industries in 1934. With few exceptions, the wages for both sexes were abysmally low. No doubt the workers would have preferred that companies like Montreal Cottons demonstrate appreciation for their employees' contributions by raising wages or granting paid vacations, rather than by giving each employee a box of chocolates at Christmas time.

All data generated regarding women's wages make it very clear that an experienced woman worker, working full-time all year long, could not have survived on her own, even if she had no dependents. By 1936 the total index of retail prices, rents, and costs of services in Canada had increased by over 5.5 percent compared to 1933 while the index of food prices had shot up by 18 percent. At the same time, the *Canadian Textile Journal* reported in October 1936 that wage rates in the textile industry had declined on average by 25 percent. Employers continued to legitimize their low wage rates on the grounds that it was an industry based on the model of the traditional family wage. By continuing to recruit entire families and to hire family members as they became old enough to work for wages, the textile companies argued that most families were doing well financially. Families with large numbers of children working in the mills potentially enjoyed the largest incomes and the greatest measure of security. The heavy reliance on a single employer nonetheless meant that the same families were especially vulnerable during times of underemployment or unemployment. Prolonged layoffs and strikes involving significant numbers of workers were particularly difficult to sustain, given the number of individuals in large families that had to be fed, clothed, and housed.

The insidious impact of the minimum-wage legislation on women wage earners partially explains its replacement in 1937 by the provincial Fair Wages Act covering both female and male employees. The only categories of workers not covered by the new law were farmers, farm hands, and domestic servants. Like its predecessor, however, it allowed for a special scale of wages for workers under eighteen, for those engaged in seasonal work, and for employees with physical or mental disabilities. Judge Ferdinand Roy assumed the role of chair of the new board created in September 1937 to enforce the act.

The bad publicity generated by the Turgeon Commission, coupled with improved economic conditions in the early part of 1937, led Dominion Textile to issue a 5 percent bonus to most of its workers in April that year. This improvement came on the heels of an earlier 5 percent increase that had taken effect in December 1936. These measures notwithstanding, the new Fair Wages Board launched an investigation of labour conditions in Dominion Textile's mills following the August 1937 strike. Under the board's conciliation powers, an eight-person committee composed of four Dominion Textile managers and four labour representatives worked out a new agreement concerning working conditions, hours, and wages. The result was Ordinance No. 8 issued by the wage board in May 1938, covering all Dominion Textile plants, Montreal Cottons, and the Drummondville Cotton Company. A separate regulation, Ordinance No. 4, applied to all other textile companies including Wabasso. Minimum wages established under the board's new schedules continued to set levels according to the size of the community in which a company operated. Ordinance No. 8 also stipulated a basic workweek of fifty hours for both day and night shifts. If companies needed to operate more than 120 hours per week, they had to utilize three shifts of workers. Workers defined as apprentices could not remain in this category for more than a year and could not exceed 5 percent of the mill workforce. The net result for wage increases, however, was negligible. The *Canadian Textile Journal* reported at the end of May 1938 that, "it is estimated that a majority of the ten thousand workers involved would receive the same rates of pay as at present."

In October 1939, the Fair Wages Board called upon cotton manufacturers to be as generous as possible with their workers. It pointed out that the impact of any wage increases would be minimal, since companies had the right to be compensated for the full costs of production, including labour costs. They could also build in a certain level of profit for war contracts. *Le Progrès de Valleyfield* reported on October 12 that the board warned "the textile companies would be wrongly advised to oppose in principle a readjustment of salaries, given that they will not bear the burden themselves." Within two weeks, Blair Gordon, general manager of Dominion Textile, announced a 10 percent wage increase for all eleven thousand of his company's employees.

A week before Canada had officially entered the war a month earlier, in September 1939, Mackenzie King's government created the Wartime Prices and Trade Board to prevent a reoccurrence of the war profiteering, high levels of inflation, and resulting social unrest experienced during World War I. Federal legislation passed the following year, in December 1940, set all industrial wages at 1926-29 levels. If wages were lower than this, employers could raise them by a maximum of 5 percent in a given year. The legislation also mandated periodic wage increases when the rate of inflation exceeded certain levels.

Ottawa took the additional step of creating the National War Labour Board and five regional boards to monitor wages and working conditions a year later, in November 1941. The national board and its regional counterparts were given sweeping powers to control industrial wages and working conditions and to arbitrate labour relations. Using data collected by the Dominion Bureau of Statistics, they could order companies to make periodic cost-of-living adjustments to their employees' pay. In an additional move to curb inflation, in 1943 the government restricted the national board to approving increases only in cases where it could be documented that workers were earning significantly less than others in the same industry and that the employer had the ability to pay more. To prevent disruptions to wartime production, the federal government also imposed a system of compulsory arbitration to be administered by the regional war labour boards.

Montreal Cottons Managing Director Aird, in his April 1942 report to shareholders outlining the previous year's results, stated that as a result of mandated wage increases and cost-of-living bonuses, Valleyfield workers' salaries had risen by 27.8 percent since the beginning of the war, whereas the cost of living had increased by only 14.9 percent. A year later, in his address to the corporation's directors, President Gordon blamed rising wages for some of the problems the company was having in keeping the mill running at full capacity. "Our employees," he maintained, "have not been immune from the tendency towards absenteeism and slackening of efforts which accompanies increased hourly earnings, but on the whole have shown a very creditable application to their duties."

A comprehensive survey of wages in the Canadian textile industry prepared by the federal Department of Labour also revealed that wages in the Quebec cotton industry improved significantly during the war years. In 1943, while Ontario wages continued to be the highest in the nation, Quebec workers' average wages surpassed those paid in the Maritimes in nearly all cases. Using similar data for March 1944, Dominion Textile placed advertisements in a number of Montreal daily newspapers entitled "The Truth About Quebec Textile Wages." It claimed that the per capita average weekly earnings for its factory workers, including those of women and beginners, amounted to $24.51, while corresponding wages in Ontario and Maritime mills were $23.39 and $22.89 respectively. A report published in the *Canadian Textile Journal* later that year concluded that such statistics would help counteract accusations "levelled against the Quebec textile industry for many years, to the effect that its wage rates were very much below those of mills in other parts of Canada" and predicted that wages would remain at the same level as those of Ontario well into the post-war period. What was not clear from the data presented was whether the average hours worked by employees in each region to achieve the reported earnings were the same. Quite likely, in fact, Dominion Textile's employees put in longer hours than their counterparts in Ontario and the Maritimes.

The increased strength and militancy of labour unions in the industry during the war and post-war periods did result in improved wages for cotton workers of both sexes. The collective agreement the FNCT signed with Dominion Textile in 1941 provided for overtime payments of time-and-a half for workers after they put in forty-eight hours a week. Similarly, the agreement negotiated between the UTWA and Montreal Cottons following the 1946 Valleyfield strike contained a number of key provisions regarding wages. Earnings were to be paid weekly, as opposed to the traditional biweekly basis, and nearly all workers were accorded an hourly increase of 5 cents over the course of the next year. Overtime work was also now compensated at a rate of time-and-a-half for any hours worked above forty-five a week by day-shift workers, or fifty hours by night-shift workers. Employees were also entitled to one week's holidays with pay equal to 2 percent of their gross earnings for the previous twelve months. By 1950, a sliding vacation pay scale was in effect ranging from 2 percent (for employees with under one year's service) to 6 percent (for those with twenty-five years of service or more).

The UTWA was also able to win additional paid holidays for most workers in its 1946-47 agreement with Montreal Cottons. They included New Year's Day, Good Friday, Saint-Jean-Baptiste Day, Dominion Day, Labour Day, the Feast of the Immaculate Conception (December 8), and Christmas Day. Employees required to work on those days received a supplement of 50 percent of their regular pay rates. Recognition of the importance of major Catholic feast days also led to the inclusion of a clause that no work would be conducted between 6 a.m. and 9 a.m. on Epiphany (January 6) and All Saints' Day (November 1) so that workers could attend early morning mass. The following year, however, the number of paid holidays was reduced to six. Immaculate Conception Day was changed to an unpaid holiday. The time on Epiphany and All Saints' during which no work was

Cleaning Spindles in Magog Spinning Room
Béatrice Pelletier cleans spindles on one of her spinning frames.
Mme Pelletier worked for Dominion Textile in Magog for forty-eight
years, between 1929 and 1977. (Courtesy of Béatrice Pelletier.)

to take place was also reduced by one hour to the period between
7 a.m. and 9 a.m. These provisions remained in place into the
1950s. The collective agreements the FNCT signed with Dominion
Textile in the post-war period, covering manufacturing plants in
Magog, Montmorency, Drummondville, and Sherbrooke, likewise
contained provisions for more paid holidays. For example, the
1950-51 contract provided for seven paid holidays and one unpaid
holiday. Workers were also entitled to up to two weeks of vacation
pay after five years of service and three weeks after twenty-five
years of employment.

Women who worked during the war and post-war years found
few, if any, opportunities to increase their wages through upward
job mobility. While experienced women workers were sometimes put in charge of teaching specific skills to beginners, this
added responsibility was not always welcome. Usually the most

accomplished workers, they were likely to be the highest-earning pieceworkers as well. When they took on roles as instructors, they were routinely put on straight hourly wage rates and consequently found that they actually earned less. Zépherina, who worked at various jobs in the folding department of the Magog print works before being transferred to an office job, reported that she lost wages as a result of her "promotion" to clerical work. She had been on the bonus system when she was on the factory floor, whereas she earned only a modest hourly wage as a clerk.

Supervisory positions such as assistant foreman and foreman remained tightly in men's control. As "Rose" explained, "At that time [1948-55] we did our work, we didn't think about promotions. There was no question of a woman becoming a foreman." The one exception to this rule was the Colonial department of the Magog print facility. Created when the Colonial mill closed in Montreal and the equipment was moved to Magog, it comprised some two hundred women who transformed cotton cloth into drapes, sheets, and pillow cases. Eugénie was offered instruction in how to be a forewoman and was promoted to this position along with three other women workers. At first, she was reluctant to assume the position, fearing she might make enemies among her co-workers. However, she took on the added responsibilities in return for an increase of $1 per hour. Her hourly salary as a supervisor in 1946 was $2.30, "a lot for the time," she recalled. The forewomen also received a small bonus of $5-$6 a week if they were successful in pushing those under their supervision to exceed their production quotas. As a supervisor, Eugénie found the most challenging aspects of her work pressuring the employees under her to work harder, reassigning those who were not able to meet their production quotas, and dealing with occasional disputes among workers. The bonus plan almost ensured that there would be competition, strife, and some hard feelings. In the early 1950s, eight new employees arrived from the Beauce who, according to Eugénie, "were not afraid of work. They went at it and then we had problems—the others couldn't keep up to them." Zépherina also reported that she encountered some problems with jealous co-workers because she was such a dedicated and hard worker. For

"Jocelyne" a major concern was that "there was always a certain jealousy among the employees. There were some who were conscientious and others who weren't too."

Corporate Welfare Measures

Mill managers liked to point out that while wages and working conditions might be less than ideal, their companies were leaders in providing other benefits and amenities that should be viewed as supplementing salaries and enhancing workers' lives. Such benefits included wage support during illness, medical insurance plans, and pensions. Testimony before the Turgeon Commission focused on the provisions Dominion Textile and Montreal Cottons made for employees who had accidents, required other medical attention, or retired. Some long-term employees of the companies were eligible for pensions, paid for in full by the company, and all employees were covered by a group life-insurance plan into which both they and the company paid. In Montreal Cottons' case, the company deducted 10 cents a week from workers who earned between $7 and $9 per week to provide group insurance to partially offset lost wages. In the event of illness, the worker was entitled to a weekly wage of $5 for a maximum of thirteen weeks. Workers earning more than $10 paid more into the plan and were eligible for higher rates of compensation, should they be unable to work. All employees were obliged to pay into the plan once they had been with the company for three months.

Montreal Cottons also provided limited medical services through yet another deduction from workers' wages. Every two weeks, individuals earning less than $8 per week were charged 5 cents, while those earning $8 or more had 10 cents deducted. Before April 1936, however, it was never stated what the medical insurance was to cover. Starting that year, the company entered an agreement with three Valleyfield doctors to care for workers who suffered from accidents or illness occurring in the mill, as well from some illnesses not directly related to the workplace. The company also paid for any medications prescribed in connection with the foregoing situations. In cases where hospital or medical services were required outside the city, the worker was responsible for paying the resulting costs. Other expenses not covered by the company included treatment associated with venereal disease or pregnancy, and the company-retained doctors had discretion in deciding whether to charge extra for treating "women's diseases." Clearly the exceptions with regard to pregnancy and problems associated with the female reproductive system could result in women employees being deprived of needed medical attention.

The company's retirement provisions worked even more overtly against women. Montreal Cottons provided a limited number of retirement pensions, but only to those who had at least forty-five continuous years of "good service." As General Manager Aird admitted, no explicit pension policy or any actuarial calculation dictated what the exact amount the employee, if deemed to be worthy, would receive. The company determined the pension amount, according to its assessment of the employee's worth and need. When asked if women who worked continuously for forty-five years might apply for a pension, Aird responded in the affirmative. However, all of the ensuing discussion around pensions referred only to male employees since fewer women during this time period would have worked for the company for forty-five years without interruption. Given that no designated pension fund existed, individuals wanting to draw pensions were on a waiting list and, according to Aird, the company could not afford to pay more than the $30,000 per annum it was already allocating for this purpose. When Judge Turgeon asked him how the company decided who would get a pension, he replied, "Some of those gentlemen are getting quite old and they pass on and when they pass on then their pensions are used for somebody else." Clearly there was no provision whatsoever for the employees' survivors to receive any continued assistance.

In their attempts to attract and maintain workers, particularly during the war years, Quebec's cotton companies continued to expand their corporate welfare schemes. These included the provision of health and first-aid facilities, cafeterias and lunchrooms, sports facilities and clubs, training classes, long-service clubs, and improved insurance and pension plans. Dominion Textile installed cafeterias at its Montmorency and Merchants facilities, and in 1943, it opened a "health restaurant" at its Magog site. Supervised by trained dieticians, this facility offered employees a three-course hot meal at a cost of 25 cents. In an attempt to reduce industrial accidents and lost hours of work, the company added doctors and nurses to its staff and provided first aid and resting rooms. Dominion Textile also continued to promote company hockey leagues and bowling leagues, and nearly all of its mills had interdepartmental athletic activities including softball, bowling, and hockey. At its Magog facility, a two-storey recreational clubhouse was available to the company's employees. In Valleyfield, Montreal Cottons offered workers participation in company-sponsored softball and hockey leagues and use of its MOCO clubhouse for tennis, lawn bowling, curling, and card tournaments. However, as previously pointed out, the clubhouses remained largely the preserve of English-speaking managers, foremen, and skilled workers.

Montreal Cottons created its first personnel office in 1944. *Le Progrès de Valleyfield* noted on June 1 that the goal of the new administrative unit was "to consider workers as individuals and to treat their problems as such." Available to workers from 7 a.m. until 6 p.m., the office was headed up by Lawrence Lyons, a young local man whom the company had sent to McGill for training in human resource management. Clearly the role of the office was to act as a liaison for workers, their foremen, and department superintendents. Given the pressures of wartime production, it is not surprising that the company saw the addition of trained personnel officers as a means of reducing shop-floor friction and resolving confrontations between workers and their immediate supervisors. At the time of the announcement of the new office, the company also signalled its intention to appoint a woman officer with authority to deal with "all female problems." For male employees, the company also provided on-the-job training that made use of French-language textbooks devoted to the cotton-manufacturing process. In addition, men workers who had the potential to be promoted to supervisory positions were sent to a special textile institute in Saint-Hyacinthe where they took classes in various technical and management specialties. No such opportunities existed for women workers.

Although the textile companies initiated more modern management techniques such as the creation of personnel departments in the 1940s, strong currents of paternalism and discipline persisted in corporate policies and practices. For example, a Montreal Cottons employee handbook published in the late 1940s stressed the importance of timeliness, good personal hygiene, and compliance with the company's regulations. It warned workers that lateness would be penalized by deductions from their wages, and habitual tardiness by a three-day layoff or dismissal. Employees were not allowed to leave their own departments unless they received a special pass to do so. In the Magog mill, workers in each department had their own distinctive colour-coded uniforms so that it was easy to spot anyone who had strayed from their own unit. A red light signalled the end of the shift, and the employees were not supposed to stop working before this light went on. A number of the women interviewed vividly remembered these various rules and recalled standing impatiently "like sheep" by the light waiting for it to signal the end to their day of confinement in their departments.

Favouritism and Sexual Harassment

Women's earning power continued to be jeopardized by unsympathetic or vindictive second hands and foremen. Until the 1940s, the foremen both hired and fired workers—a powerful control mechanism. As the husband of mill worker "Colette" explained, "If you wanted a job, you had to run after the foremen and the big bosses, go to their houses or the Union Hotel. . . . If, for example, my father had bought a foreman's house or a foreman's building lot, or rented a place in a housing unit owned by a foreman, then the whole family could get jobs, there was work for everyone." "Lucie" offered an even more graphic description:

> The two bosses [assistant foreman and foreman] might just as well have been bishops. . . . If the pope had gone past, it would have had the same effect. . . . We were fearful, afraid of losing our jobs. . . . For

a certain period of time, we were prohibited from bringing in snacks, a sandwich to eat in the morning and the afternoon. We hid them so we could eat them, and then hid our wrapping papers because they went through our garbage to check.

A significant number of the women interviewed who began working in the interwar period complained about the preferential treatment accorded to other women workers that cost them and their co-workers both financially and emotionally. In some cases this favouritism was related to romantic attachments but, in others, to family connections. Workers were particularly upset when their bosses assigned their machines to another employee. "It was unjust," stated Catherine. "When a foreman went out with a girl, he gave her the best work. . . . When I had to go to replace [someone] elsewhere, I made a little less for my salary. I didn't make as much as at my usual work because I was less accustomed [to the new work]." In the case of "Roberta," her boss played favourites with a woman newly arrived from Montreal by reassigning Roberta's machines to her. Luzina similarly recalled an incident when the second hand decided to give the sides of the spinning frame she was tending to another woman. Because he was the son of the department's superintendent, she had no recourse. Since piecework wages were directly affected by how well their equipment ran, workers liked to operate their own machines and did their best to keep them in top working order.

Other women talked about problems resulting from bosses favouring their girlfriends. For Clémentine, the issue was directly related to her being laid off:

At the print works, I started at 16¢ an hour [in 1929] —it wasn't a gift. In the first few years we worked September, October, November. . . and in April, they laid off us because there wasn't enough cotton [cloth].

The one who was the boss's girlfriend took my place. She was a separated woman—at that time they were rare, we could count them on our fingers. I asked the boss [about my situation] because my father was sick and we had to pay for the house. He replied in English that it wasn't a problem, and that she [the separated woman] didn't have a husband to support her and that I had my sisters. . . .It was like that, there was no justice and no union. We couldn't defend ourselves.

In Zoé's case, problems with her supervisor's girlfriend resulted in her being fired at one point. "There was a girl who was the boss's girlfriend—she, her sister, and two others in her gang created a lot of misery for us. She ran the boss and the boss believed everything she said. . . . She got favours—on her machine she only worked half the time." One day when his girlfriend incorrectly reported to the boss that Zoé had caused the sink in the department to back up and overflow, he fired Zoé on the spot. She managed, however, to get her job back within half an hour by complaining to the English-speaking departmental superintendent, using the company nurse as a translator.

There is good reason to question whether some of the foreman-worker liaisons were entirely voluntary on the woman's part, given the enormous power differential between the two parties and women's acknowledgement of the existence of sexual harassment. When asked about the treatment of women and men in the Magog mill, Colette's summary of the situation was most revealing:

> Well, that depends—if the foreman liked someone or if he had something against him or her, he wouldn't let anything by and lots of times the employee suffered. Myself, I lost my job in the office because I wouldn't accept the foreman's advances. . . . At that time there was no union, nothing to protect us. There were lots of girls who were the support for their family, and they were obliged to accept the advances.

While Stéphanie shared similar experiences about the negative impact of preferential treatment, her problems arose from her foreman's family connections:

> My boss was *Monsieur X.* I worked with his three sisters and three brothers. We were watched everywhere by the six. We were punished if we talked too much or if we stayed too long in the toilet. It was hard to work with all the boss's family, hard to hold one's tongue, they were always watching us. We couldn't even laugh—they said we were laughing at them. X told me I was laid off for three weeks because they told him I spent my time talking to others. . . . After three weeks, I went back and asked the reason for my work stoppage—he didn't want to tell me, so I stayed away for another week. After that, they called me back.

Women who began working in the industry in the 1940s continued to identify preferential treatment and sexual harassment as principal problems they encountered. Several noted that foremen treated women differently than they did men. According to Hélène, "The bosses had ambitions, they were rougher on the women." As earlier generations of workers had discovered, being the foreman's *préférée* (favourite) carried distinct advantages. "The foremen gave preferential treatment to their favourites—they gave the higher-paying yarn to their pets," "Marthe" contended. When a woman worker refused to accept the foreman's advances, however, life often became more difficult. Laure asserted that she was replaced by other spinners with five years' experience, while she had been spinning for thirteen years, because the others were the foreman's favourites. "That's when the squabbles started between me and my boss. I didn't have any more seniority." With the boss always on her back to produce at ever-higher levels, she decided it was time to quit.

Other workers gave even more graphic accounts of sexual harassment in the workplace. "The boss's fingers were sometimes too busy. I once had a blouse ripped by a boss who was too forward," recalled Françoise, while Célestine reported the following: "One time I was fired because the boss's fingers were a little too active, and I wouldn't let him do what he wanted. He was a good boss, but he was like lots of others—they tried. . . . I was okay until the boss realized that he didn't have any chance with me, then he arranged to fire me. He said that I was going to the washroom to talk."

Clearly sexual harassment continued to be a method that some foremen used to reinforce their personal control over the women employees under their supervision. It also illustrates the ongoing patterns of patriarchal relationships on the factory floor that were intended to keep women subordinate and their positions tenuous.

CHAPTER SIX

STRUGGLING FOR CHANGE
IN A MAN'S WORLD

For young women in the cotton industry in the 1920s and 1930s, the worlds of home and work were marked more by continuity than by change. Fathers and mothers expected them to be dutiful daughters who contributed to the household economy through their wages and domestic labour. Bishops and priests expected them to remain devoted Catholics who practised their religion on a daily basis. Mill managers and foremen expected them to be thankful for having a job, to work hard, and to avoid getting involved in labour disputes. And society at large expected them to marry, leave the workforce, and raise large families.

It took another war before noticeable changes occurred in women cotton workers' domestic and work experiences. Signs of greater autonomy among teenaged workers appeared in the 1940s with regard to their living arrangements and their social activities. Patterns regarding when and whom they married also changed as they began to wed earlier and with men from outside the cotton industry. Significantly more married women were working in the mills not only during World War II but after as well. Women cotton workers, like other women throughout Quebec society, began to practise more modern family limitation techniques and to have fewer children. As a result, and with their husbands' support, more of them continued to bring home a paycheque even after they became mothers.

While most of the workplace problems that earlier generations of girls and women had confronted were still present, new opportunities to resolve them were available thanks to a re-energized labour movement. In the 1930s, the Confédération des travailleurs catholiques du Canada (CTCC; Confederation of Catholic Workers of Canada), forerunner to today's Centrale des syndicats nationaux (CSN), worked to organize Quebec's textile workers, including women, and led a province-wide strike in 1937. While its influence waned following the few gains that strike achieved, it continued to represent workers in a number of mills throughout the 1940s. The major labour development in the industry during World War II, however, was the greatly strengthened international union movement in the form of the United Textile Workers of America (UTWA). Having transformed itself from an organization representing only the most skilled mill workers, it now actively recruited men and women workers of all skill levels. Led by a new generation of militant leaders, it took on the industry giant, Dominion Textile, in the iconic Valleyfield strike of 1946.

The work of both the Catholic and international unions led to some major improvements for workers with regard to hours, wages, and working conditions. For many women workers, however, active involvement in their local labour organizations remained problematic. Gender stereotypes, unions' structures and priorities, and a lack of time to engage in union activities were still major obstacles to women's engagement. Many women workers continued to consider individual action or collective protests with others in their department as the best ways to resolve their workplace issues, but the scope for these traditional methods had significantly narrowed. The implementation of binding collective agreements meant that disputes were now subject to regulation by union shop representatives rather than settled by workers fending for themselves. As well, the percentage of women employed in occupations that were central to cloth production, such as spinning and weaving, had declined markedly so that they had less leverage to bring about desired changes.

The Ideal Woman and Real Working Class Girls and Women

Embittered by Canadian involvement in what they considered a British imperialist adventure and by the deeply divisive conscription crisis, Quebec's political, social, and intellectual elites renewed their commitment to preserve the French language and the Roman Catholic religion following World War I. The war had accelerated industrialization in the province, and the federal census of 1921 indicated that for the first time since Confederation the majority of the province's citizens—56 percent—now lived in urban areas. For a society that had long extolled the rural way of life, this trend was a disconcerting one for many political and social leaders.

Key to the campaign to preserve the French-Canadian nation were its women. By rejecting the egocentric choices that nationalists equated with Anglo-American feminism, they could reinforce the family, the foundational unit of French-Canadian society. By marrying and bearing large numbers of children, they could keep French Canada numerically strong. The climate of opinion regarding the employment of married women took a decidedly sharp turn following World War I and was reflected in the official reports of the provincial ministry of labour. In 1921, Louis Guyon, by now deputy minister of the department, referred to women working outside the family as "one of the saddest novelties of the modern world: it is a real social heresy. Woman outside the home seems to us an uncentered, disoriented being." He continued his diatribe against this modern evil by linking the female worker with the rise of feminism: "Obliged to work like a man to earn her bread, often alongside men in the promiscuity of the factory or workshop, like man, she shouts out her demands—this is feminism." Fortunately in Quebec, he concluded, there were few married women working in factories, and most were there because their husbands had deserted them. Consequently, he believed there was no need to introduce any new legislation concerning maternity leaves, such as existed in several European and Latin American countries.

Guyon's opposition to women's waged labour was not restricted to married women. While acknowledging the economic necessity for single women's labour, he nonetheless fervently hoped that "society, one day or another, could find an economic formula capable of suppressing it." Like Guyon, most middle-class French Canadians, expected girls to be pious, obedient, helpful, and modest, and subsequently embrace their responsibilities as dutiful, moral, self-sacrificing Catholic wives and mothers. It was impossible for girls and women to escape such messages about their duties since they were widely broadcast from the pulpit, at school, in the Catholic organizations to which they belonged, and in newspapers and periodicals.

Given the continuing social and political power of the Catholic Church in Quebec, its stance on the duties of girls and women was bound to be influential. The clergy vehemently denounced feminism, with its emphasis on greater female autonomy and equality, and constantly reminded women of their Christian duty. In an article published in Montreal's *La Presse* in early January 1930, Monsignor Georges Gauthier, coadjutor archbishop of the Diocese of Montreal, stressed the importance once again of woman's proper role as "queen of the home, creator of the race" and as the social and moral guardian of the nation.

Another article published in *Le Progrès de Valleyfield* in June 1933 vividly captured the idealized concepts of girlhood and womanhood widely circulated in inter-war Quebec:

> As she grows up under the eye of her mother and guardian angel, she [the girl] is submissive and respectful to her parents, and affectionate toward them and her brothers and sisters. Raised in this atmosphere of peace and saintly joys, she loves Jesus and seeks to please him. After working hours, the whole family has fun together, with singing, music, and tasteful readings. Following the example of her mother, who does not follow fashion, [but] only what is decent, comfortable, and of good taste, she is modest in her clothing at home as well as outside, respecting others and making herself respected.

The message was clear and consistent in both clerical and lay publications. Women's work outside the home, other than volunteer activities, was highly undesirable for it drew married women away from their primary duties in the home and led single women into temptation. A noteworthy article expressing the latter perspective appeared in the July-August 1931 edition of *La Bonne Parole* (The Good Word), the official publication of Quebec's largest middle-class women's organization, the Fédération nationale Saint-Jean-Baptiste. The two women authors warned that industrial work was particularly dangerous, since it caused nervous strain "that created the need for exciting distractions, a desire for cars and cinema, dancing, drugs and cigarettes." Moreover, young women in industrial settings were exposed to the "habitual promiscuity of young men, especially if they are not rigorously supervised." The factory, too often, was a "place of perdition."

With the economic and social upheaval of the Great Depression came increased pressure on all women—married and single—to stay at home, perform their familial duties, and avoid competing with men in the labour force. This viewpoint culminated in a bill put forward in Quebec's Legislative Assembly in 1935 by Minister of Labour Joseph-Napoleon Francoeur. Officially endorsed by Premier Louis-Alexandre Taschereau, it proposed that no woman should be employed unless she could prove that she needed to support herself or her family. The bill's supporters claimed that a tragic reversal of traditional gender roles was under way, with young women and wives going off to work while young men and husbands stayed at home and looked after children. Although it had the support of leading members of the government, the motion was defeated by a vote of forty-seven to sixteen.

Despite the economic upturn and the unprecedented expansion of Quebec's manufacturing sector during World War II, public attitudes even towards single women factory workers remained ambivalent at best. One columnist, writing in *La Presse* in April 1943 under the patriotic pseudonym of De Maisonneuve, raised the spectre of young French-Canadian women unnecessarily sacrificing their health and their morality as increasing numbers of them flocked into industry. "How will this delicate flower [the woman worker] retain her freshness if she is not surrounded by the protective hedge of family virtues?" In the case of married women, especially those with children, the vast majority of commentators were downright hostile. A loss of female virtue, the undermining of paternal authority, a falling birth rate, growing numbers of latch-key children, and rising rates of juvenile delinquency were but some of the purported nefarious effects of married women going to work in factories. *Relations,* an influential Jesuit publication, highlighted an American Roman Catholic bishop's opinion that the war would be lost if the home were destroyed, and warmly endorsed his call to put women with children back in their proper place—in the home. At its annual convention in 1942, the CTCC voted to lobby the government to discourage the employment of women in factory work unless all male labour had been depleted and to prohibit the night-time employment of women.

Public discourse about the need for French-speaking Catholic girls and women to continue to fulfill their traditional obligations to their families and the French-Canadian nation would undergo little change until the mid-1960s. Even the more egalitarian view of the family espoused by progressive elements of the Catholic social action movement did not approve of married women working outside the home. Instead, wives and mothers should use their position, complementary with men's, to play an expanded role in the psychological and social development of their families. Catholic reformers embraced measures such as minimum wages for men workers and collective bargaining through Catholic unions to raise men's wages and thereby reduce the necessity for married women to work outside the home.

What is difficult to determine is the extent to which working class girls and women internalized and conformed to these messages. Given the frequency with which both lay and clerical spokespersons felt compelled to expound on women's appropriate roles and behaviour, their messages appear to have been frequently ignored. In each of the interwar decades, Quebec was second only to Ontario among Canadian provinces in terms of the percentage of the total workforce represented by women. By 1951, that number had reached 24.5 percent compared to 26.1 percent for Ontario and 23.6 percent for Canada. Married women accounted for 17 percent of all women workers in Quebec, a significant increase from the 7.5 percent they represented just a decade earlier. Similarly, 17 percent of women cotton workers in 1951 were married. In this and a number of other ways, the conduct of girls and women working in the cotton mills stood in marked contrast to the idealized versions of women's behaviour so widely crafted for them.

Working Daughters

Living at home and contributing to the family income remained standard practice for most women textile workers. Among those interviewed who began working during the interwar period, nearly all lived with their parents until they married or, if they remained single, until their parents' deaths. As in previous generations, the vast majority handed over all or most of their wages to their parents until shortly before they wed. In return, their parents housed, fed, and clothed them. In some families, unmarried daughters continued to hand over all their wages as long as at least one parent was alive, most likely a widowed mother. Such was the situation of Clémentine, who explained, "I have always lived here. I gave my pay to my parents. I never knew what it was to pay room and board. That's uncommon, isn't it? I always gave my salary to my parents to pay for the house. They didn't ask us for it, but we felt obliged to give it. During the early years, we had 25 cents a week. We were content, very happy with that." She contributed her entire pay from the time she began working in 1926 until her mother's death in 1935. After that, she and her sister shared the expenses of living in the same home. In other families, once an unwed woman reached a certain age, she and her parents concluded a new arrangement whereby she paid a certain sum for room and board. Pierrette gave all her wages to her parents between the ages of fourteen and thirty. "At the age of thirty," she explained, "I said to Papa, 'Don't you think that it would be reasonable for me to keep my salary?' and he agreed." For "Béatrice," there were three distinct phases to how much she contributed to the family coffers. Until the age of thirty-seven she gave her entire salary to her mother; then one-half; and in the final years of her mother's life, she paid room and board.

Women workers of the 1920s and 1930s regarded surrendering their wages to their parents as a completely normal practice that in no way affected their own sense of personal identity. In many cases, the daughter passed over her pay envelope unopened and in return received a small amount of spending money. "I gave my pay to my mother," Stéphanie specified. "I didn't even open it. Children today wouldn't do that. We had everything, we had good parents. I gave my pay to my mother until my marriage. Before I got married, my mother let me keep a few pays. I felt free to give it [my pay] to her." Lucie's experience in the 1930s was identical. "We came home at lunch hour on pay day and put our sealed packet on Mama's plate. Mama opened our envelopes and sometimes gave us the change."

Many of the women commented on the enormous pride they felt in making a material contribution to their family's welfare. The more money they were able to hand over every second week when they arrived home with their pay envelopes, the greater their satisfaction. Adèle's comments are typical: "I gave my wages to my parents until I was twenty-one years old [age at which she married]. I felt obliged to help them—the more I brought home, the greater the pride I felt." Similarly, "Camilla" explained: "We gave our wages to our parents and we were happy. My mother gave us the change. Sometimes it was 10 cents, sometimes 15 cents. We had cans that our mother made for us and we put that [the change] in them. The girls [at work] said 'You're not coming to the movies?'—'No, we don't have any money.' If our parents needed money, we took it from our little banks with a knife and we gave it to them. We felt happy."

Some noticeable changes occurred in young cotton workers' living arrangements by the 1940s. More were boarding away from their parents' homes, often living instead with sisters or in a relative's home. This was the case for nearly 25 percent of individuals who were unmarried when they started working in the cotton industry during this decade. As a sixteen-year-old in 1949, Jocelyne paid $10 weekly rent to stay in her uncle's home for one year, then found her own furnished apartment for $12 a week. She kept her own salary but sent some of her wages back to her family in her hometown. When Réjeanne moved to Magog in 1947 at the age of nineteen, she also opted to board. Others who did live at home paid room and board to their parents from the time they started working, rather than initially handing over all of their wages. Such living arrangements indicate that young women in this cohort were starting to establish more autonomous relationships with their parents compared to their predecessors.

At least 40 percent of individuals who started working in the 1940s nonetheless handed over all or a major portion of their wages to their parents during their initial years of employment. "In my time," recalled Rose, who began working in Valleyfield in 1948, "we gave our salary to our parents. I always gave my pay to my parents, and it was always with pleasure that I gave it to them. When we needed something, my parents bought it for us." This arrangement stayed in place until she married at age twenty-four. After that she kept $15 from each pay to cover the cost of her clothing. Huguette reported that she gave her wages to her parents from the age of eighteen until she married at the age of twenty-seven, keeping only a certain portion for pocket money. Unlike earlier generations of workers, however, she and some of her contemporaries expressed some dissatisfaction with this traditional arrangement. "I felt dependent," she said. "I couldn't talk about paying room and board for it would seem like I was trying to break away from them. . . . If I had to do it again, I would not do the same thing." Claire found paying room and board to her parents "ridiculous. I felt tied to them." Aline, who paid room and board from the beginning of her employment, shared that she did so because she wanted to be a bit more independent and to have money in her own pocket.

The age at which women cotton workers in Valleyfield and Magog married in the interwar period also reveals some significant changes. Best examined through birth cohort analysis, women who were born between 1905 and 1914 wed on average at twenty-six years of age, three years later than the average for those born between 1899 and 1904. This difference is a testimony to the negative impact the Great Depression had on household formation as couples struggled to accumulate enough savings to strike out on their own. On the other hand, it meant that many were able to contribute for a longer period to their parents' households. They did so, on average, for just over ten years, compared to the eight years of support women of the previous cohort had given. Women of the third birth cohort (1915-24) reached marriage age in the late 1930s and 1940s and wed on average when they were twenty-four. This two-year reduction compared to the previous cohort reflects the improved economic conditions they experienced as the country moved into wartime prosperity. For their parents, this situation translated into even fewer years of receiving their daughters' important contributions to their household budgets. On average, young women in this birth cohort who married worked for only seven years before they wed. The average marriage age for women in the fourth birth cohort (1925-34) was even lower, for it fell to twenty-two. Given the strong employment opportunities of the post-war era, rising wages, an increase in housing stock, and the expansion of government social programs including family allowances, marrying at a younger age became not only economically feasible but was also socially and culturally encouraged. Women in this cohort contributed on average less than six years' worth of wages while they lived at home before marriage.

The length of service recorded by women workers born after 1905 who remained single was truly remarkable. The mill whistle summoned them to work, on average, for just over thirty-eight years. They were often able to state the exact date they started at the mill and the exact date they ceased employment there. Some of the women also recalled with some bitterness the months or even years of employment that the company did not recognize, their resulting lost seniority, and forced retirements. "Géraldine" worked at the Magog complex for fifty years and nine months between 1927 and 1978, but was credited with only forty-nine years of service and therefore was denied her gold watch. For her, "Dominion Textile was pretty much the most ungrateful of companies."

Women who started working in the 1920s or 1930s were more likely to choose marriage partners who worked in the cotton industry than did those who began in the 1940s. Nearly 75 percent of the 1920s group and 65 percent of the 1930s group wed men who were also employed in their mills. This is not surprising given that the cotton factories were major employers of men as well as women in both Magog and Valleyfield. Among the 1940s group, however, only 36 percent of women mill workers married men who were also in the employ of their company. This trend reflects the diversification of the local economies as a result of the war and men's ability to find alternative employment in higher-paying industries.

How women became acquainted with their husbands also varied according to the decade in which they started work. Only 20 percent of the 1920s group and none of the 1940s group first met their husbands at the mill. For women who started working in the 1930s, 45 percent reported meeting their future husbands on the job. These variations may well reflect shifting opportunities for women and men to mingle in the mills. In the 1920s, a marked degree of gender segregation related to the various stages of cotton manufacturing was observable, while in the 1930s work that had been previously the purview of women, such as doffing and spinning, was assigned to men. This practice would have made it more likely to meet a future spouse on the job. Nonetheless, the majority of women workers in all decades met their future spouses away from the workplace since so many of them continued to work in all-female departments.

Across all three decades the most frequent ways women were introduced to their future husbands were through leisure activities or through friends. The socialization patterns of small-town working class women were changing from earlier times, as they were increasingly meeting and dating young men in public spaces such as the park, café, or skating rink. Despite the central role the family continued to play in young women's working and living arrangements, it was now friends and co-workers, rather than family members, who were more likely to introduce women mill hands to their eventual partners. This situation undoubtedly fed into the fears of those concerned about the endangered morals of working class girls and fuelled their diatribes against female employment.

Working Wives and Mothers

More than half of the eighteen women who started their employment in the 1920s and subsequently wed continued to work outside the home following marriage. For some, especially those who
did not subsequently have children, being a mill worker remained
a defining component of their life experience for another four
decades or more. For others, especially those who married during
the 1930s, their period of employment following marriage was
relatively short due to the prejudice against married women working. Francine, "Mathilde," and Roberta all stated that they wanted
to continue to work but the company dismissed them because of
their changed marital status. Married in 1938, Francine managed
to retain her job for just one month after her wedding. "Then they
laid off the married women," she explained. "I didn't have a
choice." Théodora initially left the workforce when she wed in
1933 "because it was not fashionable to work when one was married." Two years later, however, she was back in the mills because
her husband was getting only eight hours of work a week. Asked
about the effect that her paid employment had on her marriage
(which eventually produced three children), she replied that it
had a positive impact since her husband accepted it. "There was
more love between us," she stressed. Régina also bore three children and worked in the Montreal Cotton mills intermittently following their births in order to help her ailing husband. Unlike
Théodora's husband, however, Régina's husband was not happy
about her working outside the home.

Only six of the fourteen married women who began working in
the 1930s continued even though most of them wed after 1940
when there were more opportunities for married women in the
labour force than there had been during the Depression. The most
common reason for continued employment among the six was the
desire to supplement their husbands' earnings and to save toward
the cost of a home. Among the eight women who were not employed
following marriage, half cited their husband's opposition to them
working outside the home as their reason for retiring from the
workforce.

A different pattern of employment among married women was noticeable a decade later. Among the sixteen married women who started in the mills in the 1940s, eleven continued working following their marriages, most of which took place in the late 1940s and early 1950s. All but two eventually had children, and some women noted that their work was intermittent, spaced before, between, and after their children's births. In other cases, especially when they had fewer than three children, women chose to stay at home for a few years before re-entering the labour force on an ongoing basis. Most, such as Huguette, cited economic reasons for their continued employment: "We wanted to buy a house. We had lived with my mother-in-law for nine years in Montreal." All of the husbands whose wives continued to work were supportive, in large measure because it was economically advantageous to have a double income to meet the costs associated with the rising living standards of the post-war period. "My husband was in agreement, because he knew that I was going to bring in money," said Estelle. "Marguerite" indicated that she had not only her husband's approval, but also his assistance in looking after the housework. "He always helped me. That [my working] did not seem to bother him." For such couples, working on two different shifts—the husband on the first shift from 7 a.m. to 3 p.m. and the wife on the second shift from 3 p.m. to 11 p.m.—was a mechanism that allowed the wife to combine paid labour and her domestic duties.

The phenomenon of combining family responsibilities with paid employment was clearly becoming more widespread and accepted in this working class milieu by the 1950s. Some women explained that by this time it was their own desire to remain wage earners that motivated them to keep working. "Angélique," who married at age twenty-eight in 1950 and bore three children, explained, "I wanted to return to work and since they were short of experienced hands, I told them I would come back. I wanted a change." Similarly, Laure, who wed in 1954 and had one child, reported that her continued employment for a number of years following her marriage was due to her desire to remain active and to have social contacts.

New trends were also emerging regarding family size and the use of birth control among the women interviewed. Whereas those born between 1895 and 1904 who bore children had on average close to ten children, women in the second cohort (1905-14) who gave birth had an average of fewer than four. Only three of the twenty-one women in the second group gave birth to more than five children. For the most part, women in this cohort were starting their families in the late 1920s and the 1930s. For them, as for women elsewhere throughout Quebec and Canada, the devastating economic conditions of the Depression had a direct, negative impact on their family size. The dramatic decline in the average number of births was primarily the result of delayed age at marriage. In contrast to women in the first birth cohort who married on average at twenty-three years of age, those in the second cohort were twenty-six years old and already past their years of peak fertility. As well, material conditions were no longer conducive to the creation of large families. Stricter enforcement of child-labour legislation and increased competition for scarce jobs in the 1930s meant that children were increasingly a liability rather than an economic asset for industrial working class families.

Only one of the married women in the second birth cohort reported using any method of birth control other than abstinence. In her case, her husband practised *coitus interruptus*, supposedly at the insistence of his mother with whom they lived. "It was my mother-in-law who controlled me," recounted Camilla. "She told me that if I had any children, she would kill them. I told this to the priest at confession." Although four other women indicated that they were aware of the calendar method of controlling conception, none utilized it. Overall, then, the birth-control practices of this group seem to have closely resembled those of women of the first birth cohort. Yet the end result, the number of live births per woman, was vastly different.

It was the third birth cohort of interviewees, those born between 1915 and 1924, who reported the highest usage of birth control, primarily in the form of the Ogino-Knaus method, commonly referred to as the calendar or rhythm method. Of the fifteen women in this group who were able to bear children, seven, or just fewer than 50 percent, reported using Ogino-Knaus techniques to space their births and to limit their family size. Awareness and practice of the rhythm method of birth control grew steadily in Quebec starting in the 1930s, thanks in large measure to the actions of the Catholic Church. Seeking to deal with the economic and social chaos of the Depression, the church hierarchy rolled out a multi-faceted program of social action designed to draw the province's youth more directly into the life and work of the church and hopefully protect them from the dangerous forces of secularism, fascism, and communism. Within the Catholic social action movement, leaders and members discussed and debated more modern concepts of marriage.

Central to these discussions were issues related to sexuality, reproduction, and whether a couple should be able to space the births of their children to keep the psychological and emotional state of their marital relationship on a solid footing. By 1943, such questions were being formally addressed in courses for young couples offered by the Service de préparation au mariage (SPM; Marriage Preparation Service) under the auspices of Jeunesse ouvrière catholique (JOC; Young Catholic Workers). It was in this forum that many young women acquired knowledge of the Ogino-Knaus method. Although significant numbers of clerical and lay leaders still considered it unacceptable for Catholic couples to try to limit the size of their families, SPM's largely lay instructors found the rhythm method an acceptable, natural form of family planning that incorporated the church-sanctioned practice of abstinence.

Despite their relatively high use of the rhythm method, with an average of four live births each, the third birth-cohort women still had larger families than their counterparts in the previous cohort. No doubt an earlier average age at marriage—twenty-four as opposed to twenty-six—had an impact by increasing the number of years of high fertility. As well, the worst of the Depression was over by the time these women were forming their families, and post-war prosperity made it easier for couples to support children financially.

Married women of the fourth birth cohort, those born between 1925 and 1934, wed, on average, even earlier, at just over twenty-two. Nonetheless, women who became mothers did not have larger families than women in the previous cohort, since they also had an average of four children. A possible explanation is that a significant proportion of them were practising family limitation; however, that was not what the women reported in interviews. Only one of the seven women shared that she had used the rhythm method, while the rest stated that they took no steps to prevent pregnancies. The average number of births for this group may be artificially low due to its small size. Other demographic studies have indicated that nearly 60 percent of Quebec women born between 1926 and 1930 were using some form of contraception to control the timing and number of births.

For married women who never had children, or for those who became widows and sole-income supporters, workforce attachment resembled that of single women. Unless company officials were reducing the workforce by letting married women go, these women spent decades following their marriages in paid employment. For example, Carmen, who married in 1921, continued to work at the Magog mill for the next fifty-two years. Cases like this challenge the stereotypes of married women as short-term employees for whom the workplace was of passing interest.

Recreation and Leisure

The amount of time both single and married workers had at their disposal for leisure activities during the 1920s and 1930s remained extremely limited given the many hours they spent in the mills and performing chores at home. Although Géraldine never married, she found it virtually impossible to take part in Magog's associational or recreational life. In addition to labouring up to ten hours a day, as well as overtime hours some evenings, she was expected to help out at home. Her parents were poor, and her mother took in boarders to help balance the family budget. As a result, this millworker always had plenty of domestic chores to perform. Time restraints, parental control, and a shortage of funds put severe limits on social activities for many young women. "I didn't go out at that time," commented Hermione, another woman who began working in the 1920s. "My parents were strict. We had to be home before 9 p.m. During my leisure time I knit for my trousseau. With the small salaries that husbands earned, we had to have a trousseau." For workers whose parents were less strict, Saturday night movies or dancing provided a welcome diversion from the grinding everyday routine. Leisure activities were confined for the most part to the home or to activities that did not require money. Walking and skating were the most frequently cited outdoor activities, while reading, knitting, and embroidery were some of the indoor pastimes.

Women who began working in the 1940s were less likely to cite parental disapproval and poverty for their lack of involvement in recreational activities. On the other hand, there was a familiar refrain to their reasons for staying home. "Solange," who started in 1942, explained that, even though she remained single, she was too tired after work to do anything else. For Colette, it was a lack of spare time that prevented her from participating. This group of women was also attracted to activities similar to those named by the older groups of workers, such as walking, handicrafts, and movies. The amount of time spent socializing with co-workers they reported differed significantly, however, from that noted by their predecessors. Among women who entered millwork in the 1920s and the 1930s, almost half said that they socialized with their co-workers. Special occasions such as a birthday or an engagement provided the basis for celebrations, and workplace friendships were reinforced through attending dances and movies together. By contrast, only one-third of women who started in the 1940s reported spending leisure time with colleagues.

While both Montreal Cottons and Dominion Textile liked to emphasize the various recreational facilities they offered their workers in the form of company-sponsored golf, tennis, and curling clubs, these facilities were the preserve of the managers and the elite English-speaking men workers. One former English-Canadian employee observed that, "Most clubs in almost every aspect of Magog were almost all management and were all English too. It was just one of those things that the French didn't seem to partake of. We did get some of the younger French people in, but basically in those days, as you know, plant managers right down to floor boss were English."

The rate at which the women who were interviewed joined non-work-related organizations was virtually identical across the decades, with one-third from each decennial group reporting that they did not belong to any associations. The principal organizations in which the remaining women participated were religious in nature. Nearly one-half of women in each post-1920 decade belonged to the Enfants de Marie (Children of Mary) while they were girls. A new opportunity for single women's involvement in church-related organizations came in the wake of the Catholic social action movement. Drawing on ideals of collaboration and collective action, Quebec's bishops promoted the creation of specialized associations, headed by chaplains, for rural youth, students, and young workers across the province. The first group for women workers, was launched in May 1931 under the banner of Jeunesse ouvrière catholique féminine (JOCF). By November of the same year, plans to establish Jeunesse ouvrière catholique (JOC) for young men were also underway. As with the other Catholic youth organizations, young men and young women met in separate groups but came together for some shared activities. From the beginning, women outnumbered men in the social action groups. By 1939, through its 170 clubs, JOC offered its members a variety of programs including employment counselling, aid to unemployed youth, savings and loan services, educational courses, libraries, and sports and leisure activities.

JOCF chapters were active in both Valleyfield and Magog, and according to Rita, the Magog group held weekly meetings that were well attended. The association offered opportunities for young women to study workplace issues and to develop leadership skills by taking on executive positions. JOCF involvement was highest among women born between 1915 and 1924, with approximately one in three claiming membership compared to one in five of those born a decade later. Three married women also reported belonging to the Ligue ouvrière catholique (LOC; Catholic

Workers' League), the JOCF equivalent for married women. The less socially engaged Dames de Sainte-Anne (Ladies of Saint Anne), however, remained the most frequently named group to which married women in the post-World War II era belonged. Its popularity appears nonetheless to have been declining, since only one in five women in the fourth birth cohort reported belonging to this organization, compared to one in three for women in the three previous birth groups. This drop in participation stemmed most likely from the fact that more women were continuing in some sort of paid work following marriage and therefore had even less free time than their predecessors.

Women remained strongly attached to the church through their religious practices. All those interviewed who began working between 1920 and 1950 reported high levels of church attendance. In addition to attending weekly mass, they went to services on all obligatory feast days, even if that meant going to church at 5:30 a.m. before their regular day shift. Friday mornings, especially the first Friday of every month, found most respondents in church praying their novenas. Several women also indicated that they went to mass every morning before work during Lent, and some made yearly retreats. This frequency of church attendance was not unusual among Catholics in Quebec at this time. Early in the 1950s, one study of Quebecers' religiosity indicated that 90 percent of young workers attended weekly mass, while 60 percent of the men and 80 percent of the women reported that they went to confession at least once a month.

Union Developments in the Interwar Period

Had they had more time to get involved in labour organizations, women textile workers had little opportunity to do so in the 1920s. Quebec had experienced extensive industrial unrest and renewed union activity in the immediate post-war period, as had the rest of Canada. It was of short duration, however, and the decade after World War I proved largely a quiescent one across the nation for organized labour, with fewer than 10 percent of all Quebec workers claiming union membership. Efforts to engage cotton workers in union activity came from two very different sources—the older international secular labour movement represented by the United Textile Workers of America (UTWA) and the nascent Catholic workers' organization, the Confédération des travailleurs catholiques du Canada (CTCC).

In addition to reasserting its presence in Dominion Textile's Montreal mills in the spring of 1919, the UTWA tried to organize workers at Montreal Cottons in Valleyfield. But when union organizer H.-A. Foucher asked permission to hold a public meeting of mill employees at city hall, the municipal council denied his request. When his efforts to rent other facilities in the town failed, he attempted to hold an outdoor meeting. A May 22 account in *Le Progrès de Valleyfield* indicated that he was also unsuccessful in this endeavour since local police ordered people who showed up to go home and advised Foucher to leave town. While UTWA's efforts to sign up workers in Valleyfield appear to have been thwarted, the union was successful in demonstrating its presence in other mills outside of Montreal. One of its affiliates initiated a work stoppage at the Montmorency mill on July 28, 1919 that resulted in all eleven hundred employees walking off the job in an attempt to win higher wages and show support for the Montreal strikers. The strike lasted ten days and did result in a wage increase.

Four years later, Local 2003 of the UTWA confronted Dominion Textile management yet again, this time at the Saint Anne branch in Montreal. A dozen loom fixers belonging to the union walked off the job on May 15, 1923 to protest increased workloads after the company sought to reduce their number to nine while insisting that they accomplish the same amount of work. While only these 12 skilled workers were directly involved, the conflict brought work to a halt for 62 other men workers and 241 women workers. As the negotiations with the company continued, the union put forward another grievance, namely the work performed by women during the lunch hour. Within a week it reached an agreement with management that saw the company back down on its plan to reduce the number of loom fixers but allowed men to replace girls and women on looms that continued to run during the noon hour.

The loom fixers' regular hours and wages remained the same as they had been before the dispute arose.

This particular dispute was telling, for it clearly underlined that the UTWA was still first and foremost a union dedicated to protecting the interests of skilled men workers such as machinists and loom fixers. This orientation is hardly surprising since it belonged to the American Federation of Labor, a federation of craft unions. In keeping with the opinions of its parent body, its leaders considered female workers to be unskilled and therefore a direct threat to the work and wages of skilled male workers. UTWA organizers feared that management would increasingly take advantage of new technologies to reduce the skill level required for many jobs, and consequently replace men by cheaper women workers. While the potential for such changes clearly existed and was realized in some instances, such as the replacement of mule spinning by ring spinning, the union's dire predictions did not materialize. The sex-based hierarchy of labour in the mill remained firmly in place since both union leaders and managers agreed on the principle of men's entitlement to work and men's right to monopolize the most skilled and remunerative positions.

The UTWA continued to make its presence known from time to time in the 1930s. Men in Trois-Rivières walked off the job in August 1935 to protest Wabasso's practice of replacing older married men workers by lower-paid teenage boys and women. After the city's mayor intervened, they returned to work when management promised to give hiring preference to married men and to set up a joint management-worker committee to deal with other issues. Frustrated with the company's subsequent failure to implement changes, some UTWA members left their jobs in February 1936, demanding union recognition along with increased wages. Despite the mayor's and federal labour officials' efforts to achieve a settlement, the company refused to negotiate with the union. The strike was called off on March 2 when the workers were promised that the recently established royal commission studying the textile industry would review their grievances.

Determined resistance to the UTWA's efforts to win workers to its cause came not only from the textile companies but also from a growing Catholic trade union movement. Drawing on Pope Leo XIII's encyclical, *Rerum Novarum* (1891) and the turn-of-the-century European Catholic social action movement, the Quebec episcopacy became increasingly public in its opposition to foreign-controlled secular unions. It considered them to be tainted by Protestant, liberal, socialist, and even communist ideals. They were also opposed to the social and political programs that international unions endorsed, such as the provision of free public education and the nationalization of certain public services. What was needed were local Catholic unions that, while improving the plight of workers, would shun individualism and materialism and promote harmony and mutual respect between owners and their employees.

By 1915 five Catholic unions had been established in various parts of the province. The real impetus to the spread of the movement came, however, with the massive industrial unrest during and immediately following World War I. Events such as the Winnipeg General Strike and the rise of the One Big Union movement created a mood of heightened anxiety, if not panic, within the political, business, and religious establishments. Like many other Canadians, the Quebec bishops concluded that Bolshevism was on the rise and that they must do their part to stem the tide. Founded in 1921 at Hull, the CTCC represented a new stage in the Catholic Church's battle against international unions. Wherever there were at least twenty Catholic workers prepared to accept a constitution that conformed to the moral and social teachings of the church, the CTCC was prepared to accept them as an affiliate. Each local was required to have a priest named by the bishop to serve as its chaplain. Appearing a decade later before the Turgeon Commission, Abbé Georges Côté, named by Cardinal Villeneuve to serve as chaplain to Catholic unions in the diocese of Quebec and to the CTCC, explained that chaplains were to be moral advisors to union locals and ensure that their activities conformed to the social doctrine of the church. However, their principal role "was to seek collaboration with the employers to put in place a regime of peace in industry."

The movement's growth was slow over the next decade, owing in large measure to the slowdown in many sectors of the Quebec

economy. The number of affiliates claimed by the new organization scarcely changed over the next decade, with 120 locals
reported in 1921, and 121 in 1931. Estimated total membership
also remained static at approximately fifteen thousand members.
Nonetheless, by 1931 CTCC affiliates represented approximately
30 percent of all labour unions and 28 percent of all unionized
workers in the province of Quebec. By 1926, it also counted within
its ranks a federation representing textile workers, the Fédération
nationale catholique du textile (FNCT; National Catholic Textile
Federation), presided over by Émile Ouellette, a former president
of the now defunct Fédération des ouvriers du textile du Canada
(FOTC; Federation of Textile Workers of Canada). From the perspective of women cotton workers, the FNCT represented a new
organization that might militate on their behalf. Like its predecessor, the FNCT was a form of industrial unionism, composed of
locals seeking to represent various groups of Catholic workers—
skilled and unskilled, male and female, French and English.
Unfortunately, the paternalism and misogyny that characterized
international unions such as the UTWA were also frequently
manifested in the policies and practices of the Catholic unions.

At the CTCC's founding congress in 1921, delegates adopted a
resolution calling for a minimum wage for women workers only.
While participants in the 1922 congress endorsed the fifty-hour
workweek for all textile industry employees, in 1926 delegates
voted in favour of the eight-hour day, but only for women workers.
Although presented as a means to protect women, this measure
made them less competitive from a hiring perspective. As the economic crisis of the 1930s worsened, the resolutions adopted at
annual CTCC conventions reflected the misogynist temper of the
times. In 1935, the attack on women's employment was more direct than previously. Congress delegates considered a motion that
linked unemployment with the "exaggerated development of
women's work" and called on the provincial government to restrict
women's employment to "fair proportions." The resolutions committee recommended an amendment that called upon the government to start with the firing of married women, and the revised
proposal was passed.

Four years later, a lengthy diatribe against women working outside the home formed part of a resolution proposed by the central council of Catholic unions in Trois-Rivières, and this time single women bore the brunt of the attack:

> This system [of women's employment] facilitates too great an emancipation of young women, so much so that a good number of them free themselves from their parents' supervision to go and live completely free in action and often in behaviour, which leads to a host of grave moral consequences. Women's labour works to hinder marriage ... the natural environment for the exercise of their activities. These young girls and women replace youths and men, and keep alive an era of low salaries, obliging conscientious employers to engage a female workforce in order to challenge their competitors. And the vicious circle continues. Women's labour disrupts the employment market and this state of affairs calls for yet more women's employment.

The motion following this denunciation called for legislation to restrict employment to only those women in economic need and was adopted as presented.

Opportunities for women union members to voice formal opposition to such motions at CTCC conventions were extremely limited. Women appear to have attended conventions for the first time in 1934 when the presence of four women "visitors" from the Quebec district was noted. Four women were also present as observers in 1935, but it was only in 1936 that the first woman delegate attended, along with one woman visitor. In 1937, there were two women delegates [one from Quebec and one from Jonquière] and one woman visitor in attendance. In August the same year, a local was formed in Trois-Rivières to represent Wabasso workers, and Mademoiselle M.-L. Chandonnet was elected vice-president. The following year, 1938, she was one of the Catholic labour representatives at Valleyfield's union day. When the strongly worded motion against female labour was passed in 1939, only one woman delegate was present at the convention.

Despite the striking underrepresentation of women among CTCC delegates, resolutions sponsored by women sometimes made it onto the convention agenda. In 1937, a number of resolutions were introduced on behalf of the women's inter-professional union of Jonquière. One of them called for the forty-eight-hour workweek for all workingwomen, except for those engaged in domestic labour. This stance might suggest that women shared their union brothers' perspective that only women's hours needed regulation, but it is impossible to determine if their motivation was exactly the same. Had they accepted the argument that women were undermining men's labour and thus jeopardizing the married man's ability to provide for his family? Or were they simply seeking to make it easier for women to combine paid work with their family responsibilities? Since the same local also proposed that provincial labour laws be amended to require one week's paid vacation for all working women with one year's experience, and two weeks for those with two year's experience or more, it may well have been the latter consideration that was foremost in its members' thinking.

The deterioration in working conditions and wages that occurred during the Depression greatly increased the need for workers of both sexes to engage in collective protection. Charles Plourde, a machinist and the business agent for the Association des travailleurs catholiques de Salaberry-de-Valleyfield (ATCSV; Catholic Workers' Association of Salaberry-de-Valleyfield), testified before the Turgeon textile enquiry that he had recruited about eight hundred women and men mill workers in 1932. He identified the improvement of working conditions and the elimination of competition from workers who resided outside Valleyfield as the union's two primary objectives. The union wanted mill managers to stop hiring people from Magog and Trois-Rivières at the expense of the town's workers. Plourde also reported that he had met with W.G. Aird, general manager of Montreal Cottons, to discuss the formation of the Catholic union. According to Plourde, Aird had stated that he did not care whether workers joined the union or not—that was their concern, not his. While indicating his willingness to address workers' grievances, Aird acknowledged that he had been instructed by head office "to oppose certain things."

In June 1933, the Valleyfield association announced in the local newspaper its intention to represent the interests of employers as well as employees and invited Montreal Cottons to contact its business agent if it needed workers. Citing its adherence to Catholic social doctrine, it denounced the view that bosses and workers were enemies. It claimed to represent more than eight hundred workers from various industries and professions, including construction workers, mechanics, unskilled workers, grocery clerks, and textile workers. A subsequent newspaper account declared the first organizing meeting for female textile operatives a success, with over three hundred girls and women in attendance. The organizers outlined the advantages of having a well-organized, strong union and announced that general assemblies of women textile workers would take place the first and third Monday evenings of every month. However, unlike men who formed their own sections and held their own weekly meetings in addition to general assembly meetings, women do not appear to have formed their own local.

Despite the promising beginning, the association had some difficulty in continuing to attract women to its meetings. A notice of a general meeting to be held on July 17, 1933, featuring a number of prominent Catholic union organizers from Montreal, made a special appeal to girls and women to attend. *Le Progrès de Valleyfield* subsequently reported, however, that the speakers consistently addressed the gathered audience as "Sirs," a salutation that would seem to indicate that few, if any, women were in attendance. Although the association held its meetings in the basements of the town's Catholic churches, a familiar venue for women workers, they were held in the evening. As noted earlier, both single and married women workers had demanding household responsibilities that prevented them from easily finding time for evening sessions.

The Catholic unions, in stark contrast to the overt opposition encountered by the UTWA in its organizing attempts, were enthusiastically promoted not only by the clergy but also by local and provincial politicians who frequently showed up on the speakers' lists at union events. This increased momentum of the

Catholic workers' movement, however, only steeled the resolve of Dominion Textile's president, Blair Gordon, not to allow any unions into his mills whatever their national or ideological provenance. Trefflé Leduc, a Montreal Cottons loom fixer who was elected vice-president of the Valleyfield Catholic workers' association in 1933, revealed the lengths to which mill management would go to keep unions out when he testified before the Turgeon Commission. Leduc, who had started working for Montreal Cottons when he was ten and given the company forty-two years of service, was fired on May 9, 1935 with no explanation. That same day, three other executive members of the Valleyfield Catholic workers' association also lost their jobs.

The following year, efforts were made to shore up the weakened Catholic union movement in Valleyfield through the creation of a new textile local. Alfred Charpentier, president of the CTCC, was the principal speaker at the founding meeting held on June 17. He thanked the nearly four hundred men and women workers in attendance for showing up as requested by the local parish priests. He reported that he had met with General Manager Aird, who reiterated his position that he had no objection to workers joining the Catholic union. Aird's seemingly conciliatory attitude was in marked contrast to that expressed by the editor of the *Canadian Textile Journal* in September 1936. "In Quebec," he wrote, "the French-Canadian has been the victim of his own folly. The textile industry has been a major influence towards emancipation of Quebec youth out of political and secular despotism.... The most anomalous aspect of the textile labour troubles among French-Canadian workers is the witness of radical influence in their heritage of Roman Catholicism."

Despite Charpentier's optimism, the new Valleyfield union grew slowly. Speakers at a meeting held in April 1937 to elect a new executive stressed that all workers had a duty to join Catholic unions to protect their religion and urged women workers to attend meetings and join the union. An announcement for a meeting to be held on a Sunday afternoon the following week called upon both men and women to attend. It is impossible to tell how many women attended that meeting or similar occasional general assemblies held on Sunday afternoons. Speakers at subsequent meetings emphasized the role of the Catholic unions in preserving the faith and constantly reassured workers that they would not lose their jobs if they joined the Catholic union. These approaches undoubtedly reflected a strategy on the part of the textile federation's leadership to draw more women into union ranks.

The growing militancy on the part of workers and their willingness to take job action spoke not only to their desperation but also to the church's legitimization of workers' rights to obtain greater justice. The exposé of the terrible working conditions in the province's mills by the Turgeon Commission and the resulting widespread sympathy for the workers acted as powerful stimuli to increased job action. A heady mixture of religion and nationalism combined to stoke public resentment in Quebec and led to widespread denunciations of mill owners and managers as greedy English, primarily Protestant capitalists mercilessly exploiting defenceless French-Canadian Catholic workers. Starting in the early 1930s Catholic Church leaders had dropped their insistence on the individual worker's right to negotiate his own terms and conditions of labour, and come out wholeheartedly in support of collective bargaining. They also grudgingly recognized that strike action was a legitimate weapon of last resort.

Throughout Canada, 1937 witnessed the most widespread labour unrest since 1919. Workers were extremely frustrated, as they had failed to secure any immediate benefits from the economic recovery that had begun the previous year. Quebec was not spared the growing confrontation between capital and labour. Union recognition, collective bargaining, and wage increases were the main issues underlying the massive province-wide strike of cotton mill workers that began on August 2, 1937 and continued for twenty-four days. Orchestrated by the FNCT, it involved some ten thousand workers—six thousand men and four thousand women—employed at nine mills operated by Dominion Textile and its affiliates, Montreal Cottons and Drummondville Cottons. As the strike dragged on, increasing numbers of workers felt compelled to cross the picket line, but even among those who returned

Mount Royal Plant, Montreal During The 1937 Strike
Taken outside Dominion Textile's Mount Royal facility, this photo shows
a group of picketers being watched by a contingent of police with
motorcycles. The province-wide strike, led by the Confédération des
travailleurs catholiques du Canada, involved some 10,000 cotton mill
workers and lasted for twenty-four days. (BAnQ, P48,S1,P1511)

to work, over half were getting less than twenty-four hours of work
a week. With workers enduring increased hardship and negotiations in a stalemate, the union leadership accepted an offer by
Premier Maurice Duplessis to mediate the dispute, and called off
the strike.

On December 27, 1937, a committee of unionized and non-
unionized workers reached a settlement with management providing for a 5 percent general wage increase covering the period
from August 31 to December 18. The new contract provided for
additional wage increases for specific groups of workers, including pieceworkers. The workweek was also to be reduced for most
workers from fifty-five to fifty hours. Thanks to the direct intervention of Cardinal Villeneuve, archbishop of Quebec, the settlement also included acceptance of the principle of collective

bargaining by Dominion Textile's management. No provision for a closed union shop was included, however, and either party could terminate the contract within six months.

It was, in fact, the FNCT that took advantage of the termination clause to signal its desire to bring the existing contract to an end in May 1938, as it wished to amend it to provide additional improvements. Dominion Textile refused to negotiate and declared that it was no longer bound by the contract. It chose instead to distribute pamphlets to all of its employees, inviting them to air any grievances they might have with the joint company-union work committees. The FNCT, knowing it was not strong enough to lead yet another strike, requested that the provincial Fair Wages Board act as mediator.

The settlement the board produced contained many of the same elements as the 1937 contract with the notable exception that the union lost even the partial recognition it had won. The new agreement provided once again for the establishment of shop committees, each composed of six members. The number of committee members the FNCT could appoint depended on the union's ability to sign up members. If it could establish that 50 percent of mill workers were dues-paying members, it could name two of the three workers designated to sit with the company's three representatives; otherwise, it could name only one. In Valleyfield the union called a meeting on July 6, 1938 at which it attacked Dominion Textile's creation of such work committees as a violation of provincial and federal labour laws, and it pleaded with both men and women workers to support the union. It was already apparent, however, that much of its strength had been sapped, for the reported attendance was considerably smaller than it had been at previous meetings.

Labour strife, unsurprisingly, continued in the industry. Between 80 and 150 spinners walked off the job at the Montmorency mill on July 11, 1938 to protest what they considered to be an increase in workload without any commensurate increase in wages. Federal officials estimated that the work stoppage affected from 700 to 1,800 additional mill employees indirectly. Although the FNCT had a Montmorency local, it was not directly involved in the dispute because the company would not recognize it. The workers refused to return to work until Blair Gordon agreed to meet with them in person. When Gordon declined to settle the matter on the spot, a group of workers invaded the office where he and the assistant manager had taken refuge and roughed them up. During the brief melee, Gordon was hit on the head with a large inkwell, while the assistant superintendent was hit over the head with a telephone. In Gordon's own words, "What with the blood and the red ink I was a hell of a mess." A faint forehead scar served as a permanent reminder of this encounter.

The following March, it was the turn of the drawing tenders in the Mount Royal mill's carding department to confront the company when it attempted to reduce piece work prices by some 8 percent. The dispute, involving twenty men and ten women, was resolved within an hour when management agreed to keep the existing wage rates. The overall fate of the FNCT was less auspicious. Despite the union's efforts to convince workers that it had won better wages and working conditions for them, memberships and attendance at meetings plummeted. By 1939, all of its affiliates, with the exception of the Montmorency chapter, had either disbanded or were inactive.

The vast majority of women interviewed who were employed in the 1930s reported that they did not know of any union activity in their mills before 1935-36. Even after Catholic unions became more active in their towns, some women indicated that they were not aware of them. Ignorance of unions and their goals is not particularly surprising, given the union's weakness during most of this period and the gender dynamics of the workplace and of the labour organizations. Lucie recalled that, "It [the union] was not a force, not strong. At that time many things were hidden. There were meetings but we weren't informed about that at work. We knew about them by reading the newspaper." Since the union was anathema to the company, unions could not post notices of their activities in the mills before 1938. "Rosa" and Colette also described the Catholic union as weak since it was not obligatory for people to join, and they did not attend meetings because they were not members.

Colette's husband recalled that initially meetings in Magog consisted of only five or six workers gathered in the evening in workers' kitchens so that the foremen would not find out. Workers belonged first and foremost to departments and, in most cases, the circle of their mill acquaintances did not extend beyond the workers in their own sections. Unless either a family member or a co-worker was a member of the union, employees would have found it difficult to garner detailed knowledge of the organization.

Most women who were aware of the existence of Catholic unions understood that their principal aims were to improve wages and working conditions. Some also mentioned ensuring greater justice and protecting workers from arbitrary dismissal as key union objectives. A small number indicated that they had not only joined their local FNCT affiliate but regularly attended its meetings as well. "Laurentia" recalled that she went to meetings to find out what was going on. "It was an outing," she said, "a whole gang of us went." When Marcelle entered the mill at the age of fifteen in 1937, she immediately joined the union. "I was active because you have to look after yourself," she stated. That involvement proved to be but the start of many years of participation in union activities, including serving on the executive of her local in the 1950s. Louisette talked about Trefflé Leduc's efforts on behalf of the FNCT in the mid-1930s and about how some workers asked him to intervene on their behalf to help resolve problems.

For women workers, the Catholic union movement of the 1930s offered some distinct advantages over the UTWA of the 1920s. To begin with, it had the approval of church and local civic figures, its leaders spoke French and were Catholic, and it sought to represent employees of all skill levels. Women nonetheless had fewer reasons than their men co-workers for seeking to channel their energies through such unions. As noted earlier, union leaders demonstrated blatantly paternalist attitudes at annual CTCC conventions during the 1920s. The massive unemployment of the early 1930s and the resulting fierce competition for jobs turned this paternalism into outright hostility toward women workers. Alphonsine, who worked because of her husband's ill health, was upset with the Catholic union's stance on married women workers. "I sometimes went to the meetings and the union wanted to have married women dismissed. When they wanted to collect dues from me I said 'No, I won't pay so that you can put me out.'" Union representatives took their campaign door-to-door in Magog and asked people to sign a petition in favour of the dismissal of married women. When she voiced concern about her own situation, union leaders assured Alphonsine that she would keep her job since they knew her husband was ill. By promising to safeguard her job, they convinced her to take out a union membership. Another married Magog worker, Roberta, heard about the union, but she maintained that married women were not involved in it. She lost her own job shortly after the 1937 strike when married women were let go.

Single women also expressed their concern over male dominance of the Catholic unions and the lack of encouragement for women to assume active roles in them. According to Clémentine, "Men didn't have any confidence in women—a married woman was made for her little work at home, and the girls were young." She remembered the union chaplain attending meetings and speaking out against strikes: "He said 'Try to resolve things so that there is no strike. What will your families do [if there is a strike]? They will starve and you will be left with debts.'" She also pointed out that the union chose men representatives at the departmental level, even though some workrooms were overwhelmingly staffed by women. Other reasons that women cited for not getting involved in the union included fear of company reprisals, low interest in union activities, parental opposition to unions, lack of time due to other family obligations, difficulty in securing transportation to get to meetings, and an absence of any personal grievances. A number of women also expressed the opinion that the union could not help them address their most important workplace concern, namely which machines they were assigned to operate.

While few women expressed outright hostility to unions, many were critical of strike activity, contending that subsequent wage gains never made up for wages lost as a result of work stoppages. The fact that the FNCT won a bigger increase in its 1937 contract for hourly workers, who were mostly men, than it did for piece workers, who were overwhelmingly women, may also have under-mined their confidence. The differential was at least 25 percent and potentially much higher, since there were bonuses for night work that only men could perform.

Only two women claimed to have actively participated in the 1937 general strike by walking the picket line. Others reported that they accepted the union's request to make sandwiches for the strikers. In return for this work they received goods-in-kind and a small amount of money to help see them through the strike. Yet others used the strike as an opportunity to rest up or spend time on leisure activities. Géraldine stated that she stayed quietly and sensibly at home, and Pierrette and "Catherine" reported doing the same. According to the latter, neither the church hierarchy nor the chaplain got involved in the conflict, other than to pray for the return of industrial peace. For her part, "Arthurine" took advantage of the work stoppage to visit Montreal.

Union Organization during World War II

During the early years of World War II, the FNCT was able to stage something of a comeback. Federal labour documents reported in 1941 that the FNCT had twelve locals representing cotton-mill workers in Montmorency, Magog, Trois-Rivières, Shawinigan Falls, Drummondville, Valleyfield, and Sherbrooke. It nonetheless had lost ground to the UTWA in Dominion Textile's important Montreal mills, a development that led company management to exhibit a more collaborative attitude toward the Catholic unions, since it considered them to be the lesser of two evils.

While the Catholic union movement became increasingly professional in its management and bargaining processes, its stance on women's labour issues remained decidedly conservative. The massive entry of women into Canada's war economy created grave concerns in many quarters, and nowhere were they more heatedly aired than by Quebec's political, clerical, and social elites. Their worries focused on several aspects of women's work including long hours, unhygienic working conditions, a lack of adequate work breaks, and the hiring of married women with young children.

Proposed solutions to the "social scourge" of married women's paid employment included calls for provincial laws implementing the forty-hour workweek and prohibiting mothers with children under the age of sixteen from working in factories. By far the most vehement opposition, however, focused on the employment of women with children on night shifts. A 1942 study of women's industrial night work undertaken by the CTCC and reported in *Relations* in May that year argued that married women with young children should not be permitted to work in war industry and certainly not on the night shift. "The primordial task of our mothers is to raise their children well," declared Alfred Charpentier, the CTCC's president.

Despite this opposition, women's labour-force participation grew and a number of work stoppages involving women occurred at mills where the FNCT represented the workers. Federal labour officials noted in February 1940 that 150 women cone winder tenders and 50 of their male colleagues had walked off the job in Montmorency to protest a reduction in the piecework rate. The dispute lasted one week and indirectly affected up to 600 workers. The protesters returned to work after being guaranteed an hourly salary of 31 cents per hour and a promise that the province's fair wages board would review their existing wage rates. Two months later, 56 women and 5 men from the same department stopped work for five hours to protest the company's posting of piecework rates to be used for test purposes while the guaranteed rate of 31 cents was still in effect.

Two years later, in September 1942, 40 women working in one of the Montmorency spinning rooms and 48 of their male co-workers walked out to protest the promotion of a helper fixer from another department to the position of fixer in their department. The dispute, lasting two days, was resolved when their regular fixer, who had been away for medical reasons, returned to work. Another major work stoppage occurring in 1943 involved a show of solidarity around the observation of an important Catholic feast day. To protest the firing of 37 of the nearly 300 who had not reported to work on Epiphany (January 6), 260 women and 100 men doffers and spinners walked off the job. This work action

258 THROUGH THE MILL

had a direct impact on all 2,000 of the mill's employees and lasted for six days. The dispute ended when both sides agreed to submit the case of the fired employees to the local selective service officer. Another labour dispute, this time over the lack of a collective agreement, was sparked when some 800 workers, including doffers, spinners, weavers, and loom fixers walked off the job in April 1943. Half of the protesters were women. The workers returned to work three days later after the company agreed to meet with the executive of the FNCT to negotiate a settlement.

Women workers in other mills also took militant action during the war years. In Sherbrooke, for example, fifty women and four men walked away from their machines on March 6, 1945 to protest the transfer of employees from one occupation to another, and called for the dismissal of a foreman with whom they were dissatisfied. The protest came to an end two days later with an agreement that the workers' grievances would be settled sometime later.

In their efforts to represent textile workers across the province, Catholic union leaders faced intense competition from the UTWA. Beginning in 1942, left-wing labour activists Kent Rowley and Madeleine Parent, working on behalf of the UTWA, became fully engaged in a drive to organize Dominion Textile's Montreal mills and its subsidiary, Montreal Cottons in Valleyfield. By the early 1940s the UTWA had been transformed from a traditional craft-style union, representing only the most skilled male textile workers such as machinists and loom fixers, to an industrial union representing workers of all skill levels and both sexes. Wartime conditions in the textile industry were especially propitious for a major union membership drive. From 1940 to 1943 the mills ran twenty-four hours a day, seven days a week, and Dominion Textile's profits reached record levels.

A federal order-in-council introduced in February 1944, P.C. 1003, greatly facilitated union recruitment by enshrining the principle of compulsory collective bargaining and providing a framework for reaching first contracts. The same year the provincial Quebec Labour Relations Act mandated a certification procedure for employers and unions to follow for provincial industries that were not classified as war industries. It based union recognition on workers' signing cards, with the law initially requiring that the union had to sign up 60 percent of employees in order to gain official recognition. The threshold was soon changed to a simple majority. A union could request that a secret ballot be held if fewer than 50 percent of the workers had signed cards, but there was strong interest in organizing in that locale. If a majority cast ballots in favour of the union, it could then apply for official bargaining unit status.

Although cotton workers' wages rose appreciably during the early war years, they still lagged behind those of other war industries. In 1941, average annual earnings for men employed in the cotton cloth and yarn industry in Quebec were $845; in munitions, $905; and in the aircraft industry, $1090. The UTWA leadership made the cotton industry's continued low wages, long working hours, and stressful conditions the key focus of their organizing efforts. By 1943, Rowley's and Parent's recruitment efforts resulted in two organizations—Local 102, covering Dominion Textile's four Montreal plants, and Local 100 at Montreal Cottons in Valleyfield. In February 1943, Local 100 received its charter from UTWA's American headquarters, and by mid-month local officials were reporting that 199 members had remitted their semi-monthly dues of 50 cents. Union records contained in the Rowley-Parent Collection held by Library and Archives Canada indicate that the number of paid members fluctuated significantly from pay period to pay period, with the highest number being 233 in April and the lowest, 77 in August. The major obstacles organizers encountered included the fierce hostility of management, high rates of turnover among employees who sought better-paying jobs in other war industries, and competition from the Catholic textile unions. In 1943, the FNCT claimed to represent some 8,600 workers spread over sixteen locals.

The UTWA nonetheless made serious inroads, as illustrated in its success in replacing the FNCT in some of Dominion Textile's most important mills. The UTWA's various appearances before the regional and national war labour boards provided it with a public platform to paint itself as the true defender of cotton workers' interests. In a brief presented to the National War Labour Board (NWLB) in May 1943, UTWA officials contrasted the harsh reality of work in the mills—shifts of ten to thirteen hours, speed-ups, unhealthy working conditions—with the unprecedented prosperity enjoyed by Dominion Textile and Montreal Cottons. Economic justice for French Canadians was a major theme running throughout the entire document, particularly during a time when national unity was a necessary condition to winning the war. "The Turgeon Commission," it maintained, "demonstrated that our people in Quebec have lived and worked under conditions economically inferior to the rest of Canada. As long as these conditions prevail, one cannot talk of true national unity. A real unity is a unity of equality."

The UTWA further linked its campaign for better working conditions and higher wages to the success of the Canadian war effort by arguing that low wages and poor working conditions were leading to high turnover rates of personnel and undermining the morale of those workers who remained in the industry. Why, union leaders asked, were wages in the same industry consistently and significantly lower than those in Ontario? The UTWA also drew attention to the large numbers of young people under the age of sixteen who were working in the mills "during long hours, at work that is often too hard and too strenuous for bodies that are not yet formed."

Ten UTWA representatives, including Parent and another woman, were back before the national labour body in September 1943 to appeal the limited wage increases that had been approved by the regional board. During a two-week period before the hearing, Parent and the Liberal premier, Adélard Godbout, had been exchanging telegrams. Godbout concluded one message by saying "I hope that you will obtain better recognition of your rights in an orderly and peaceful way." In her reply, Parent indicated that Godbout's intervention had been reported to union meetings in Montreal and Valleyfield and that workers there had consequently voted against striking for at least two weeks while awaiting the results of the NWLB hearing. She concluded her message with an expression of appreciation for Godbout and his deputies.

The subsequent labour-board hearings focused on the workers' entitlement to higher wages and paid vacations. In her testimony, Parent emphasized the large number of women in the industry,

Madeleine Parent, circa 1950

Madeleine Parent was one of the most important textile union organizers in Canadian history. She and her partner, Kent Rowley, started to organize cotton workers in Quebec during the Second World War under the aegis of the United Textile Workers of America. They led the 1946 strikes that closed down Dominion Textile's Montreal plants and Montreal Cottons in Valleyfield. (NAC, 93837.)

and their low level of earnings despite longer hours and increased production rates: "You have apprentices, drawing-in tenders, apprentice weavers, apprentice spinners—I must say these are girls; there are a tremendous number of workers on piece rates who are women and girls—at 25 cents an hour." In fact, some new doffers were earning as little as 22.5 cents per hour. By comparison, according to the union's data, the average industrial wage in 1943 was 37 cents per hour for women and 62 cents for men. Once again Parent complained about injustice to French Canadian workers, arguing that "the majority of employees are French Canadian. For national unity they should be paid equal wages.

There is no reason why, with Dominion Textile making something like $12 million in profits, besides reserves, our French-Canadian people should work for 25¢, 30¢ or 35¢ an hour."

In the end, the UTWA's request to the national labour board for two-week vacations with pay, a general increase of 10 cents per hour, and a full cost-of-living bonus was not granted, and so the union resorted to other tactics such as slowdowns and encouraging workers to report in "sick." Since the provincial federation of labour, to which the UTWA belonged, was opposed to strike action during the war, it was a challenge for Rowley and Parent to keep workers motivated to join a union whose scope for effecting significant change was so limited.

Still, recruitment efforts picked up in 1944. By March, Parent reported in correspondence with Anthony Valente, secretary-treasurer of the UTWA in Washington, that in Valleyfield "...some fifty odd workers... [were] actively signing up members in homes, in the shop and all over the town." Throughout the spring, between two and three hundred workers were paying monthly dues despite what Parent called the intimidation tactics of the company. Getting women into the union was one of Madeleine Parent's major objectives. When she and Rowley first started to organize the Merchants mill in Montreal, she met resistance from the skilled men workers when she told them that it was important to recruit women. She persuaded them to name some of the women who had been active in the strike of 1937, visited those individuals in their homes, and convinced them to join the union. She believed the women at the Hochelaga mill in Montreal played an important part in building up the union as well: "Recruiting didn't start with the skilled tradesmen this time and that was already an important evolution. ... With the women came the young people because women know better how to speak to young people and gain their confidence."

Two extant lists of Local 100 members indicate that the number of dues-paying women members of the Valleyfield local, at least initially, was also noteworthy. They represented nearly 30 percent of paid-up members in November 1944, at a time when women represented approximately 40 percent of the workforce.

By the following spring, however, they represented less than 10 percent of the membership list. It is, of course, impossible to ascertain how representative these lists were since the numbers of contributing members fluctuated from month to month. They may reflect the changing employment situation for women by war's end and the increased challenge that change created for union organizers wanting to recruit them. Cotton textile production was already slowing down in 1944, and both Dominion Textile and Montreal Cottons responded by downsizing their workforces. Women, especially married women who had been hired during the war to deal with the manpower shortage, were the first to be dismissed.

The UTWA activists also had to contend with renewed efforts by the clerical and lay supporters of the Catholic trade union movement to rescue it from its moribund condition. The FNCT began organizing meetings in which it attacked the UTWA leaders as communists who were bent on installing a "company union" in Valleyfield that would benefit only American workers and the textile trusts. *Le Progrès de Valleyfield* reported on August 24, 1944 that Catholic union leaders had extended a special invitation to young women to attend local meetings as "the union takes special care of them." Madeleine Parent claimed that Dominion Textile actively assisted the Catholic union movement in its efforts to re-establish its presence by bringing in a paid organizer from the union's ranks. In a letter to Valente written on March 14, 1944, she concluded however, "the Church campaign is not so bitter as we expected; namely, I think, because of the fine feeling among the workers. And consequently the Syndicates [Catholic unions] campaign and their full-time organizer is [sic] a complete flop."

Perhaps it was their frustration at the FNCT's lack of success that led some Catholic youths to ransack the UTWA's Valleyfield offices in June 1944 and to storm city hall where a union meeting was being held. Rowley, Parent, and some of the other union members had to barricade themselves there for several hours before the hostile crowd dispersed. The UTWA leadership blamed Paul-Émile Léger, vicar-general of the diocese of Valleyfield and later archbishop of Montreal and cardinal, for inciting the young people to demonstrate their patriotism by protesting against the presence of the international union. On the other hand, the election of Trefflé Leduc, a former vice-president of the Valleyfield Catholic textile union, as president of Local 100 helped legitimize the international union for the town's workers. He had been a key witness during the Turgeon Commission hearings and his testimony vividly detailed the various tactics managers at Montreal Cottons had used to prevent the unionization of workers. In his speeches to Local 100's membership, he stressed the importance of involving women. The local executive elected in February 1944 did include a woman, Thérèse St.-Onge, who served as secretary, and another woman was elected to the eleven-person executive council.

Despite the various obstacles placed in its path, the union continued to gather strength. The issue of whether Local 100 had the right to speak on behalf of Valleyfield's cotton workers remained nonetheless contentious. Union officials argued that Judge Alfred Savard, who had headed a federal commission of enquiry into industrial disputes, had recognized them in December 1943 as a legitimate negotiating agent. It had been his opinion that, if a vote had been held at that time, a substantial majority of workers would have voted for the UTWA, and he advised the company to negotiate an agreement with this union. His ruling was not binding, however, and the company flatly refused to bargain.

The Godbout government adopted a new labour-relations act in February 1944, six months before it was defeated by Maurice Duplessis and the Union Nationale. Godbout's legislation required unions to demonstrate that 60 percent of workers had voted by secret ballot in their favour before the union could be certified. The right of the UTWA to represent workers in Dominion Textile's general machine shop and the Merchants, Mount Royal, and Hochelaga mills in Montreal was established in this manner, but no confirming vote was held in Valleyfield. Union leaders orchestrated a one-day stoppage by 440 men and 420 women at the Hochelaga mill in September 1945 to support their demands for a general wage increase, certification of the union as the sole bargaining agent for the Montreal plants, and negotiations on working conditions. The workers resumed their duties after Antonio Barrette, the Union

Nationale's provincial minister of labour, persuaded them to pro-
ceed with their grievances in a legal manner. Three months later,
approximately 180 women and 260 men belonging to Local 102 and
drawn from all three Montreal mills walked off the job again, this
time to protest the size of a regional war labour board wage adjustment. The disruption lasted three working days and indirectly
involved nearly two thousand employees.

Dominion Textile's managers did not stand idly by while the
international union sought to organize their workers. As federal
ministry of labour documents reveal, they used a combination of
their own mill security police and informers to keep tabs on
UTWA activists and to report back on union strategies and activities. For example, one informant described a midnight meeting
that the UTWA had convened at a Greek restaurant in Montreal
in early June 1943 attended by some twenty-five people including
Madeleine Parent, Kent Rowley, and Azélus Beaucage, president
of the Merchants local. The report, submitted to Dominion
Textile's chief security officer, indicated that some fourteen individuals had signed their cards, with the strongest show of union
support coming from the card room. The same informer reported
on another meeting involving twenty men and five women, each
representing different departments at the Merchants branch. In
another report, he noted:

> Miss Lemon (or Lehmon) from Mount Royal Branch - Card Room,
> stated the employees of Mount Royal Branch are fed up with waiting
> and have set the date for a general walk-out at Mount Royal Branch
> for Monday, January 17th 1944. Miss Parent was the next speaker.
> She asked the members from all Branches if they would be willing to
> help out in getting new members for Hochelaga Branch by going to
> the employees' homes at night.

Interviews conducted with sixteen women who were employed
at Montreal Cottons during the time that the UTWA was organizing that mill revealed that four regularly attended local meetings and were generally supportive of the union and of Madeleine
Parent. Renée, for example, declared that "Madeleine Parent was
an educated woman. Her speeches made good sense." On the other
hand, two women stayed clear of the union because they had

trouble identifying with the leaders' radical politics and they accepted the Catholic clergy's depiction of Parent as a communist and a woman of loose morals. Célestine confided that she had no involvement whatsoever with the union: "We were rather afraid because it was said that they [the union leaders] were communists." Similarly, "Nicole" reported that she did not participate because "We were afraid of Kent Rowley's union—we were good Catholics." Parent also reported that her opponents, in their attempts to discredit her, accused her of all types of aberrant sexual behaviour. As a result, when she passed by the local school playground, the supervising nun rang the bell and made the children go into the school.

The Valleyfield Strike of 1946 and Beyond

By 1946, union leaders and members were thoroughly frustrated by the complex federal and provincial labour bureaucracies and the continuing refusal of Dominion Textile to enter into negotiations. Although federal wartime price and wage controls would remain in effect until that November, workers across Canada feared rising levels of inflation would soon eradicate any wage increases gained during the war. Job security was another major preoccupation as wartime industries closed and thousands of workers lost their jobs. Management typically aimed to reduce labour costs by decreasing the number of employees and increasing the productivity of those who remained through improved technology and higher production quotas per worker. From coast to coast, labourers in such diverse industries as logging, mining, manufacturing, and transportation walked off the job to gain union recognition, improved working conditions, and higher wages.

In keeping with this trend, UTWA officials declared on May 31, 1946 that approximately six thousand mill workers—three thousand in Montreal and another three thousand in Valleyfield—would walk off the job the following day to protest the continued refusal of the company to negotiate with the union. The principal demands were a union contract, a general wage increase of 25 cents an hour,

Picket Line, Merchants Mill, Montreal
This group of strikers walks the picket line outside Dominion Textile's
plant in Saint-Henri. The date is not recorded but the photo may have
been taken during the 1946 strike. (NAC, 93879.)

and a forty-hour, five-day week. Four days later, Labour Minister
Antonio Barrette announced that the strike in Valleyfield was
illegal because the union had followed neither required provincial
certification procedures nor compulsory conciliation and arbitration measures. He also argued that the strike violated sections of
federal Privy Council Order 9384 (1943) that set out the procedures
unions and companies had to follow relative to wage increases. It
also prohibited strikes as a means to secure such increases. By contrast, he declared that the Montreal strike was legal because the

UTWA had followed all the required legal procedures before calling for the walkout, save appealing a regional labour board decision regarding wages to the national board.

Anxious that labour strife not detract from Quebec's reputation as an attractive location for big business, Premier Maurice Duplessis took an early and active interest in the strike. In what would become standard procedure in subsequent major strikes in Quebec, he issued a widely circulated communiqué in which he characterized the strike as a communist plot with little or no support from the vast majority of workers. In his capacity as attorney general, he also dispatched a contingent of Quebec provincial police to Valleyfield, even though the situation there was entirely calm. He justified this action on the basis of protecting workers who wished to continue to work and were choosing to cross the picket line. This show of state force was also designed to send a strong message to left-wing activists. *Le Devoir* reported on June 6 that Duplessis had proclaimed "Communists and their leaders need to know that there is no place for them in the province of Quebec." The mayor of Valleyfield, Robert Cauchon, expressed his vehement opposition to the premier's decision to send in the provincial police on the grounds that they were not needed and that their presence would perhaps lead to violence. In addition, Cauchon demonstrated his support for the strikers by allowing them to use city hall for their meetings.

Various newspaper accounts described the situation in Valleyfield in the early days of the strike as calm. The day after the Duplessis announcement, fewer than one hundred workers reported for work. They met no resistance from the approximately two hundred picketers and crowd of some 1,500 supporters and onlookers who had gathered outside the mill gates. The same day, over one thousand workers attended a general strike meeting at city hall, and the following day, only fifteen employees showed up for work. In an attempt to encourage more workers to return to their jobs, management obtained an injunction to stop all picketing. On June 12, reporters for *Le Devoir* claimed that only seven girls and two men showed up to work while more than one thousand persons attended another strike meeting at city hall.

A month into the strike, Barrette revealed that he had been pressing Dominion Textile to negotiate a collective agreement with the Montreal local and openly expressed his sympathy for the textile workers. He issued a statement to the local Valleyfield newspaper on July 4 that was quite stunning in light of the premier's highly publicized condemnation of the strike as a communist plot. "I did not pronounce on the legitimacy of the workers' demands," he explained, "but only on the illegality of the procedure followed. Let us admit that textile industry workers do suffer grievances, let us admit that relations between workers and foremen are not always harmonious, let us admit that salary levels need to rise given the increase in the cost of living and the opportunity to raise the standard of living for textile workers. Let us admit all of these things."

The company continued to try to break the strike, and as it dragged on, the strikers' solidarity was sorely tested. Representatives of the Quebec Provincial Federation of Labour (QPFL), the labour body with which the UTWA was affiliated, started talks with the company without Rowley, Parent, or any worker representative from Valleyfield being present. They reached an agreement on June 22 on behalf of the Montreal workers and announced that the strike was over at the four company properties in that city. Four days later, Local 102 signed a contract with Dominion Textile. In a gesture of support that also allowed local leadership in Valleyfield to save face, a meeting there attended by some five thousand Montreal Cottons workers and their supporters passed a resolution approving the signature of the Montreal contract. It was obvious nonetheless that the settlement of the Montreal strike posed a serious threat to the continued work stoppage in Valleyfield.

To add to Local 100's problems, Albert Wallot, publisher of *Le Progrès de Valleyfield* and vociferous opponent of the UTWA and its leaders, wrote an editorial urging the textile workers to form a new independent union. Calling itself the Association des employés du textile de Salaberry-de-Valleyfield (AETSV), the new group announced its formation in Wallot's newspaper on August 7 and stressed its autonomy from outside control of any sort. While claiming that it would defend the interests and rights of textile workers, it promised to co-operate with management through the creation of permanent joint committees. The UTWA leaders and many of the strike supporters promptly dismissed it as a creature of the company since it included many foremen.

For his part, Blair Gordon sought to use the Montreal settlement to undermine Rowley's and Parent's leadership by stressing that the company would not negotiate with the "radical" leaders who had been excluded from the Montreal negotiations. The resumption of production at the Montreal plants also meant that Dominion Textile could carry on without its Valleyfield operation for at least some time into the future. The company also attempted to break the local strike by contacting individual workers directly. It conducted a referendum by mail, asking its employees if they were willing to return to work under the same conditions and for the same wage levels as existed before the strike. Within two days, the company announced that nearly 100 percent of the returned questionnaires indicated that the workers wanted to return to work and retain the fifty-hour week, rather than adopt the forty-hour week the Montreal workers had ratified. Unsurprisingly, the actual number of questionnaires that had been returned remained a secret.

Tensions mounted noticeably following the company's release of the referendum results. In a press release Blair Gordon went on the offensive once again, blaming the continuing impasse on Rowley and Madame Bjornson [sic]. His use of Parent's foreign-sounding married name was intentional, designed to undercut her credibility with the overwhelmingly French-Canadian workforce. Treating the returned questionnaires as a vote in favour of a return to work, Gordon announced that the company was inviting workers to report for duty on August 12. He stressed that it was the mayor's duty to call upon the provincial police or federal authorities if the municipal force were unable or unwilling to ensure the protection of returning workers.

Mayor Cauchon's response was immediate and angry. He lectured Gordon on his own duty to address the unsatisfactory conditions and wages in his mill. Furthermore he scoffed at the company's repeated assertions about the widespread intimidation in which the strikers were engaging. Cauchon concluded with a scathing denunciation of the company's attempts to break the strike, which included calling for the provincial police when they were not needed; announcing that a high-ranking company official had visited Saint-Lambert to see if the mill might be relocated there; and having Trefflé Leduc, a respectable citizen who had worked forty-eight years for the company, arrested. While it is difficult to determine the extent to which local citizens approved of their mayor's stand, there were multiple indications of support for the strikers. The women interviewed about the strike recalled that many local merchants extended credit to the workers, their own families included. Montreal's *Le Devoir* similarly reported on the large amounts of credit that Valleyfield's storekeepers had advanced to the strikers and their families in its August 15 coverage of the strike. One merchant reported that he was owed $3,000 while another claimed that his unpaid accounts were in excess of $6,000.

On the morning of August 12, some 150 workers did obey the company's order to report for duty. When they left the mill that day they were met with a hail of insults, tomatoes, and rotten eggs. In the ensuing pandemonium, members of the provincial police hurled tear gas into the crowd. Despite these unsettling events, the next morning a few hundred employees arrived for work under the protection of the provincial police. This renewed attempt to reopen the mill evoked yet another demonstration of community solidarity for the strike. Wives and mothers of striking workers sent out word by phone and door-to-door through milk-, bread-, and ice-delivery men that everyone should show up at the mill's main entrance at noon.

When some of the returned workers left to go home for lunch, they were greeted by a hail of stones and tomatoes. The wrath of the crowd, numbering several thousand, was seemingly provoked by the actions of the company's private police force. By 3 p.m., a full-fledged riot was underway. The dozen or so provincial police on the scene called in reinforcements from Montreal, but the arrival of that detachment only exacerbated the situation. The crowd went on a rampage, tearing up paving stones, damaging

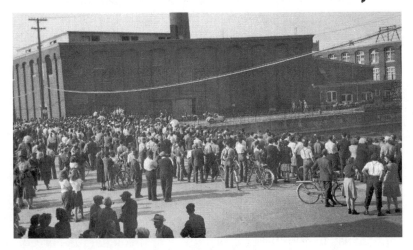

Valleyfield Strike, 1946
These photos, were taken on August 13, 1946, the day of the riot at
Montreal Cottons. The first photo shows strikers and their supporters
gathered outside the Gault mill, while the second is a view of the crowd on
Dufferin Street, near the Empire mill. The bitter labour conflict in
Valleyfield raged for over three months, but finally culminated in formal
recognition of United Textile Workers of America's right to represent
Dominion Textile's workers in Valleyfield.
(Le MUSO — Musée de Société des Deux Rives)

cars, and breaking windows. The police responded with tear gas, and tried to evacuate the employees inside the mill in small groups, but that attempt only reinflamed the crowd. The following day *La Presse* reported that, "On the second attempt [to exit the mill]... a young girl from Champlain Street, hooted at by her pals, delivered a vigorous cuff to a female spectator. The next instant they were in a good dust-up and it took the strength of two security agents to protect the young woman." At this point the remaining workers refused to leave the mill and were evacuated only later under cover of darkness. By 10 p.m., after Rowley, Beaucage, and two women from the strike 'auxiliary' negotiated a truce with police, calm was restored but the strike was unbroken. The terms of the truce included the withdrawal of the company police from Valleyfield and the re-closure of the factory.

The following night, August 13, the strike committee called another meeting at city hall, but it was fairly small, with only three hundred in attendance, and relatively calm. The reporter from *Le Devoir* focused on the behaviour of some of the women following the meeting in his report published two days later. Alleging that they were mainly women the union had brought in from Montreal, he shared with his readers his discomfort with their scandalous conduct. "After the assembly," he wrote, "some women belted out crude songs in the town square against the company containing words that no one would dare repeat in public. But the crowd did not even head in that direction and it was a lost cause."

It is impossible to determine from newspaper accounts what proportion of those who attended strike meetings and walked the picket line were women. According to a report filed by the company with federal labour officials, one-third of the Valleyfield strikers were women. Some surviving union picket lists contained in the Rowley-Parent papers indicate that approximately one in every seven workers assigned to picket duty was a woman. In one instance, however, twenty-seven of thirty-two strikers assigned to picket outside the Old Mill were women. Former employees' opinions about the level of women's involvement were often conflicting. Some claimed that few women took an active role in the strike while others maintained that they participated by the hundreds and in a highly visible manner. Not surprisingly, their memory of women's role was very much coloured by their own behaviour during the strike. Some said that they did not want to get involved, because they were afraid of losing their jobs. Others were also afraid, but of the men from outside the community who had come to support the strike. Three of the sixteen women interviewed who were employees during the strike cited the need to support their families for their decisions to take jobs elsewhere during the strike. Only two reported that they regularly attended the strike meetings and actively supported the strike, while two others admitted to either crossing or attempting to cross the picket line.

Madeleine Parent's own recollection of the strike was that women workers were among its most active supporters and demonstrated their resoluteness throughout the prolonged conflict. The demonstrations of militancy by some women were all the more notable, given the active role that the local clergy played in trying to undermine the strike. Renée recalled seeing a priest leading a group of women in an attempt to cross the picket line, a manoeuvre that Parent maintained happened with some frequency. According to her account, Vicar Léger and local parish priests encouraged workers to show up for early morning mass and, when their numbers were sufficiently large, to head toward the picket line and attempt to cross it. Given that Monsignor Joseph-Alfred Langlois, bishop of Valleyfield, had just received a contribution from the provincial government to expand the diocesan seminary and was lobbying Duplessis for another grant to construct a bridge—that now bears his name—to join the two sides of his diocese, it is not surprising that the city's clergy did not want to be viewed as abetting the UTWA in any way. Reports that Montreal Cottons provided free cotton goods to all diocesan institutions free of charge also circulated.

In the wake of all the dramatic and widely publicized events in Valleyfield, the provincial minister of labour was under increased pressure to intervene and negotiate an end to the strike. After consulting with Gordon, Antonio Barrette proposed that employees return to their jobs, with the company reserving the right not to take back any workers found guilty of criminal offences committed during the strike. Once they were back at work, the minister promised to conduct a secret ballot to determine which labour organization would represent them. Montreal Cottons would negotiate a collective agreement with whichever organization gained a majority of the workers' support. Questions relating to wages and working conditions would be presented before the regional war labour board, and any changes it approved would be made retroactive to the beginning of the strike. On the recommendation of their leaders, the strikers rejected the minister's proposal because it did not guarantee a return to work for all strikers.

On August 23, Premier Duplessis went on the attack once again, repeating his charges that the Valleyfield troubles were the work of communists acting on orders from Moscow who were bent on destroying democracy, freedom, and the Catholic religion. Describing the brave workers of Valleyfield as victims of cunning agents who disguised themselves as labour leaders, he announced that he had issued warrants for the arrest of Rowley and Beaucage on various charges related to the riot and had instructed prosecutors in Montreal to refuse bail for them. During the following week, Antonio Barrette attempted to negotiate a settlement that would have met some of the UTWA demands regarding salary increases equal to those paid in other Canadian mills, voting by secret ballot to establish which union would be recognized by the provincial labour board as representing workers, and voluntary dues check-off. Before accepting the minister's latest offer, the strikers insisted that Barrette give his assurance that all workers would be taken back and that an arbitrator would be available to ensure the successful negotiation of a collective agreement. When the minister agreed that all workers, except those whose cases were before the courts, would be taken back, the strikers voted unanimously to accept the offer.

The company announced the mill would reopen on September 9. However, only eight hundred of the approximately three thousand employees were able to resume work immediately. The rest were sent home until repairs could be made and enough work generated to require all hands. Two days later, Rowley and Beaucage

276 THROUGH THE MILL

were finally released on bail, but on condition that they not leave Montreal, refrain from speaking about the Valleyfield strike, or undertake any action connected to it. Then, on September 18, just one day before the scheduled crucial vote on union representation, a summons was issued in Montreal for the arrest of Madeleine Parent, on the grounds that she had tried to bribe three teenagers not to testify in the upcoming trial against Rowley and Beaucage. Parent claimed she had merely warned the boys, whom she maintained had been paid by the company's police to testify against the union leaders, that giving false testimony was a serious matter and that they should think about it. Subsequently they refused to testify.

After the warrant for her arrest was issued, Parent went into hiding with a local worker's family but managed, through a messenger, to continue to direct negotiations about how the secret vote would be conducted. Meanwhile the union's lawyers arranged for a Montreal judge to read the charges against her and set bail. Leaving Valleyfield in the back of a taxi in the late afternoon, Parent managed to appear before the judge and be back in Valleyfield for an evening strike meeting. Needless to say, her presence there caused a great stir since the news of her arrest had been widely circulated. After this assembly, accompanied by some three hundred chanting women, she marched to the hotel where Lawrence McCall, the official appointed by the provincial government to oversee the vote, was staying and demanded a meeting. During this encounter, Parent got him to agree to have two union scrutineers at each mill polling station, in order to balance the presence of two others—one appointed by the company, and the other, by the recently created rival labour group, the Association des employés du textile de Salaberry-de Valleyfield. In addition, she negotiated the addition of more polling sites and a longer voting period and secured a commitment to ensure that the count would take place while the scrutineers were present and before any ballot boxes were removed.

The results of the vote on September 19 constituted an overwhelming victory for the UTWA and its leaders. With just over 92 percent of eligible workers casting ballots, the UTWA garnered more than twice as many votes as the AETSV (1,477 to 707). While it is impossible to determine precisely if men and women workers voted in equal numbers for the UTWA, an analysis of the poll-by-poll results contained in the Parent-Rowley collection suggests that there was no significant gender gap in the vote. Members voted at eight polling stations, each combining some predominantly men's and some predominantly women's departments. Poll results varied, with 57.5 percent to 75 percent of workers favouring the UTWA. Poll Three, which included several departments with large numbers of women workers, recorded a 66.6 percent approval rating for the UTWA. This result was nearly identical to the 67.6 percent endorsement received for the entire mill.

In the wake of the UTWA's decisive victory, company officials were finally obliged to enter into negotiations, but it took until November 29 before they signed a first contract with the union. The agreement called for an increase of 3 cents an hour retroactive to September 9, with another 2-cent wage hike after February 23, 1947. Both parties justified these low wage hikes, compared to the hefty increases the union had originally demanded, on the basis of the small increases that the regional wage labour board was willing to grant. Day workers were to receive overtime wages for work beyond forty-five hours per week, while night workers were eligible after fifty hours. In addition, the company was to provide for a revocable automatic dues check-off. The most significant achievement of the strike, however, was the recognition of the union, the establishment of legitimate grievance procedures for workers, and seniority lists. For women workers, this change was especially welcome since many had suffered from the arbitrary decisions of foremen that all too often were connected to various forms of sexual harassment.

Both Rowley and Parent continued to pay dearly for their part in the strike in the form of a six-month prison term for him and charges of seditious conspiracy against her that were dropped only in 1954. Yet the strike demonstrated that even the weakest segments of the French-Canadian working class could bring a powerful English-Canadian corporate elite to terms. Just over a year later, in November 1947, it was the FNCT's turn to take on

Dominion Textile to win better wages and working conditions for the 4,100 men and 1,900 women employed in its Magog, Montmorency, Sherbrooke, and Drummondville mills. Well-known Catholic labour leader Jean Marchand led the weeklong stoppage, and the principal negotiator for the union was Gerard Picard, another highly visible labour activist. The resulting collective agreement recognized a reduction in the standard work-week from forty-eight to forty hours, with time-and-a-half paid for any additional work, automatic check-off for union dues, two weeks of paid vacation for workers with more than five years of service, and a general wage increase of 20 cents per hour. Subsequent agreements in 1949 and 1950 contained not only improvements in general wages and vacation pay but also an increase in the number of paid holidays to seven per year.

The UTWA continued to represent cotton workers in Dominion Textile's Hochelaga, Merchants, Mount Royal, and General Machine Shop operations through Local 102, while Local 100 spoke for Montreal Cottons employees in Valleyfield. As a result, it negotiated separate collective agreements for the two organizations. In September 1949, a new agreement signed on behalf of Local 102 set the regular work day at eight-and-a-half hours with a half-hour reserved for a lunch break, and provided for six paid holidays and a later start time on the feast days of Epiphany, Ascension, and All Saints. The company also agreed to provide one week of paid vacation for each employee and an additional week at its discretion. Benefits under the agreement included life insurance, sickness and accident benefits, as well as some defined hospital services.

One year later, the UTWA signed a new agreement covering Local 100 employees in Valleyfield. In addition to negotiating wage increases, the union settled on a five-day workweek and a new workday consisting of three shifts: 7 a.m.–3 p.m., 3 p.m.–11 p.m., and 11 p.m.–7 a.m. No provision was made for a meal break on any of the three shifts since workers were now expected to eat on the job. The change in work hours had a noticeable impact on the pace of daily life in the town, as the mill whistle now sounded for the different shift times. "It is strange," wrote a local columnist, "not to see the streets crowded at noon and at 6 p.m. as in the past."

For women workers, the contracts that organized labour negotiated in the 1940s resulted in many decided improvements in
their wages and working conditions. In particular, they would
have appreciated the establishment of a standard workweek of
eight-hour days, paid holidays and vacations, and new health
benefits. At the same time, their interests were not always protected in negotiated agreements. For example, in the 1950 agreement between the FNCT and Dominion Textile, the guarantee of
100 percent base salary for pieceworkers during time trials to
establish new rates of pay was reduced to 90 percent. Since most
women workers were paid on a piece rate basis, they would have
been directly affected by this reduction.

The Catholic union movement also continued to demonstrate
contradictory tendencies toward women workers. On the one
hand, provincial leaders still issued indictments against women
working outside the home while, at the local level, union organizers courted both single and married women to join their ranks.
At the annual convention of the CTCC in 1946, delegates approved
a resolution that linked "alarming rates" of juvenile delinquency
to the continued presence of married women in Quebec factories
and called on provincial authorities to enact any and all measures
to encourage married women to return to the home. Two years
later, the CTCC convention endorsed yet another resolution that
called on the government to amend its labour legislation to limit
work for girls and women to seven hours per day and thirty-five
hours per week. The preamble to the resolution cited the increase
in female employment and the need to protect the physical health
of young women "who are called to become the wives and mothers of tomorrow" as the underlying rationale for this motion. Not
surprisingly, it was male delegates who moved and seconded such
resolutions. Indeed, evidence of a significant presence of women
at the annual meetings of either the textile federation or its parent body, the CTCC, is rare.

While the UTWA under Rowley's and Parent's leadership did
not enunciate the same negative attitudes toward women's paid
employment, one of their collective agreements reflected prevailing social norms regarding married women. In Local 102's 1949

contract, male employees' hospital benefits could also cover their wives and unmarried children under nineteen. The same provision was made for the children of widowed employees, but married women workers could not claim the same benefits for their husbands or children. The underlying assumption was clearly that women would be covered by a male breadwinners' benefit package. If a married woman worker was so unfortunate as to be divorced, separated, or have an unemployed husband, her dependents were at a distinct disadvantage.

By 1948, under the provisions of collective agreements covering Dominion Textile's Quebec operations, all mill workers were automatically represented by either the UTWA or the FNCT and had to pay dues to their respective locals. Most of the women workers interviewed, however, did not take an active part in their local's activities, regardless of whether they were represented by a Catholic or an international union. Only Marguerite, a Valleyfield weaver, and Jocelyne, a Magog weaver, indicated that they regularly participated in union activities; Jocelyne eventually became a member of her local's executive. When she was asked whether most women workers were interested in the union, Jocelyne firmly replied that they were not. According to her, one of the primary reasons for their lack of involvement was that they felt uncomfortable making requests or asking questions at the meetings. She also shared that she thought the union should have focused more on basic work issues such as speed-ups rather than on wage increases.

Those who did not participate regularly in union meetings gave similar reasons for their non-involvement, including a lack of personal interest, lack of time, and the belief that the union was not woman-friendly. Although Réjeanne went to the occasional meeting, she found them boring and overly long. Similarly, Reine complained that the meetings were too long, and she resented being cooped up in a room especially on a Sunday when the meetings were often held. Moreover, she expressed the view that "the men had more freedom to speak. The women were supposed to listen to what the others said. If a woman stood up to speak, she was laughed at."

Outside the Union: Women's Activism on the Factory Floor

Given the relative weakness of the textile unions in the interwar period, it is not surprising that women employees continued to rely on their own strategies in the 1920s and 1930s to cope with the injustices and other stresses they encountered on the job. They formed friendships, sometimes lasting for decades, that resulted in mutual encouragement and support. When asked about workplace problems, Emma replied, "Between us, it [work] went well. We helped each other. . . . There were some who cried, who got discouraged—I went to help them to put their machines in order." Lucie also recalled the solidarity among women workers in her department: "We worked [hard] but I want to say that there was a joyful spirit among us, we didn't work in a state of revolt. There was a fraternity that prevailed because the employees didn't change every day. . . . We lived as a family." Indeed, these close relationships were often based on family ties. "When I had some free time," explained Géraldine, "I would help others, my sister who was slow, I would leave my department on the third floor to go and help them."

In some instances, this mutual support assumed more assertive expressions. Florida remembered a time in 1923 or 1924 when workers in her weave room walked off the job to demonstrate their support for a foreman that the company wanted to let go. The 1928 annual report of the clerk of the provincial conciliation and arbitration board provides another example of this type of action by women. When Dominion Textile sought to increase production at its Hochelaga mill by replacing daily wage rates by piece rates for fifty-six women workers, twenty-two of them objected and stayed off the job for three days. It was only after the said provincial official intervened and held discussions with management that the problem was resolved. The employees all returned to work within forty-eight hours. Clémentine provided another example of a group of women taking action, this time much less successfully. "There was a girl who worked with me," she reported. "She said, 'We're all going to go home.' It was in the spinning room, and she found that

At "The Sink", Magog Mill

This photo demonstrates one of the ways women workers defied the tight
control they experienced in their workplace. The sign above the towel
holder reads "It is forbidden to loiter in this area during work hours."
Women workers were accused of spending too much time on toilet breaks
and thus slowing the pace of production. Note the uniforms that
identified each worker according to her department. (Courtesy of Pauline
Provençal, who began working in 1948 at the Magog mill.)

they [the bosses] weren't treating her fairly.... A dozen or so [work-
ers] left, but they were obliged to return after they were watched.
The one who began it all was fired. They didn't give her back her
job and she was blacklisted."

It is difficult to imagine that individual women could successfully assert themselves given the lack of job security for employees
and the extensive power of foremen. Yet they sometimes did. Zoé

vividly recounted the exchange with the foreman who fired her as a result of a complaint about her lodged by his girlfriend: "I told him that if he fired me, I'd smash his face in. He was a little guy and he knew it. I told him 'Yes, it's true. If you fire me, it's not just my fingers that you're going to have, but something much more than my fingers. I am the woman to give it to you.'" Refusing to accept her firing, she appealed to the superintendent who soon had her reinstated at her machine. Like Zoé, several women reported that they went directly to the plant superintendent to have their issues resolved.

Flore's story provides another example of the feisty spirit that helped women exert a measure of control over their working conditions:

> When we first entered [the mill], we were a little timid, but we had to defend ourselves. I got angry one time... and decided to leave because the work was going so badly—the threads weren't staying attached and everywhere it [the work] was falling. I told my fixer who was also our second foreman, "If you don't give me other frames, I'm leaving." He didn't want me to leave and told me I didn't have the right to go...I left and he ran after me, swearing. The next day he called me and said, "You're coming back to spin?"— "Are you going to give me other work?" — "Yes," he said, "right."—"I'll go back." I said, "If it makes sense, I'll stay, but if not, I'll return home." He gave me other frames and you would never know I was the same spinner. It went first class and I stayed there until I got married.

Even after union shop representatives were in place, some workers expressed a lack of confidence in the stewards' ability to make meaningful improvements in their daily working conditions. Aline claimed that she never went to the union steward in her department when she had a problem, preferring instead to address the issue directly with her foreman. Huguette explained her lack of involvement in the union by its failure to remedy a major injustice she had experienced. As previous generations of women workers had done, women in the 1940s exhibited their agency when dealing with issues on the factory floor. When Bernadette found the work she was performing too boring, she complained to her foreman and threatened to quit unless she was reassigned. She was sent to see the director of personnel, who arranged to have her assigned to another department.

Another major consideration in explaining women workers' low level of involvement in formal union activities was their resiliency and ability to cope with challenging conditions. Like their counterparts in the first cohort, the vast majority of women interviewed who worked in the mills between 1920 and 1950 expressed high levels of job satisfaction. When asked about workplace problems, a significant proportion initially stated that they personally had not encountered any. It was only when they were asked more specific questions about working conditions that they brought up issues such as the heat, humidity, dust, and noise, and made reference to the exhaustion and medical problems that led some of them to take extended periods of time away from their work. Workers who reflected positively on their work experiences frequently made reference to the fact that they had bosses who treated them well, thereby demonstrating once again the importance of foremen and mill managers to women's work experience. Many also spoke with great satisfaction about the machinery they operated, using the possessive term "my machines," and about the excellent quality of the work they produced. Not only did they express great pride in their ability to do good work but also in their role as wage earners.

CONCLUSION

Léa, Emma, Pierrette, Aline—all French-Canadian women, all devoutly Roman Catholic, all former cotton-mill workers, but each with her own unique life story. Léa, the eldest, was born in 1892, while Aline came into the world more than three decades later in 1927. Two of the women resided in Magog and two in Valleyfield. Their years of entry into the industry spanned several decades, from 1906 to 1942. Two were fourteen when they first walked through the mill gate, while the other two were fifteen. Two married and two remained single. Only one eventually had children—twelve, to be exact. Together they represented over a century of service to the cotton industry. The stories of these four individuals, along with those of the other eighty women interviewed, provide valuable insights into the work and life experiences of women cotton textile workers in Quebec before 1950. This body of oral history, taken together with primary and secondary source materials, allows us to chart significant continuities and changes in how they lived their lives both inside and outside the mill. Their voices help to illuminate the complex interplay of demographic, economic, political, social, and cultural factors that fashioned individual women's opportunities, choices, and ultimately, lives.

From the late nineteenth century to the middle of the twentieth century, the cotton textile industry remained one of the most important Canadian manufacturing enterprises. Conceived by English-Canadian commercial capitalists, with the National Policy as its midwife, it fed on abundant water-generated power sites and surplus rural populations. By the end of World War I the industry had transformed from a number of enterprises scattered across the country to one dominated by a few large corporations located mainly in Quebec. Cotton cloth and yarn production there ranked in the top ten in terms of the value of products and number of employees, and it was second only to the garment industry in terms of the numbers of women it employed. Cotton mills were imposing architectural structures that dominated several Quebec communities for generations, reflecting the economic, political, and social power of the corporations that built and managed them. By the mid-twentieth century, Dominion Textile, along with its affiliate Montreal Cottons and its much smaller rival, Wabasso, had a virtual stranglehold on Canadian cotton goods manufacturing.

Women played a key role in the establishment and development of Canada's cotton textile industry, not as investors and managers, but as consumers and producers. It was Canadian homemakers, with their purchase of a broad range of cotton fabrics, clothing, and household goods, who provided the manufacturers with a viable domestic market. The availability of seemingly limitless supplies of impoverished French-Canadian girls and women hungry for wages was a major component of the cotton textile industry's success in Quebec. Before 1920, women workers accounted for more than half of the province's cotton cloth and yarn production workforce. The fact that they laboured outside their homes seems to have raised few objections, for it was generally assumed that they worked out of financial necessity to support themselves and their working class families. By their attitudes and actions, mill managers, Catholic Church leaders, and heads of families created an environment conducive to women's employment and enabled working class daughters to play a significant role in the early industrialization of Quebec.

Before World War I, few women cotton mill hands in Quebec were wives or mothers, and those who were married were usually widowed, separated, or had husbands unable to provide for their families. The manpower crisis of World War I did lead to a short period of employment opportunities for married women in the industry, but those with employed husbands were let go once peace returned. Using women as an inexpensive reserve labour pool became a well-established corporate practice to offset the endemic volatility in the cotton industry. During the depths of the Depression, management fired or laid off both single and married women in order to trim the size of the workforce and to give priority to men. By this time, the concept of a household income earned by several family members was losing ground to the ideal of a family wage achieved entirely by a male breadwinner.

As World War II progressed, the supply of workers needed to meet rising production levels melted away as men signed up for the armed forces or sought better-paying jobs in essential war industries. The textile manufacturers responded to this situation by hiring women once again to take up the slack. Initially they relied on single young women but, as the labour shortage worsened, they had to engage increasing numbers of married women. After 1944, like most other manufacturers, the cotton companies initially laid off married women, only to bring many of them back when they needed experienced workers to meet burgeoning post-war consumer demands and military orders during the Korean War. Many of the married women who continued to find employment worked afternoon and evening shifts that allowed them to combine their domestic duties with paid labour. In this way, they reflected a new trend among increasing numbers of women who worked after marriage, before they had children, and then returned to the workplace once childcare arrangements had been put into place. By 1951, 17 percent of Quebec's women cotton workers were married. Overall, however, women's presence in the industry had declined, since they now accounted for only one-third of all cotton textile workers in Quebec.

The way in which girls and women found their way into the industry had also changed, mainly as a result of the Great Depression. Throughout the late nineteenth and early twentieth centuries, Quebec's cotton companies relied extensively on family recruitment methods, sending their agents into poor rural areas with promises of employment and company housing for those willing to migrate to the textile centres. That approach was largely abandoned in the 1930s. With high unemployment rates and fierce competition for existing jobs that pitted local residents against any and all outsiders, the companies no longer needed to invest resources in recruitment campaigns. The creation of personnel departments and formal hiring procedures in the 1940s also put more emphasis on individual applications as opposed to the old informal practice of foremen engaging members of families they knew. As a result, the phenomenon of several members of the same household entering the mill together and working alongside each other became rarer. Still, the overwhelming majority of women workers in the industry were French Canadians.

At first glance, it appears that the girls and women who form the basis for this study conformed in large measure to prevailing views of appropriate feminine behaviour. They were dutiful, obedient, hardworking, economical, and devout, and family and faith continued to be significant touchstones in their lives. They nonetheless deviated in important ways from the idealized concepts of womanhood promulgated by Quebec's clerical and social elites. To begin with, some chose not to marry, preferring to live their lives as single working women. Others continued to work after marriage and, increasingly, after having children. When they did not continue their employment, usually due to company policy, many expressed regret that they were forced to leave their paid work. It is in the area of family size, however, that women who began working after 1930 demonstrated the greatest difference from their predecessors and from the model of bountiful motherhood touted by French-Canadian nationalists. The straitened economic circumstances they encountered during the Depression led them and their husbands to practise family limitation, albeit in a manner endorsed by leaders within the Catholic Church. Smaller families made it more feasible for them to combine paid labour with their domestic duties.

The gender dynamics of the workplace, however, changed very little over the decades. With the exception of new opportunities during the two world wars for a very small number of women to perform tasks traditionally designated as men's work, occupational segregation on the basis of gender was the norm. The physical geography of the mill, composed as it was of overwhelmingly women's or men's departments, reinforced the segregation.

Only in a few workrooms did women and men work side by side, and, even when they did, they rarely interacted. Men ate with men, women with women. When men were present where women worked, they were usually foremen, assistant foremen, or machinery repairmen. With the exception of becoming an overseer in an all-woman department, such as one where women sewed cotton cloth into sheets, drapes, and other household goods, there was no vertical occupational mobility available to women.

One noticeable trend with regard to the division of labour on the basis of sex was an erosion of both the quantity and quality of women's work. In the late nineteenth century, women workers had initially benefited from technological innovations such as ring spinning that made it possible for them to take the place of skilled male mule spinners. By the 1930s, however, continued improvements in textile machinery led to a deskilling of the work involved in many jobs and a reduction in the level of manual dexterity needed to perform these tasks. Technological innovations, along with a relentless drive toward rationalization and increased profitability, enabled manufacturers to produce greater quantities of goods with fewer workers. Particularly affected by these changes were machine tenders, such as carders, spinners, and weavers, whose work could be classified as semi-skilled.

At the same time, the unprecedented economic crisis created by the Depression reinforced patriarchal beliefs about men's responsibility to provide for their families and their entitlement to whatever paid labour was available. With minimum-wage laws that covered only women, it became less costly to employ men than women in many instances. Manufacturers took advantage of this confluence of political, economic, and social factors to hire men for jobs that had previously been considered women's work. By 1950, the proportion of women employed in less-skilled work such as cloth inspection, folding, and packaging had increased, while their presence among semi-skilled workers had noticeably declined.

In spite of government efforts to improve working conditions in Quebec's cotton mills between 1885 and 1950, many of the problems that women such as Léa encountered in the early twentieth century remained unresolved. The greatest improvement was the elimination of child labour, but that was due primarily to a reduced need for underage workers in the wake of technological changes and the institution of free, compulsory education in 1943. Over the years, the cotton manufacturers did invest substantially more effort and resources into improving lighting, ventilation, and hygiene, and making their mills more modern. The machinery was less dangerous, and there were fewer serious accidents. When accidents did occur, better in-house medical facilities and insurance programs were available to deal with them. Nonetheless, as reports published in the late 1940s noted, mill hands continued to experience major health issues as a result of physically demanding working conditions. Of specific concern to women workers was the problem of foremen's abuse in its many forms—physical, psychological, and sexual. This mistreatment remained an ongoing problem for women given the reproduction of patriarchal social relations within the mill and the resulting imbalance in male-female power relations.

The young age at which most women entered mill employment was not an inherent obstacle to developing a strong sense of attachment to their workplace and an interest in labour issues. On average, even those who married had nearly a decade of work experience before they wed. They worked in the same mills, and frequently in the same departments, as older members of their nuclear and extended families. Outside factory hours, they socialized with other mill girls who usually worked alongside them. Thus there were many opportunities to develop worker solidarity. Women who did not marry frequently continued as mill workers for decades, and being a mill worker remained a core feature of their identity. They had a vested interest in protecting their livelihoods and seeing that working conditions improved. These were not the temporary workers with low levels of attachment to the labour force so often portrayed in historical accounts of women's labour-force participation.

From the cotton industry's earliest days in Quebec, adolescent girls and women fought collectively and individually to improve the conditions under which they laboured. They were the driving force behind the industry's first strike in Hochelaga in 1880 and *la Grève des jeunes filles* of Valleyfield in 1900. These were major work stoppages that brought production in the mills where they occurred to a halt. Women and girls also played a visible role as rank and file members of the first province-wide industrial union for textile workers, the Fédération des ouvriers du textile du Canada, and in the many work actions it spearheaded between 1906 and 1908. As carders, spinners, and weavers, their work was central to the production process. Consequently, when they walked off the job, large sections of the mill were forced to close, thereby providing them with considerable leverage in addressing workplace issues.

By the 1930s, the Confédération des travailleurs catholiques du Canada (CTCC) was actively involved in the recruitment of mill workers of both sexes through its affiliate, the Fédération nationale catholique du textile (FNCT). Given women workers' strong attachment to Roman Catholicism, as exemplified by the Magog and Valleyfield interviewees, this new union organization should have had great appeal for them. However, many of the obstacles to women's involvement in earlier labour organizations persisted. They included personal challenges (a lack of free time to attend union meetings due to family responsibilities), structural issues (an absence of union representatives in female work departments), social constraints (women feeling intimidated to express their opinions in male-dominated meetings), and ideological obstructions (gender bias against women working for wages endorsed by the union leadership). In spite of these problems, some women did actively participate in union activities, especially those who were also members of Jeunesse ouvrière catholique féminine. Nonetheless, when the CTCC led a month-long strike of cotton workers across the province in 1937, it was guided by traditional gender roles in assigning duties to its members—women were in church basements making sandwiches for men who walked the picket lines.

In the following decade, women played a more active role in the union drives orchestrated by a revitalized, more radical United Textile Workers of America. Leaders Madeleine Parent and her partner, Kent Rowley, made specific and strategic efforts to recruit women into their organization. During the 1946 strikes in Montreal and Valleyfield, women workers who supported the work stoppages walked the picket lines along with men and demonstrated at public meetings in support of the strike. In doing so, they garnered criticism for their "unladylike" behaviour. The Valleyfield Strike, like the Asbestos Strike that would occur three years later, was an early manifestation of the swirling economic, social, and political forces within French-Canadian society that would culminate in massive change in the 1960s. It was a significant testing of existing power relations, as relationships between women and men, union leaders and rank and file members, workers and townspeople, parishioners and priests, and business and government were all brought into question. Hundreds of men and women openly defied their church leadership by continuing to support the UTWA throughout the prolonged strike. This assertion of the right of individual Catholics to make up their own minds on purely secular matters was a touchstone of Quebec's Quiet Revolution.

With the success of the FNCT and the UTWA in signing collective agreements covering Quebec's cotton mills in the 1940s, the need and opportunity for workers to undertake militant action on their own greatly diminished. Union negotiation with management replaced spontaneous walkouts as the preferred method for resolving workplace issues. As well, women workers were increasingly employed in areas that would not directly affect production if they were to strike. Individually, however, they continued to take matters into their own hands when it came to problems that were uniquely connected to their gender, such as foremen's preferential treatment of certain women workers and sexual harassment. They did so in a number of time-honoured ways, such as slowing the pace of production, taking their complaints to the foreman's superiors, and, if necessary, walking off the job.

By 1951, cotton workers were putting in fewer hours each week, receiving supplementary rates for overtime work, having more paid holidays, and enjoying annual paid vacations. Although male cotton workers' average annual wages were less than those earned by all men employed in Quebec manufacturing, female cotton workers earned just over 10 percent more than the average wage for women in the province's manufacturing sector. For women workers, the pervasive piece-rate system offered both advantages and major challenges. For highly motivated, experienced workers, the bonus system made it possible to earn wages that were high in relation to those of women in other industrial sectors and occupations. Certainly many women interviewed who were working in the early 1950s commented positively on their weekly earnings. At the same time, they underscored how much more stressful their work had become as a result of machinery speed-ups, increased production quotas, and demanding foremen. Women of all four cohorts spoke with considerable pride about their ability to perform the tasks assigned to them and to produce work of excellent quality. They regarded the machines they operated as their own, taking care to ensure that they were clean, well-maintained, and in top running condition. Since their wages as piece-workers were directly affected by the state of the equipment they operated, the women's possessive relationship to their machines was completely logical.

In reflecting on their working lives, many of the women interviewed provided surprisingly positive assessments of their experiences. While they acknowledged the harsh conditions under which they laboured, they took great satisfaction in the work they had accomplished and in their identities as paid workers. Only two women regretted their years as mill workers. Positive evaluations of their working careers were common among women in both Valleyfield and Magog, among members of all birth cohorts, and among those who had been employed for varying lengths of time. Agathe, who worked for seventeen years in the sample and folding departments in the Magog print works, stated, "I loved my work. If I were young, I would like to go back." Adelima, a thirty-one-year veteran of the Valleyfield finishing department, explained that she only left her job in 1969 because that department closed. "I would like to have worked until the age of seventy-five," she confided. "I loved my work." Pierrette, who worked for forty-seven years as a spinner in Magog, had similar feelings about leaving the mill. "Believe it or not," she remarked, "it pained me to quit. I loved it." For Françoise, the primary reason for quitting her job as a spinner in Valleyfield in 1953, after just five years of employment, was insufficient work to provide her with full-time employment, so she took a job elsewhere. "I really liked being a spinner a lot. I used to sing while I worked." Perhaps Clémence, a twisting machine operator for more than three decades in Valleyfield, summarized these prevailing sentiments best of all. "If it were to be done all over again, I would love to return to the same place. I really loved my work. It was my life."

The Interviewees:
A Brief Introduction

Cohort 1 (Born 1895-1904)

Agathe

Magog worker, 1909-26. Born in 1897 in Bonsecours, QC. Worked in the sample and folding rooms in the print works, as a spinner in the grey mill, and briefly as a weaver in the Sherbrooke mill. Married in 1926. No children.

Alphonsine

Magog worker, 1923-68. Born in 1904 in Wotton, QC. Worked as a weaver. Married in 1927. One adopted child.

Clémence

Valleyfield worker, 1916-50. Born in 1902 in Valleyfield, QC. Worked on twisting machines. Single.

Desneiges

Magog worker, 1914-64. Born in 1900 in Roxton Falls, QC. Worked as a doffer and spinner. Single.

Florida

Magog worker, 1916-66. Born in 1902 in Wotton, QC. Worked as a weaver and cloth inspector. Single.

Gabrielle

Magog worker, 1916-25. Born in 1903 in Magog, QC. Worked as a battery hand and weaver. Married in 1925. Nine children.

Hortense

Magog worker, 1915-24. Born in 1902 in Magog, QC. Worked as a doffer and a spinner. Married in 1924. Twelve children.

Léa

Magog worker, 1906-09. Born in 1892 in Magog, QC. Worked as a doffer and spinner. Married in 1910. Twelve children.

Marie-Berthe

Magog worker, 1918-21. Born in 1901 in Saint-Côme de Beauce, QC. Worked as a doffer and spinner. Married in 1921. Sixteen children.

Philomène

Valleyfield worker, 1918-52. Born in 1904 in Valleyfield. Worked as a hand twister and drawing-in operative. Single.

Rachel

Magog worker, 1910-17. Born in 1893 in Beauce, QC. Worked as a weaver. Married in 1917. Five children.

Ursule

Valleyfield worker, 1915-62. Born in 1903 in Valleyfield. Worked in the carding room. Married in 1928. No children.

Véronique

Valleyfield worker, 1908-18. Born in 1893 in Valleyfield. Worked as a hand twister and a machine twister. Married in 1919. Eleven children.

Zoé

Magog worker, 1928-65. Born in 1899 in Sainte-Luce-sur-Mer, QC. Worked in the print works as a napping machine and folding machine operator. Married in 1919. Three children.

Cohort 2 (1905-14)

Adèle

Magog worker, 1924-34. Born in 1910 in Saint-Adrien de Ham, QC. Worked as a doffer and spinner. Married in 1934. One child.

Adelima

Valleyfield worker, 1938-69. Born in 1908 in Valleyfield. Worked in the print works as a sewer and packer in the finishing room. Married in 1922. Two children.

Amélie

Magog worker, 1926-36. Born in 1912 in Magog. Worked as a doffer, spinner, and shuttle filler. Married in 1936. Eight children.

Arthurine

Valleyfield worker, 1922-41. Born in 1906 in Valleyfield. Worked as a spinner. Married in 1953. No children.

Aurélie
Magog worker, 1929-70. Born in 1905 in Saint-Joseph de Beauce, QC. Worked as a tacker, sample maker, labeller, and wrapper in the folding room in the print works. Single.

Camilla
Magog worker, 1922-74. Born in 1909 in Saint-Lazare-de-Bellechasse, QC. Worked as a doffer and card room operative in the grey mill and as a folder and inspector in the print works. Married in 1926; separated. No children.

Carmen
Magog worker, 1921-73. Born in 1905 in Saint-Victor de Beauce, QC. Worked as a doffer in the card room and as a cloth inspector. Married in 1926. No children.

Catherine
Magog worker, 1930-46. Born in 1913 in Magog. Worked in the sample room and in the folding room in the print works. Married 1941. Two children.

Clémentine
Magog worker, 1926-54. Born in 1912 in Wotton, QC. Worked as a doffer and spinner in the grey mill and as a sewing machine operator in the print works. Single.

Elmire
Magog worker, 1947-76. Born in 1911 in Magog. Operated a napping machine and then made samples in the print works. Single.

Emma
Valleyfield worker, 1924-66. Born in 1909 in Valleyfield. Worked as a doffer, spinner, machine shop employee, and finally as a roller buffer. Single.

Évangeline
Magog worker, 1947-77. Born in 1914 in Magog. Operated a napping machine, bundled towels, folded sheets, and worked as a first aid officer in the print works. Single.

Flore
Magog worker, 1928-37. Born in 1912 in Saint-Côme de Beauce, QC. Worked as a spooler and spinner. Married in 1927. No children.

Francine
Magog worker, 1928-38. Born in 1914 in Saint-Côme de Beauce, QC. Worked as a doffer and spinner. Married in 1938. Two children.

Géraldine
Magog worker, 1927-78. Born in 1913 in Saint-Élie d'Orford, QC. Worked as a doffer and spinner in the grey mill, a sewing machine operator in the print works, as a sample packer in the warehouse, and as a cloth inspector and colour verifier in the print works. Single.

Hermance
Magog worker, 1928-70. Born in 1905 in Saint-Côme de Beauce, QC. Worked as a folder, cloth inspector, and spot checker. Single.

Hermione
Valleyfield worker, 1925-38. Born in 1908 in Valleyfield. Worked as a cloth inspector. Married in 1937. Four children.

Laurentia
Magog worker, 1937-42. Born in 1913 in East Broughton, QC. Worked as a cloth inspector and sewing machine operator in the print works. Married in 1943. Three children.

Léda
Magog worker, 1939-73. Born in 1910 in Saint-Jacques de Leeds, QC. Worked in the folding room and then as a payroll clerk. Single.

Louisette
Valleyfield worker, 1932-38. Born in 1914 in Valleyfield. Worked as a battery hand, weaver, and spot checker. Married in 1938. Eight children.

Luzina
Magog worker, 1923-33. Born in 1911 in Chesterville, QC. Worked as a spinner. Married in 1933. One child.

Marie
Valleyfield worker, 1918-29. Born in 1905 in Valleyfield. Worked as a spooler. Married in 1929. Five children.

Marielle
Magog worker, 1935-45. Born in 1912 in Magog. Worked as a clerk. Married in 1941. Two children.

Mathilde
Magog worker, 1926-34. Born in 1912 in Magog. Worked as a doffer and spinner. Married in 1933. Two children.

Régina
Valleyfield worker, 1928-57. Born in 1913 in Valleyfield. Worked as a doffer and spinner. Married in 1939. Three children.

Renée
Valleyfield worker, 1923-46. Born in 1910 in Valleyfield. Worked as a spooler and cone winder. Married in 1951. No children.

Roberta
Magog worker, 1928-37. Born in 1914 in Notre-Dame-des-Bois, QC. Worked as a frame cleaner, doffer, and spinner. Married in 1936. Two children.

Stéphanie
Magog worker, 1921-29. Born in 1908 in Saint-Côme de Beauce, QC. Worked as a doffer and spinner. Married in 1928. Nine children.

Suzanne
Valleyfield worker, 1926-78. Born in 1913 in Valleyfield. Worked as a hand twister and drawing-in hand. Single.

Théodora
Valleyfield worker, 1923-33. Born in 1909 in Valleyfield. Worked as a doffer, shuttle filler, and weaver. Married in 1933. Three children.

Cohort 3 (1915-24)

Andrée
Magog worker, 1929-77. Born in 1916 in St-Louis de Ha! Ha!, QC. Worked as a doffer and spinner. Married in 1943. Two adopted children.

Angélique
Valleyfield worker, 1937-53. Born in 1922 in Valleyfield. Worked as a bobbin spooler. Married in 1950. Three children.

Béatrice
Magog worker, 1942- still employed in 1980. Born in 1923 in Saint-Gabriel de Stratford, QC. Worked as a bobbin filler, battery hand, weaver, smash piecer, and cloth inspector. Single.

Claire
Magog worker, 1941- still employed in 1980. Born in 1921 in Magog. Worked in the print works as an inspector of paint rollers, then engraver, and in the finishing room measuring and hand-pressing cotton pieces. Single.

Colette
Magog worker, 1939-53. Born in 1922 in Magog. Worked as a cloth inspector and clerk. Married in 1953. One child of her own and four stepchildren.

Ernestine
Valleyfield worker, 1940-68. Born in 1919 in Valleyfield. Worked as a harness maker and at various tasks in the drawing-in room. Single.

Eugénie
Magog worker, 1938-56. Born in 1922 in Windsor Mills, QC. Worked in the cafeteria as a cook and cashier, then as a sewing machine operator, and finally as one of four female overseers of the Colonial department in the print works. Married in 1951. Three children.

Éveline
Magog worker, 1939-46. Born in 1921 in Waterloo, QC. Worked as a wrapper in the folding room. Married in 1946. Three children.

Florentine
Valleyfield worker, 1940-44. Born in 1915 in Valleyfield. Worked as a spooler and then in the finishing room. Married in 1944. Ten children.

Ghislaine
Valleyfield worker, 1940-47; 1952-58; 1962-still working in 1980. Born in 1923 in Ormstown, QC. Worked as a doffer, cleaner, and operator of roving frames in the card room. Married. Four children.

Guylaine
Magog worker, 1930-39; 1941-42. Born in 1917 in Saint-Côme de Beauce, QC. Worked as a doffer, cleaner, and spinner. Married in 1939. Four children.

Henriette
Magog worker, 1938-42; 1958-still working in 1980. Born in 1922 in the United States. Worked in the print works as a roller painter and pantographer and in the folding and sample rooms. Married in 1942. Two children.

Isabelle
Valleyfield worker, 1940-44. Born in 1923 in Valleyfield. Worked as a warp spooler. First marriage in 1943. Second marriage in 1952. Five children.

Janine
Magog worker, 1947-still working in 1980. Born in 1915 in Eastman, QC. Worked as a spinning frame cleaner and spinner. Married in 1932. Four children.

Jeannette
Valleyfield worker, 1940-47. Born in 1923 in Laprairie, QC. Worked as a doffer and spooler. Married in 1946. Four children.

Josette
Magog worker, 1939-still working in 1980. Born in 1922 in Magog. Worked in the slash room, as a battery hand, and then as a weaver. Single.

Lucie
Valleyfield worker, 1936-41. Born in 1922 in Valleyfield. Worked as a doffer and spinner. Married in 1943. Eleven children.

Marcelle
Magog worker, 1937-47, 1952–still working in 1980. Born in 1922 in Magog. Worked as a cleaner and spinner. Single.

Marthe
Valleyfield worker, 1941-44. Born in 1923 in Valleyfield. Worked as an office clerk and twisting machine operator. Married in 1942. One child.

Nicole
Valleyfield worker, 1935-44, 1946-49. Born in 1919 in Valleyfield. Worked as a shuttle filler, doffer, and spooler. Married in 1948. Four children.

Pierrette
Magog worker, 1932-79. Born in 1918 in Lac-Mégantic, QC. Worked as a shuttle filler and weaver. Single.

Rita
Magog worker, 1940-still working in 1980. Born in 1923 in Magog. Worked as a cleaner and spinner. Single.

Rosa
Magog worker, 1929-79. Born in 1915 in Magog. Worked as a bobbin stripper, cleaner, doffer, and spinner. Single.

Solange
Magog worker, 1942-still working in 1980. Born in 1918 in Magog. Worked as a battery hand, weaver, and cloth inspector. Single.

Sylvie
Magog worker, 1941-76. Born in 1921 in Magog. Worked as a cleaner and spinner. Single.

Zépherina
Magog worker, 1941-80. Born in 1915 in Saint-Méthode, QC. Worked in the print works as a folder, cutter, cloth inspector, wrapper, labeller, and time clerk. Single.

Cohort 4 (1925-34)

Agnès
Magog worker, 1943-still working in 1980. Born in 1926 in Magog. Worked in the print works as a folding machine operator, cloth inspector, sewing machine operator, and in the engraving room as a roller painter and pantographer. Single.

Aline
Valleyfield worker, 1942-44, 1948-53, 1954-55. Born in 1927 in Valleyfield. Worked as a cleaner and spinner. Married in 1953. No children.

Bernadette
Valleyfield worker, 1945-47. Born in 1924 in Buckingham, QC. Worked as a bobbin spooler. Married in 1947. Three children.

Célestine
Valleyfield worker, 1943-48. Born in 1927 in Valleyfield. Worked as a shuttle filler and spinner. Married in 1948. Five children.

Estelle
Magog worker, 1942-44, 1945-47, 1952-still working in 1980. Born in 1925 in Thetford Mines, QC. Worked as a cleaner, doffer and spinner. Married in 1944. One adopted child.

Françoise
Valleyfield worker, 1948-53. Born in 1932 in Valleyfield. Worked as a frame cleaner and spinner. Married in 1953. Nine children.

Hélène
Magog worker, 1948-still working in 1980. Born in 1932 in Magog. Worked as a spooler, bobbin stripper, frame cleaner, and spinner. Married in 1952; divorced. No children.

Huguette
Valleyfield worker, 1942-53. Born in 1925 in Magog. Worked as a frame cleaner, spinner, and cloth inspector. Married in 1952. Four children.

Jocelyne
Magog worker, 1949-still working in 1980. Born in 1933 in Disraeli, QC. Worked as a battery hand and weaver. Single.

Laure
Valleyfield worker, 1948-61. Born in 1933 in Valleyfield. Worked as a frame cleaner and spinner. Married in 1954. One child.

Marguerite
Valleyfield worker, 1942-66. Born in 1926 in Valleyfield. Worked as a shuttle filler and weaver. Married in 1947. Two children.

Reine
Magog worker, 1942-still working in 1980. Born in 1926 in Lac-Mégantic, QC. Worked as a frame cleaner, doffer, and spinner. Single.

Réjeanne
Magog worker, 1947-still working in 1980. Born in 1927 in Kateville, QC. Worked in the print works as a sewing machine operator, cylinder painter, and pantographer. Single.

Rose
Valleyfield worker, 1948-55. Born in 1932 in Valleyfield. Worked as a frame cleaner, doffer, and spinner. Married 1956. Three children.

Notes Regarding Related Sources

The Quebec Cotton Industry

The reports and supporting documentation of three royal commissions are particularly helpful in tracing the evolution of the Quebec cotton industry. The *Report of the Royal Commission on the Relations of Labor and Capital* (1889) provides valuable insights into the mill workforce, working conditions, and the attitudes of mill managers in the late nineteenth century. Extensive excerpts of the compelling testimony can be found in Greg Kealey, ed., *Canada Investigates Industrialism: The Royal Commission on the Relations of Labor and Capital, 1889* (Toronto: University of Toronto Press, 1973). The 1908 *Report of the Royal Commission to Inquire into Industrial Disputes in the Cotton Factories of the Province of Quebec*, authored by William Lyon Mackenzie King, and the documentation his commission generated, outline the size and nature of the cotton industry's workforce, working conditions, labour disputes, and union organization in the first decade of the twentieth century. The 1938 report of the Royal Commission on the Textile Industry —popularly known as the Turgeon Commission—contains a critical assessment of the evolution of the Quebec cotton industry, management practices, and labour issues during the Great Depression. In addition, *The Report of the Royal Commission on Price Spreads* (1935), also referred to as the Stevens Commission, shines a spotlight on the cotton companies and the consequences of tariff protection for Canadian consumers. Thousands of primary documents prepared for these commissions are located in the manuscript collections of Library and Archives Canada (LAC), and hundreds were consulted for this study.

Other major LAC manuscript resources include the Dominion Textile collection containing over four hundred files, and the Madeleine Parent-

Kent Rowley collection. Access to many files in the Dominion Textile papers, however, remains restricted, with some materials closed until 2045. The Parent-Rowley collection contains many valuable records relating to the unionization drive in the cotton industry undertaken by the United Textile Workers of America during the 1940s and to the Valleyfield strike of 1946. Federal Department of Labour files, also located at LAC, contain original annual reports and documents regarding labour disputes, such as strike and lockout records. Summaries of much of this material can be found in the department's yearly publication, *The Labour Gazette,* beginning in 1903. In addition, the decennial *Census of Canada* contains many data related to the industry and to the demographic composition of its workforce, as well as to the growth of the communities in which the mills operated.

Annual provincial factory inspectors' reports remain a vital source for information on issues such as child labour, working conditions, and government legislation relating to manufacturing establishments. They can be found in the *Sessional Papers* published each year by the Quebec Legislative Assembly, as it was then called, starting in 1895. Letters and other documents generated by Quebec factory inspectors are held in the provincial ministry of labour files at the *Bibliothèque et Archives nationales du Québec.* In Valleyfield, the archives of the Diocese of Valleyfield contain materials relating to Montreal Cottons, including correspondence between Louis Simpson, an early mill manager, and Bishop Joseph-Médard Émard that shines light on the intricate relations between the company and the church.

Hundreds of articles related to the industry can be found in the *Canadian Journal of Fabrics* and its successor, the *Canadian Textile Journal.* Given the importance of the industry, major daily newspapers including Montreal's *La Presse* and *The Gazette,* and weekly community newspapers such as *Le Progrès de Valleyfield* and *La Chronique de Magog* are rich sources of information. *The Annual Financial Review— Canadian* contains the yearly financial statements of all Canadian cotton-manufacturing firms. Dominion Textile's internal publication, *Les Moulins des Cantons de l'Est* (1947-54) provides information about company programs for employees and often includes profiles of long-serving retirees.

A comprehensive treatment of the development of the cotton industry in Canada is provided in A.B. McCullough, *The Primary Textile Industry in Canada: History and Heritage* (Ottawa: Ministry of Supply and Services Canada, 1992). Over half of the book is devoted to a well-documented study of the architectural features of textile mills containing many excellent photos. Barbara Austin's dissertation, "Life Cycles and Strategy of a Canadian Company–Dominion Textile: 1873-1983," (Ph.D. thesis: Concordia University, Montreal, 1985), provides a detailed analysis of the evolution of Canada's largest cotton company, its corporate strategies, and managerial structures. Melvin T. Copeland, *The Cotton Manufacturing Industry of the United States* (New York: A.M. Kelley, 1966) contains a wealth of information relating to manufacturing processes and to structural and technological changes in the industry that are very relevant to the Canadian industry.

The *Dictionary of Canadian Biography* [online version: http://www.biographi.ca] contains well-researched articles relating to some of the important historical actors connected to the industry, including Sir Hugh Allan, Louis-Joseph Forget, Alexander Tilloch Galt, Andrew Frederick Gault, Victor Hudon, Sir Charles Gordon, Wilfrid Paquette, and David Yuile.

At the local level, Réjean Charbonneau et al. offer a brief history of the Hochelaga mill and its workers in the late nineteenth century in *De fil en aiguille. Chronique ouvrière d'une filature de coton à Hochelaga en Montréal* (Montréal: Société Saint-Jean-Baptiste et l'Atelier d'histoire Hochelaga-Maisonneuve, 1985). For Magog, see Alexandre Paradis, *Commercial and Industrial Story of Magog* (n.p., 1951) and for Valleyfield, J.D. St-Aubin, *Salaberry-de-Valleyfield, 1842 à 1872: Histoire religieuse, municipale, scolaire, commerciale et industrielle* (Valleyfield: G. Brault, printer, 1973).

A number of studies have focused on the sexual division of labour within the industry and its consequences. William Lazonik's pioneering piece, "Industrial Relations and Technical Change: The Case of the Self-Acting Mule," *Cambridge Journal of Economics*, 3,3 (1979) is a good place to start, given the importance of British technology and processes for the early Canadian industry. Gail Cuthbert Brandt has explored women's changing roles and employment opportunities in the industry in "'Weaving it Together': Life Cycle and the Industrial Experience of Female Cotton Workers in Quebec, 1910-1950," in *Labour/Le travailleur*, 7 (Spring, 1981) and "The Transformation of Women's Work in the Quebec Cotton Industry, 1920-1950," in Bryan Palmer, ed., *The Character of Class Struggle: Essays in Canadian Working Class History, 1850-1985* (Toronto: McClelland and Stewart, 1986). Two unpublished theses also deal specifically with the gender division of work in the cotton industry, namely Louise Fradet's, "L'économie familiale et le travail des femmes dans une ville industrielle: l'exemple de la Dominion Textile de Montmorency, 1940-1960" (Ph.D. thesis, Université Laval, 2004) and

Ellen Scheinberg's, "Women, War and Work: Female Textile Workers in Cornwall, Ontario, 1936-1946" (M.A. thesis, Queen's University, 1990).

For an understanding of the most important developments in labour organization within the cotton textile industry prior to 1930, Jacques Rouillard's *Les Travailleurs du coton au Québec, 1900-1915* (Montréal: Les Presses de l'Université du Québec, 1974) and his later work, *Les Syndicats nationaux au Québec de 1900 à 1930* (Québec: Les Presses de l'Université Laval, 1979) remain important studies. More recently, his *Syndicalisme québécois: Deux siècles d'histoire* (Montréal: Boréal, 2004) provides a more general account of various labour organizations' forays into the textile industry. Fernand Harvey's "Les Chevaliers du travail, les États-Unis et la société québécoise, 1882-1902," in Fernand Harvey, ed., *Le Mouvement ouvrier au Québec* (Montréal: Boréal Express, 1980) provides a good overview of the development of the Knights of Labor movement and of the opposition it encountered in Quebec. *Le Fileur (1906-1908)*, the official publication of the Fédération des ouvriers du textile du Canada, sheds light on the involvement of women in the first large-scale union movement in the Quebec cotton industry. The issue of women's early militancy has been explored in much more detail by Jacques Ferland, in his article "'In Search of the Unbound Prometheia': A Comparative Study of Women's Activism in Two Quebec Industries, 1869-1908," *Labour/Le Travail*, 24 (Fall 1989).

Alfred Charpentier, the first president of the Confédération des travailleurs catholiques du Canada, has covered that organization and its involvement in the industry in the interwar period in "Le mouvement ouvrier: la Confédération des travailleurs catholiques du Canada," *Relations industrielles/Industrial Relations*, 4, 1 (1948) and in "La conscience syndicaliste lors des grèves du textile de 1937 et de l'amiante 1949," *Labour/Le Travailleur*, 3 (1978). Another former union organizer, Jean-Paul Hétu, provides details about labour developments among textile workers in Magog from 1900 to 1975 in his brief account, *Lutte des travailleurs du textile au Québec* (Montréal: Centrale des syndicats démocratiques, 1979). A useful unpublished study of the 1937 strike is Ralph Ellis's "Textile Workers and Textile Strikes in Cornwall, Sherbrooke and St. Grégoire de Montmorency, 1936-1939" (MA thesis, University of Ottawa, 1985).

Published works relating to Kent Rowley and Madeleine Parent and their role in leading the United Textile Workers of America in the 1940s and early 1950s include Rick Salutin, *The Organizer: A Canadian Union Life* (Toronto: Lorimer, 1980) and Andrée Lévesque, ed., *Madeleine*

Parent: Activist (Toronto: Sumach Press, 2005). An interview with Parent focusing on the 1946 Valleyfield strike can be found in Gloria Montero, *We Stood Together: First Hand Accounts of Dramatic Events in Canada's Labour Past* (Toronto: James Lorimer, 1979). Denyse Baillargeon's, "Histoire des Ouvriers Unis des Textiles d'Amérique, 1942-1952" (Thèse de maîtrise, Université de Montréal, 1981) and Michel Ouimet's "L'Industrie textile et les grèves de 1946 et 1952 à la Montreal Cottons Limited, Valleyfield, Quebec" (Thèse de maîtrise, Université du Québec à Montréal, 1979) provide more in-depth analyses of the UTWA, its leaders, and the strikes it led.

Demographic, Economic, and Social Changes in an Industrializing Province

Helpful overviews of the demographic, economic, and social development of Quebec during this period include Paul-André Linteau, René Durocher and Jean-Claude Robert, *Histoire du Québec contemporain. Vol. 1. De la Confédération à la crise, 1867-1929* (Montréal: Les Éditions du Boréal, 1989), and Peter Gossage and J. I. Little, *An Illustrated History of Quebec: Tradition and Modernity* (Don Mills, ON: Oxford University Press, 2011). Gérard Bouchard's *Quelques arpents d'Amérique: Population, économie, famille au Saguenay, 1838-1971* (Montréal: Boréal Express, 1996) provides an excellent regional study of a rural area undergoing the transformative processes of industrialization, while pioneer sociologist Léon Gérin's, *Le type économique et sociale des Canadiens* (Montréal: Éditions de l'Académie canadienne-française, 1938) offers first-hand observations about rural families and the relationship between marginal farming and industrial employment.

Additional discussion of migration patterns and mill employment among Franco-American workers can be found in Tamara Hareven, *Family Time and Industrial Time* (Lanham, Maryland: University of America Press, 1993), Yves Roby, *The Franco-Americans of New England: Dreams and Realities* (Montréal: McGill-Queen's and Septentrion, 2004), and Jacques Rouillard, *Ah Les États! Les travailleurs canadiens-français dans l'industrie textile de la Nouvelle-Angleterre d'après le témoignage des derniers migrants* (Montréal: Boréal, 1985). All three rely extensively on oral interviews.

A recent vivid and engaging account of Franco-American society is presented by David Vermette in his *A Distinct Alien Race: The Untold Story of Franco-Americans, Immigration, Industrialization and Religious Strife* (Montréal: Baraka Books, 2018).

Family composition and the intersecting dynamics of ethnicity and gender are explored in Bettina Bradbury, *Working Families: Age, Gender, and Daily Survival in Industrializing Montreal* (Toronto: McClelland and Stewart, 1993) and Peter Gossage, *Families in Transition: Industry and Population in Nineteenth-Century Saint-Hyacinthe* (Montreal & Kingston: McGill-Queen's University Press, 1999). The impact of the early stages of industrialization on women's lives are also explored in Suzanne Cross "The Changing Role of Women in 19th Century Montreal," in Alison Prentice and Susan Mann Trofimenkoff, eds. *The Neglected Majority: Essays in Canadian Women's History, Vol. 1* (Toronto: McClelland and Stewart, 1977). For an early study of attitudes toward female industrial workers and their behaviour, see Susan Trofimenkoff, "One Hundred and Two Muffled Voices: Canada's Industrial Women in the 1880s," in Veronica Strong-Boag and Anita Clair Fellman, eds. *Rethinking Canada, 1st ed.* (Toronto: Oxford University Press, 1986). Michelle Lapointe provides an examination of an early unionizing effort among female workers in manufacturing in "Le syndicat catholique des allumetières de Hull, 1919-1924," *Revue d'histoire de l'Amérique française*, 38, 4 (mars 1979) while Francine Barry outlines major trends in women's work in Quebec, including unionization, for a later period in her book, *Le travail de la femme au Québec: l'évolution de 1940-1970* (Québec: Les Presses de l'Université du Québec, 1977). On changing birth patterns, see Danielle Gauvreau and Peter Gossage, "'Empêcher la famille: Fécondité et contraception au Québec, 1920-1960," *Canadian Historical Review*, 78, 3 (Sept. 1997).

Assessing the attitudes and actions of the Roman Catholic Church in relation to the industrialization of Quebec has been the focus of many detailed studies, starting with William Ryan's *The Clergy and Economic Growth in Quebec, 1896-1914* (Québec: Les Presses de l'Université Laval, 1966). At the local level, Lucia Feretti's *Entre voisins. La société paroissiale en milieu urbain: Saint-Pierre-Apôtre de Montréal, 1848-1930* (Montréal: Boréal Express, 1992) explores the role of the clergy and of local parish organizations in one industrializing Montreal parish. For the interwar period, Michael Gauvreau's comprehensive study, *The Catholic Origins of Quebec's Quiet Revolution, 1931-1970* (Montreal & Kingston: McGill-Queen's University Press, 2005) stresses the role of Catholic laity in the making of modern, liberal Quebec through their involvement in various social action programs, including the dissemination of birth control information. Louise Bienvenue, *Quand la jeunesse entre en scène: L'Action catholique avant la Révolution tranquille* (Montréal: Boréal, 2003) provides an overview of Catholic social action and its role in mobilizing Quebec youth. For young French-Canadian working class women, the organization specifically designed for them was Jeunesse ouvrière catholique féminine. The ways in which they interacted with this organization is examined by Lucie Piché in her *Femmes et changement social au Québec. L'apport de la jeunesse ouvrière catholique féminine, 1931-1966* (Québec: Les Presses de l'Université Laval, 2003).

Women's Role in Quebec Society

Syntheses of Quebec and Canadian women's history that explore many of the themes raised in this study include the Clio Collective's *Quebec Women: A History* (Toronto: The Women's Press, 1987), Denyse Baillargeon, *A Brief History of Women in Quebec* (Waterloo, ON: Wilfrid Laurier University Press, 2014), and Gail Cuthbert Brandt, Naomi Black, Paula Bourne and Magda Fahrni, *Canadian Women: A History, 3rd ed.* (Toronto: Nelson, 2011). More detailed analyses of the cultural and class underpinnings of prevailing views about women and their roles in Quebec society appear in Denise Lemieux and Lucie Mercier, *Les femmes au tournant du siècle: âges de la vie, maternité et quotidien* (Québec: Institut québécois de la recherche sur la culture, 1989) and Andrée Lévesque, *Making and Breaking the Rules: Women in Quebec, 1919-1939* (Toronto: McClelland & Stewart, 1994). Lévesque's recent book, *Freethinker: the Life and Works of Éva Circé-Côté* provides a unique perspective on major issues of religion, patriotism, feminism, and women's work in the first half of the twentieth century penned by an influential woman of letters.

Various articles featured in Marie Lavigne and Yolande Pinard, eds. *Travailleuses et féministes. Les femmes dans la société québécoise* (Montréal: Boréal Express, 1983) cover issues related to working class women and their employment. *Maîtresses de maison, maîtresses d'école: Femmes, famille et éducation dans l'histoire du Québec* (Montréal: Boréal Express, 1983), edited by Nadia Fahmy-Eid and Micheline Dumont, contains a number of early studies relating to female education and class in the nineteenth and twentieth centuries. Denyse Baillargeon's *Making Do: Women, Family and Home in Montreal during the Great Depression* (Waterloo, ON: Wilfrid Laurier University Press, 1999) demonstrates the effective use of oral history to illuminate the connections between the worlds of paid employment and household economies. For its part, *La Bonne Parole,* published by the Fédération nationale Saint-

Jean-Baptiste, reveals the preoccupations of reform-minded middle class women and their relations to working class women between 1913 and 1938.

Gender Dynamics in the Workplace

While Joy Parr's book *The Gender of Breadwinners: Women, Men and Change in Two Industrial Towns, 1880-1950* (Toronto: University of Toronto Press, 1990) focuses on the knit goods and furniture industries in two small Ontario communities, her analysis of the social construction of gender and of gender dynamics in workplaces and communities is particularly relevant to this study. Joan Sangster's *Earning Respect: The Lives of Working Women in Small-Town Ontario, 1920-1960* (Toronto: University of Toronto Press, 1995) provides a wealth of information relating to female industrial wage earners in Peterborough, Ontario, including woollen textile workers. Other studies of women industrial workers in Canada covering the century from 1850 to 1950 that are very useful for comparative purposes include Ruth Frager, *Sweatshop Strife: Class, Ethnicity and Gender in the Jewish Labour Movement of Toronto, 1900-39* (Toronto: University of Toronto Press, 1992); Mercedes Steedman, *Angels of the Workplace: Women and the Construction of Gender Relations in the Canadian Clothing Industry, 1890-1940* (Toronto: Oxford University Press, 1997); Margaret E. McCallum, "Separate Spheres: The Organization of Work in a Confectionery Factory: Ganong Bros., Saint Stephen, New Brunswick," *Labour/Le Travail* 24 (Fall 1989); and Julie Guard, "Fair Play or Fair Pay? Gender Relations, Class Consciousness and Union Solidarity in the Canadian UE, 1949-1955" *Labour/Le travail, 37* (Spring, 1996).

INDEX

St.-Onge, Thérèse (UTWA official), 264

strikes: (1880), 100; (1882), 101; (1891), 101–2; (1893), 102; (1898), 102; (1900), 103–7; (1906–07), 108–12; (1908), 114–17; (1911), 120; (1913), 120; (1918), 120; (1919), 242; (1923), 242–3; (1935), 243; (1936), 243; (1937), 250, *251*, 256, (1946), 266–76, 292

Suzanne (Valleyfield interviewee), 134

Taillefer, Edeia (mill worker), 80

tariff regulations, 36, 39, 137–8, 140–1, 144, 166

Taschereau, Cardinal Elzéar-Alexandre, 42, 67

Taschereau, Louis-Alexandre (premier of Quebec), 67, 227

Taylor, Frederick W. (American engineer), 131

Théodora (Valleyfield interviewee), 180, 234

Thériault, Mary (mill worker), 80

Trades and Labour Congress, 92, 202

Trois-Rivières, city of, 41, 129, 132, 169, 175, 246, 247

Turgeon, Judge W.F.A. (royal commission chair), 38, 129, 144, 200, 205, 216

L'Union amicale (labour union), 118

union movement: cotton workers and, 241–2; development of, 102–3, 109; federal legislation on, 264; in interwar period, 241–56; paternalism and misogyny of, 113–14, 245–7, 257; women's participation in, 110, 114, 246–50, 253–6, 262–6, 280, 291–2; *See also* entries for individual unions

United Textile Workers of America (UTWA): appearances before war labour boards, 259–62; attitudes toward women's paid employment, 279–80; collective agreements 212, 278, 279, 280, 292; competition with Catholic unions, 244, 258, 263–4; organization of strikes, 120–1, 242–3, 264–5, 266–76; victory over AETSV, 276–7; women members, 260, 262–3, 265–6, 273–4, 279–80, 224, 262, 291–2

Ursule (Valleyfield interviewee), 48, 68, 95

Valente, Anthony (UTWA secretary-treasurer), 262, 263

Valleyfield, city of: 15, 21, 32, 34, 154, 242, 268, 270–1

Valleyfield mill: See Montreal Cotton

Valleyfield Strike (1946), 266–77

Venne, Joseph (foreman), 115, 117

Verdun mill, 127, 131, 133, 139, 140, *141*, 152

Véronique (Valleyfield interviewee), 21, 93

Verville, Alphonse (member of parliament), 114

Viau, Delima (mill worker), 77, 119

Villeneuve, Cardinal Jean-Marie-Rodrigue, 244, 251

Wabasso Cotton Company: age of workers, 147; competitors, 163; dividends, 127, 143; expansion of, 41, 129; financial problems, 131, 136, 138; foundation of, 40–1, 137; housing, 40; minimum wage law, 209; modernization of, 131, 139; mule-spinning operation, 50; photographs, *70, 88, 127, 137*; profits, 41, 130, 138, 164; strikes, 243; supplementary hours, 183, 186; union activity, 246; wartime contracts, 152–3; *See also* Saint Maurice Valley Cotton Mills and Shawinigan Cotton Company

wages: average wages, 72–7, 199–201, 208, 261; bonus system, 121, 131, 190, 196–7, 198–9, 209, 214, 293; employers' manipulation of legislation on, 148, 204–5, 206–8; factors affecting, 72–4, 200, 201, 206, 213–14, 219; fine system and, 73–4, 201–2, 204; gender disparity,

MIX
Paper from
responsible sources
FSC® C100212

Printed by Imprimerie Gauvin
Gatineau, Québec